# Exodus

## GOD OUR DELIVERER

14 Studies for Individuals or Groups

D A L E  &  S A N D Y  L A R S E N

Harold Shaw Publishers • Wheaton, Illinois

ISBN 0-87788-___-6
Editor: Mary ____ _____
Cover photo © 1998 by Dick Dietrich

05  04  03  02  01  00  99  98

10  9  8  7  6  5  4  3  2  1

# CONTENTS

# INTRODUCTION

"God, get me out of this!"

How often have you said that? Are you in a situation right now that makes you say it?

When the Israelites were slaves in Egypt, they had plenty of opportunities and plenty of reasons to beg, "God, get us out of this!" They had wound up in Egypt because Joseph was sold into slavery by his own brothers. Joseph did not continue as a slave; through God's intervention and faithfulness Joseph rose to power in Egypt. Eventually Joseph's father, Israel, his brothers and their families all found refuge from famine in Egypt with him. Initially, the Israelites flourished. But later when a Pharaoh came along who knew nothing of Joseph, he saw this vast group of Hebrews as a threat and enslaved them.

The new Pharaoh may not have known about Joseph, but the Israelites knew their own history. They knew the Lord had pulled Joseph up out of humiliation, slavery, and false imprisonment. Would the Lord do it again, this time for an entire people?

In many ways we're in the same condition as the Israelites. We live under various external and internal struggles—with difficult people or situations, with our own sin and failings. We know God *can* deliver us; we know it from what we read in the Bible and have seen in our own and others' experiences. But *will* he deliver us? When? How? Is he leaving us in a difficult situation for a purpose? And what do we have to do, if anything, to help our deliverance happen?

God's deliverance comes in many different ways, as the Israelites learned. Sometimes it means miraculous rescue from trouble. Other times it means a change of heart or an internal strengthening which is equally miraculous.

So the story of the Exodus is also our story, because it is the story of God's deliverance of an imperfect people. The story doesn't always read the way we'd like. The trip is rough. Sometimes it doubles back or gets delayed. But it is always going somewhere, and most important, God is there with us at every step.

# HOW TO USE THIS STUDYGUIDE

Fisherman studyguides are based on the inductive approach to Bible study. Inductive study is discovery study; we discover what the Bible says as we ask questions about its content and search for answers. This is quite different from the process in which a teacher *tells* a group *about* the Bible, what it means, and what to do about it. In inductive study God speaks directly to each of us through his Word.

A group functions best when a leader keeps the discussion on target, but this leader is neither the teacher nor the "answer person." A leader's responsibility is to *ask*—not *tell*. The answers come from the text itself as group members examine, discuss, and think together about the passage.

There are four kinds of questions in each study. The first is an *approach question*. Used before the Bible passage is read, this question breaks the ice and helps you focus on the topic of the Bible study. It begins to reveal where thoughts and feelings need to be transformed by Scripture.

Some of the earlier questions in each study are *observation questions* designed to help you find out basic facts—who, what, where, when, and how.

When you know what the Bible says, you need to ask, *What does it mean?* These *interpretation questions* help you to discover the writer's basic message.

*Application questions* ask *What does it mean to me?* They challenge you to live out the Scripture's life-transforming message.

Fisherman studyguides provide spaces between questions for jotting down responses and related questions you would like to raise in the group. Each group member should have a copy of the studyguide and may take a turn in leading the group.

For consistency, Fisherman guides are written from the *New International Version*. But a group should feel free to use the NIV or any other accurate, modern translation of the Bible such as the *New Living Translation*, the *New Revised Standard Version*, the *New Jerusalem Bible*, or the *Good News Bible*. (Other paraphrases of the Bible may be referred to when additional help is needed.) Bible commentaries should not be brought to a Bible study because they tend to dampen discussion and keep people from thinking for themselves.

## SUGGESTIONS FOR GROUP LEADERS

**1.** Read and study the Bible passage thoroughly beforehand, grasping its themes and applying its teachings for yourself. Pray that the Holy Spirit will "guide you into truth" so that your leadership will guide others.

**2.** If the studyguide's questions ever seem ambiguous or unnatural to you, rephrase them, feeling free to add others that seem necessary to bring out the meaning of a verse.

**3.** Begin (and end) the study promptly. Start by asking someone to pray for God's help. Remember, the Holy Spirit is the teacher, not you!

**4.** Ask for volunteers to read the passages out loud.

**5.** As you ask the studyguide's questions in sequence, encourage everyone to participate in the discussion. If some are silent, ask,

#310   07-17-2012 4:18PM
Item(s) checked out to SCHULTZ, NATHAN.

TITLE: Exodus : God our deliverer : 14 s
BARCODE: 25054007581836
DUE: 08-14-12

TITLE: Exodus
BARCODE: 25054007860164
DUE: 08-14-12

TITLE: Exodus,
BARCODE: 25054006041402
DUE: 08-14-12

"What do you think, Heather?" or "Dan, what can you add to that answer?" or suggest, "Let's have an answer from someone who hasn't spoken up yet."

**6.** If a question comes up that you can't answer, don't be afraid to admit that you're baffled! Assign the topic as a research project for someone to report on next week.

**7.** Keep the discussion moving and focused. Though tangents will inevitably be introduced, you can bring the discussion back to the topic at hand. Learn to pace the discussion so that you finish a study each session you meet.

**8.** Don't be afraid of silences; some questions take time to answer and some people need time to gather courage to speak. If silence persists, rephrase your question, but resist the temptation to answer it yourself.

**9.** If someone comes up with an answer that is clearly illogical or unbiblical, ask him or her for further clarification: "What verse suggests that to you?"

**10.** Discourage Bible-hopping and overuse of cross-references. Learn all you can from *this* passage, along with a few important references suggested in the studyguide.

**11.** Some questions are marked with a ♦. This indicates that further information is available in the Leader's Notes at the back of the guide.

**12.** For further information on getting a new Bible study group started and keeping it functioning effectively, read Gladys Hunt's *You Can Start a Bible Study Group* and *Pilgrims in Progress: Growing through Groups* by Jim and Carol Plueddemann.

## SUGGESTIONS FOR GROUP MEMBERS

**1.** Learn and apply the following ground rules for effective Bible study. (If new members join the group later, review these guidelines with the whole group.)

**2.** Remember that your goal is to learn all that you can *from the Bible passage being studied.* Let it speak for itself without using Bible commentaries or other Bible passages. There is more than enough in each assigned passage to keep your group productively occupied for one session. Sticking to the passage saves the group from insecurity and confusion.

**3.** Avoid the temptation to bring up those fascinating tangents that don't really grow out of the passage you are discussing. If the topic is of common interest, you can bring it up later in informal conversation following the study. Meanwhile, help each other stick to the subject!

**4.** Encourage each other to participate. People remember best what they discover and verbalize for themselves. Some people are naturally shier than others, or they may be afraid of making a mistake. If your discussion is free and friendly and you show real interest in what other group members think and feel, they will be more likely to speak up. Remember, the more people involved in a discussion, the richer it will be.

**5.** Guard yourself from answering too many questions or talking too much. Give others a chance to express themselves. If you are one who participates easily, discipline yourself by counting to ten before you open your mouth!

**6.** Make personal, honest applications and commit yourself to letting God's Word change you.

# Ancient World
## c.1500-1300 B.C.

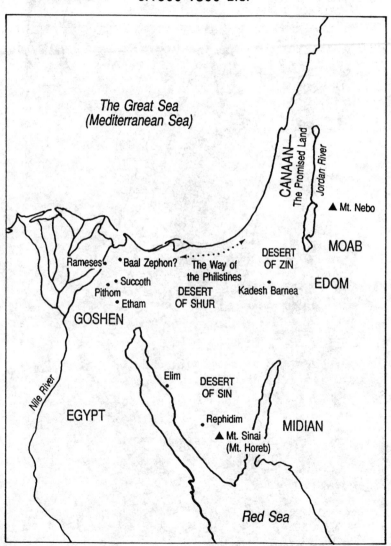

The Great Sea
(Mediterranean Sea)

CANAAN—
The Promised Land

Jordan River

▲ Mt. Nebo

MOAB

Rameses

Baal Zephon?

The Way of
the Philistines

DESERT
OF ZIN

EDOM

Succoth

DESERT
OF SHUR

Kadesh Barnea

Pithom

Etham

GOSHEN

Elim

DESERT
OF SIN

Nile River

EGYPT

Rephidim

MIDIAN

▲ Mt. Sinai
(Mt. Horeb)

Red Sea

The Tabernacle & the Encampment of the Tribes

# GOD IS ALREADY ANSWERING

Exodus 1–2; 3:1-15

The check was on the way to you, but you didn't know it. All you knew was that the rent was due and you didn't know how you were going to pay it. You looked at the calendar, saw the dreaded date approaching and tried to figure out how you would explain. And all the while the unexpected envelope was safely making its way through the postal system—being sealed, stamped, mailed, trucked, flown, trucked again, sorted, carried, and finally delivered to your door. God was at work all along—you just didn't know it.

Enslaved in Egypt, the people of Israel cried out to God for release. Had God forgotten them? No, he still cared, and he was beginning to do something to deliver them. But the beginnings of his plan were obscure.

**1.** Give an example of a situation where God was at work to help you (or someone else) but you had no idea of it until much later.

## Read Exodus 1–2.

2. Describe the changes in the Israelites' situation at the time of Moses' birth.

What might the people have been thinking and feeling (1:1-22; 2:23-25)?

3. What people were key in Moses' survival (2:1-10)?

4. From the brief glimpse we get here, what do you know about Moses' life in Egypt (2:1-15)?

What turn did Moses' life take?

## Read Exodus 3:1-15.

♦ 5. Here is the first active indication that God was going to do something about the Israelites' oppression. Describe the setting in which this announcement took place (verse 1).

♦ *Indicates further information in Leader's Notes*

◆ **6.** What do you discover about the heart of God from what he told Moses in verses 7-10?

**7.** From his responses in verses 2-6, what do you discern about Moses' character?

**8.** As God spoke the words in verses 7-10, how might Moses' mood have fluctuated?

◆ **9.** What were Moses' objections to being chosen, and how did the Lord counter each of them (verses 11-15)?

◆ **10.** In what ways can you relate to the Israelites' dilemma in verse 7?

**11.** How was God beginning to help the Israelites in Egypt, even though they didn't yet know about it?

**12.** What encouragement and hope can you draw from this passage when you face difficult situations?

**13.** How can this passage affect how you pray for yourself and others during hard times?

# THE LORD OVERCOMES DOUBTS

Exodus 4:1–6:12

Have you ever dared complain to the Lord? Maybe you do that all the time; maybe you've done it in the past but not lately; or maybe you consider it unthinkable that a human being would complain to a holy God. Yet we've all experienced times when it felt that God just wasn't doing what we expected or what we needed.

As the story of Exodus continues, Moses and his brother, Aaron, obey the Lord and appeal to Pharaoh for freedom. Immediately it looks as if the whole scheme has backfired. Pharaoh comes down hard on the Israelites, and the Israelites angrily turn on Moses and Aaron. With their promised hope of freedom apparently shattered, Moses turns to the Lord and blurts out his honest feelings.

**1.** Have you experienced a time in your life when God did not respond as you wanted him to? What did you do?

**Read Exodus 4:1-17.**

**2.** The story picks up with Moses still talking with God at the burning bush. What further doubts did Moses express about going to Pharaoh, and how did God successively overcome each doubt?

**3.** Put yourself in Moses' place for a minute. How would you respond to a task like this? Why?

How has God worked to overcome doubts or fears in your life?

**Scan Exodus 4:18–5:21.**

**4.** Moses returned to Egypt and teamed up with his brother, Aaron. What sort of reception did they receive from the Israelites?

**5.** When Moses asked Pharaoh to release the people, what chain reaction of events followed?

**Read Exodus 5:22–6:12.**

**6.** Moses proceeded to complain to God. What was reasonable or unreasonable about his complaints?

◆ **7.** How did God assure the Israelites that he would keep his promise (6:2-5)?

**8.** The Israelites did not immediately listen to Moses. As a result, what did God tell Moses to do as a next step?

**9.** Compare and contrast the people's response to Moses with Moses' response to God (6:9, 12). How are they alike? different?

**10.** What insights into God's character do you glean from his dialogue with Moses here?

♦ **11.** God reminded the Israelites of his past faithfulness. As Christians, what are some things in our corporate church history that reassure us of God's continual care?

**12.** More specifically, how can God use your own spiritual history to reassure you of his care? (That is, what are some events in your own life that you can recall to remind yourself that God is faithful?)

# THE LORD OF POWER

Exodus 7–10

Chicago's Fourth of July fireworks were coming to a close. The grand finale was cascading downward to be quenched in the dark waters of Lake Michigan. Suddenly, crack! A lightning bolt transformed night to day for an instant; then came a *wham!* of thunder. God seemed to be saying, "You think your fireworks are something? Wait till you see what I can do!"

Most people in the crowd probably didn't even think about God in that setting. Even the greatest demonstration of God's power does not necessarily make a non-believer into a believer. But for those who are open to see it, God demonstrates his power every day.

1. What are some ways you have seen God demonstrate his power? (Consider a variety of channels: in nature, in your church, in other people's lives, in your own life.)

**Scan Exodus 7–10.**

**2.** Divide into smaller groups of two or three people. As you scan the passage, chart the first nine plagues God sent and answer the following questions together:

What did each plague consist of?

Who was affected?

What was the people's response?

How did Pharaoh respond?

What were the results?

**Read Exodus 9:13-21.**

**3.** One reason God brought the plagues on the Egyptians was to persuade Pharaoh to let the Israelites leave Egypt. What other reasons are given (verses 14-16)?

♦ **4.** How could these demonstrations of power result in God's name being "proclaimed in all the earth"?

23

◆ **5.** What would make the plague of hail a particularly powerful demonstration of the power of God?

**6.** How was God's mercy shown even as the plague was announced? In other ways?

◆ **7.** What evidence do you see that the plagues were beginning to have the intended effect?

**Read Exodus 9:22-35.**

**8.** How was God's sovereignty shown in what was destroyed by the hail and what was spared? Consider both his sovereignty in Israel's history and in the world in general.

**9.** What did Pharaoh's actions reveal about the sincerity of his repentance? about his true character?

**10.** Why does even a great demonstration of God's power not completely convince a stubborn person?

**11.** In what ways does seeing God's power of behalf of his people encourage you?

**12.** How can you allow what you have experienced of God's power to lead you to deeper holiness and commitment to him?

# THE PASSOVER

Exodus 11:1–12:30

What do you use to help you remember things? Some people write big notes to themselves and stick them up in conspicuous places. Others ask friends to remind them of appointments or leave themselves messages on their home answering machines. Some people turn on their computer for their daily calendar to pop up.

Most of us need help remembering the things we should remember. The Israelites were no exception. As God acted for their deliverance, he also gave them a most effective way to recall his faithfulness. That's one purpose of religious rituals—they help us remember what we would otherwise forget.

**1.** What memory techniques or helps are most effective for you and why?

**Read Exodus 11.**

**2.** Describe the events leading up to the final plague on Egypt. Who was involved? What was the tone?

**3.** As news of the last and most devastating plague began to spread among the Egyptians and the Israelites, what may have been the prevailing mood in each group?

**Read Exodus 12:1-23.**

**4.** How were the Israelites specifically instructed to prepare for the Passover (verses 1-13)?

**5.** What were the requirements for the sacrificial animal (verses 3-5)?

♦ **6.** What significance do you see in the various things that were to be done at this first Passover (verses 5-11)?

**7.** What positive and negative actions would the Lord himself take (verses 12-13)? Why?

♦ **8.** Moses gave final instructions in verses 21-23. What was to be done with the blood, and why?

**Read Exodus 12:24-30.**

**9.** How were the Passover events made into a lasting remembrance to be kept by the people? (Compare Exodus 13:1-16) Why?

**10.** In what ways is the remembrance of Passover similar to the Christian communion service?

**11.** What part does communion play in your own experience of worship?

**12.** Through what other creative means can you celebrate and remember what God has done for you in the past?

# THE LORD LIBERATES HIS PEOPLE

Exodus 13:17–14:31

"I don't get it," a friend of ours said. "I stepped out on faith and did what I thought God wanted me to do, and so far it looks like nothing but disaster!"

Is there anything more confusing than having things apparently go wrong when we've obeyed God as best we knew how? That's the distressing situation in which Moses and the Israelites found themselves as they huddled in their encampment by the sea, with deep water on one side and the dust of Pharaoh's approaching army on the other.

**1.** Have you ever felt stuck in a situation with seemingly no way out? What happened?

**Read Exodus 13:17–14:12.**

♦ **2.** God did not lead the Israelites along the shorter route through the Philistine country (see map on page 11). What reason did he give for the longer route (13:17-18)?

♦ **3.** What things impress you about God's "guidance system" for the Israelites (13:20-22)?

**4.** How has God led or guided you recently? How did you know it was God?

**5.** God had been unmistakably leading the Israelites out of Egypt. Describe the situation in which they now found themselves (14:5-12).

**6.** How did the Israelites respond to this new emergency?

**7.** If you had been in the same emergency, what thoughts might have been going through your head? (Compare your hypothetical response with your answer to question 1.)

**Read Exodus 14:13-31.**

♦ **8.** What command and what assurance did Moses give the people (verses 13-14)?

**9.** How can Moses' advice still encourage us today when our situation seems hopeless?

**10.** What different means—natural and supernatural—did God use to intervene and deliver his people (verses 16-22)?

**11.** God also gave a hint about why he had put the Israelites in this difficult position. What reason did he imply?

**12.** Have you seen God using a similar "Red Sea" strategy in your own life or someone else's life? Explain.

**13.** God may not literally part a sea for us, but he is still a God who delivers and frees us, spiritually and physically. What stories of God's deliverance do you have to share?

# YIELDING CONTROL

Exodus 16:1-36; 18:9-27

Has it ever happened to you? You were in charge of some big event and you felt responsible for taking care of every detail and making sure it ran like clockwork. Then you got sick or some other emergency came up and you couldn't be there.

And what do you know, the event came off perfectly without you! Other people stepped in, took up the slack and did "your" job quite well. Finding out that we're not 100% necessary, and that we need help, is a humbling—but freeing—experience. Moses had to learn this lesson too.

**1.** In what areas of life do you especially like to be in charge?

**Read Exodus 16:1-36.**

**2.** After all that God had done, why do you think the people responded as they did to the hardships of the desert (verses 1-9)?

**3.** When the Israelites talked about how good it used to be back in Egypt, what were they forgetting or ignoring?

**4.** Moses told the Israelites that they were grumbling not against him but against God. When we grumble against circumstances or people in our lives, how could it be said that we are complaining and grumbling against God?

♦ **5.** By what unusual means did God provide for the people in the desert?

Why do you think God put the limits he did on gathering (verses 16-36)?

**Read Exodus 18:9-18.**

*While Moses was in Egypt, his wife Zipporah and his son were staying with his father-in-law Jethro. After the Israelites' escape from Egypt, Jethro accompanied his daughter and grandson to the Israelites' encampment in the desert. Moses reported to Jethro all that God had done.*

**6.** What do we learn about Jethro from his response to Moses' words?

**7.** Describe what Jethro saw the next day and why it disturbed him.

**Read Exodus 18:19-27.**

♦ **8.** What was Jethro's method for solving Moses' difficulty?

**9.** What qualities of character did Moses need in order to accept Jethro's advice?

♦ **10.** What would have been the risks of turning over part of Moses' responsibilities to a group of people who lacked experience?

Beyond the time saved, what were some advantages of Moses' delegating the work to others?

**11.** In what areas of your life is it difficult for you to relinquish control?

**12.** Think of the advantages of taking Jethro's advice. What do you need to do to put that advice into action?

# GOD'S PERFECT LAW

Exodus 19:1–20:21

Speed Limit 55. Keep Off the Grass. Walk/Don't Walk. No Parking Here at Anytime. No Trespassing. Use Separate Plate for Each Trip to the Salad Bar.

Regulations are everywhere, and few of us welcome them. We complain about them and resist them because we don't like the restrictions they place on our freedom. No wonder it sounds like a contradiction when God says that his laws are designed to give us freedom!

**1.** Growing up, what part did rules and regulations play in your family? How did you usually react to these?

## Read Exodus 19:1-25.

**2.** The Israelites had wandered for three months and finally stopped in the Sinai Desert. How did God encourage his people as he initiated conversation with them (verses 3-6)?

◆ **3.** Identify all the preparations that had to be made for receiving the law (verses 1-15).

**4.** What words or phrases would you use to describe the setting where the law was given (verses 16-22)?

## Read Exodus 20:1-11.

**5.** In your own words, relate the essence of each of these first four commandments.

♦ **6.** What is the overarching concern or focus of these four commandments as a whole?

**7.** What can we discern about the character of God from these commandments?

---

**Read Exodus 20:12-21.**

**8.** Identify the specific areas of life dealt with here.

What is the overall focus of these final six commandments?

**9.** What further insight do these commandments give you about God's character?

**10.** Imagine the drama of the scene in verses 18-21. What response did God's presence evoke? Why?

**11.** People often accuse the Ten Commandments of being too restrictive. Yet the Bible calls God's law *liberating* (see Psalm 119:45 and James 2:12). How would you explain the ways in which the laws of God can be liberating?

**12.** Which of these commandments have you personally found restrictive? Why?

What has helped bring you around to finding freedom through obedience to God's commands?

# LORD OF EVERY PART OF LIFE

Exodus 23:1-19

Some parts of our lives are easy to hand over to God. But for most of us there is a corner or a space—or maybe an elephant-sized room—that we'd like to hold onto and control. What's the area for you? Finances? Personal goals? Sexuality? Your job? Even church?

The Lord stakes his claim on every area of life, not because he wants to spoil our fun but because he wants to transform those areas into something holy and good. But first we have to let them go, acknowledging his ownership of every part of our lives. At Sinai the Lord expanded on the Ten Commandments and gave the Israelites specific instructions about some very close-to-home areas of life.

1. Consider an aspect of your life where you have difficulty yielding to the Lord. What fears or other emotions inhibit you from trusting God with that part of life?

**Scan through Exodus 21–22, looking for dominant themes.**

**2.** In what ways does God expand on the Ten Commandments here?

Identify some of the themes and areas of life covered by these more specific laws.

---

**Read Exodus 23:1-9.**

**3.** What common idea(s) do you see running through this section of commands? Discuss.

**4.** Our culture is very different from the nomadic culture to which these laws were directed. (Most of us don't own a donkey or an ox and don't know anyone who does.) How can the principles of these particular laws be put into practice in our own culture? Discuss some practical examples.

**Read Exodus 23:10-19.**

**5.** List the guidelines for remembering the Sabbath. (Compare with Exodus 20:8-11.)

♦ **6.** What benefits were promised for keeping the Sabbath laws?

**7.** As the people considered obeying these Sabbath commands, what possible concerns may have begun to creep into their minds?

**8.** What concerns and pressures do we face in trying to keep the Sabbath in our own culture?

◆ **9.** The people were told to celebrate three feasts. How did these feasts demonstrate God's claim on the totality of human life?

◆ **10.** How could we fulfill the intent of these celebrations today within the context of our own Christian community?

**11.** What will you do this week to celebrate and commemorate God's goodness and faithfulness?

# TIME WITH GOD

Exodus 24

It's exciting to be part of a great crowd praising the Lord together; ask anyone who has been in a worship service in a football stadium, arena, or some other vast setting. When thousands of diverse voices mingle into one chorus glorifying God, we realize that as believers we're not alone.

But there are other times we need to be alone—alone, that is, with the Lord himself. Sometimes God takes us out of the crowd so he can capture our full attention. If he needed to do that with his servant Moses, certainly he needs to do it with us.

**1.** Imagine being actually summoned by God to spend time with him. How do you think you'd react? Why?

**As background for this study, scan Exodus 23:20-32.**

**2.** In what ways did the Lord express the depth of his commitment to the future of the Israelites?

---

**Read Exodus 24:1-8.**

♦ **3.** Roughly diagram the positioning of the people at the mountain (verses 1-2). What message about God was conveyed by the arrangement?

**4.** How did the people express their attitude toward God's laws?

◆ **5.** What steps did Moses take in confirming the covenant of God with the people?

---

**Read Exodus 24:9-18.**

**6.** The Hebrew people believed that no one could see God and survive. Yet Moses, Aaron, Aaron's two sons, and the seventy elders went up Mount Sinai and "saw God" (verse 10). How do you account for their willingness to take such a risk?

**7.** Compare the description in verse 10 with Isaiah 6:1-4, Ezekiel 1:25-28, and Revelation 4:1-6. What impresses you about these descriptions?

**8.** Consider the time frame of Moses' stay on the mountain with the Lord. What would have been difficult about that lapse of time for Moses? For those waiting for him?

**9.** If you wish, describe a time when you have spent an extended time apart with God. How did it come about? What did you do?

**10.** What immediate and/or long-term results have you seen from time spent alone with God?

**11.** How does your response to God compare with the people's response voiced in verse 7? Pray together that you can respond wholeheartedly as the Israelites did.

# "HOLY TO THE LORD"

Exodus 28:1-5, 31-43; 29:1-46

Most of us like a certain degree of ceremony to mark the passages of life. Whether it's a job promotion, the granting of a high school diploma, or the inauguration of a president, we expect some kind of formal observance of the person's new position.

It wasn't that different back in the days of the Israelites. When Aaron and his sons became priests of the Lord, God outlined holy rituals and even special clothing to set them apart for his service. While much of the ancient symbolism is foreign to our culture, the ceremonial importance of what was done still shines through.

**1.** What ceremony in your life has been meaningful to you, and why?

**Read Exodus 28:1-5 and 31-43.**

*In Exodus 25–27 God gave Moses detailed instructions for the building of the movable tent of worship and the holy articles of worship. Next, God established the priesthood.*

**2.** How were Aaron and his sons to be set apart for a special type of service to the Lord?

**3.** Identify the various garments described here.

Why do you think God mandated such elaborate and ornate clothing?

**4.** Suggest how bearing a literal physical remembrance of the Israelites into God's presence might affect Aaron himself.

**5.** Suggest how knowing that Aaron bore that remembrance might affect the people.

**6.** In your own experience, what outward symbols have taken the holiness of God out of the abstract and made it more real?

---

**Read Exodus 29:1-46.**

**7.** Enumerate the various steps used in the consecration of Aaron and his sons as priests to the Lord.

◆ **8.** How did the steps of preparation show that Aaron and his sons were inadequate—humanly speaking—to serve as priests?

♦ **9.** What offering was to be made for seven days, and why (verses 35-37)?

**10.** In connection with the offerings, what promises did God make (verses 42-46)?

**11.** How did past and future come together in the consecration of Aaron and his sons (note verses 42 and 46)?

**12.** What things—in creation, in corporate worship, in religious ceremonies—serve to remind you of God's holy presence, as the priests did for Israel?

**13.** Consider further ways you can daily remind yourself of God's faithfulness to you.

# REBELLION, INTERCESSION, AND RESTORATION

Exodus 32

Sometimes God just doesn't move fast enough—at least not as fast as we think he should. When we see problems to be solved and needs to be met, it's hard to understand why God isn't doing something now.

At those frustrating times of waiting, it's tempting to take things into our own hands. We want to construct the solution that God just isn't getting around to providing. Our solutions may take many forms. For Israel, waiting at the foot of Mount Sinai, the form was an idol made of gold.

**1.** Tell about a time when you seemed to lose the sense of God's presence in your life (or when God seemed very far away). How did the experience affect you?

**Read Exodus 32:1-14.**

**2.** List the reasons the people gave for asking Aaron to make them gods.

♦ **3.** What was Aaron's creative response?

Why do you think he complied with the people's demands?

**4.** How did the people respond to having a new god?

**5.** With Moses, their representative and leader, absent for forty days, the Israelites felt at a loss. To whom or to what do you sometimes turn when God doesn't seem to be providing the help you expect?

**6.** In response to Israel's idolatry, what did God propose to do?

**7.** What does Moses' reply to God say about his character?

**8.** In Moses' prayer to God in verses 11-13, what were the various steps of the development of his appeal?

**9.** How can Moses' example further your understanding of interceding for people who have fallen into sin?

**Read Exodus 32:15-35.**

**10.** When confronted with the people's sin, Aaron made excuses. In what ways do these resemble typical excuses people make for sin?

**11.** Moses' response to the people's sin seems harsh by our standards today. Why did he take these actions (verses 25-31)?

What does this passage tell us about the seriousness of sin?

**12.** How did Moses put his own life on the line for the Israelites (verses 30-33)?

**13.** Consider people you know who need your intercessory prayers. Using Moses' example, and without revealing to the group things that should be kept private, spend time praying for those people.

# A LASTING COVENANT

Exodus 34

Sometimes it seems that nobody keeps promises anymore. From broken marriage vows to useless service contracts to ambitious politicians, people give their word lightly. Often they don't even intend to make good on what they've promised to do. It's refreshing to find someone trustworthy; a person who says "I'll do this"—and then does it.

The Lord is that trustworthy One who keeps his commitments to us. He has made an eternal promise to be faithful to his people, and he has never broken a promise.

**1.** Who has blessed you by keeping a promise?

**Read Exodus 34:1-17.**

*Earlier in Exodus 33, Moses had despaired at the prospect of being without the Lord's presence. But God assured him that he would never leave, allowing Moses to see God's glory pass by. Then God gave Moses a new task.*

**2.** In anger at the people's idolatry, Moses had smashed the original two stone tablets bearing the Ten Commandments. What do you think was the significance of those tablets being replaced?

◆ **3.** Note God's declarations as he passed before Moses. How do you reconcile the statements in verse 6 with that of verse 7b?

◆ **4.** In his covenant with the people, what did God promise to do (verse 10)? To what end?

♦ **5.** To what extreme measures were the people called to be obedient (verses 13-17)? Why?

**6.** Why do you think idolatry was such a persistent problem for God's people?

**7.** In what ways are believers today tempted to depend on something or someone besides the Lord to meet their needs?

What can we do to break down the idols in our lives?

**Read Exodus 34:18-35.**

♦ **8.** The next requirements of God's covenant with the people included three annual feasts. How could these yearly feasts help them avoid falling back into idolatry?

**9.** How did Moses' entrance into the camp differ this time (verse 29) from his previous entrance in Exodus 32:19?

How was the people's response different?

**10.** From verses 29-35, how would you describe Moses' relationship with God?

**11.** How did that close relationship enable Moses to not compromise God's laws?

**12.** Which of God's promises have meant more to you over the years? Which ones have meant more to you recently? Why?

Take time to praise the Lord together for his faithfulness to keep his promises.

# GIVING BACK TO THE LORD

Exodus 35:1–36:7; 39:32-43

"I wish I could make worship banners like she does . . . or coach softball like him . . . or write music like they do . . . or . . ." It's easy to fall into the trap of envying skills of other Christians. We look at ourselves in comparison and think we don't have much to offer.

Sometimes in the church we elevate performance gifts like music or public speaking while we downplay practical gifts like building and craftsmanship. But there is value in all the various skills God has placed within his church. When we have opportunities to offer our gifts, whatever they are, back to God, then we thrive in our faith.

**1.** What spiritual gifts or talents do you tend to consider more important than other ones? Why?

**Read Exodus 35:1-29.**

**2.** What requirements were set forth for the people who were to make the tabernacle furnishings and provide the materials (verses 2, 5, 10)?

**3.** Why would these requirements be vital for this task?

**4.** Consider the gifts and skills represented in this passage. Who do you know who possesses these or similar skills? How are they using them for service?

◆ **5.** What repeated phrases do you observe that describe how the people responded (verses 21-29)?

How does their attitude compare with your own toward giving to the Lord?

**Read Exodus 35:30–36:7.**

♦ **6.** Obviously there were many artistically gifted people among the Israelites. What set Bezalel, Oholiab, and the other, unnamed craftsmen apart?

**7.** What "complaint" did the workers make to Moses (36:3-5)?

What do you think motivated the people to give so freely?

**8.** What inhibits you from giving of your time and talents to the Lord's work?

**Read Exodus 39:32-43.**

♦ **9.** This passage puts the tabernacle together physically and in the reader's mind. How did Moses react to seeing it all?

Look at the rendering of the tabernacle on page 12. How do you think you would have reacted if you had been there?

**10.** Think about your own church building and place of worship. How does it display believers' gifts *from* the Lord and *to* the Lord (either material gifts or skills)?

**11.** Consider your own material resources. What new ways do you see to give to the Lord besides financially?

**12.** Consider your God-given skills or spiritual gifts. What new avenues can you see for using your abilities for the Lord?

**13.** Think of someone in your fellowship whose gifts or contributions tend to go unnoticed. How will you affirm that person's gifts this week?

# GOD'S PRESENCE FILLS THE TABERNACLE

Exodus 40

We have followed Moses and the children of Israel from Egypt to the wilderness to Mount Sinai. We have watched as God has miraculously delivered his people over and over again. Now as we come to the close of the book of Exodus, we find the Lord faithfully assuring his people that he will always be with them.

How many of us have wished we could see or touch God, just to be sure he was there? Israel had the privilege of watching God's very presence fill the tabernacle they had constructed. But this was no warm fuzzy experience—it was awesome!

**1.** When have you been overwhelmed by the holiness of God? Tell about it.

**Read Exodus 40:1-38.**

**2.** To prepare everything for service, what final things were done in the tabernacle?

**3.** Describe the final steps of how Aaron and his sons were dedicated to serve the Lord as priests.

**4.** What impact might all these final preparations have had on the people's attitudes toward the tabernacle and the priests?

**5.** Finally the magnificent tabernacle was done. Look again at the drawing on page 12. Then, making use of verses 17-33, label each of the nine items in the following diagram of the tabernacle. If there is time, discuss the purpose of each item to be used in worship.

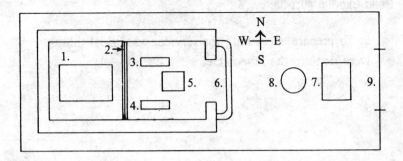

1.                              6.

2.                              7.

3.                              8.

4.                              9.

5.

**6.** When the people had finished setting up the tabernacle, how did the Lord verify that it was his?

**7.** How have you seen God manifesting himself in your church? (Consider the quiet and obscure manifestations as well as more dramatic ones.)

**8.** In the New Testament, Christian believers are called God's dwelling place, both individually and corporately (see 1 Corinthians 6:19 and 1 Peter 2:5). What difference does it make in your life to know that you are God's "tabernacle"?

**9.** As we close our study of Exodus, what main event or themes from this book have fixed themselves in your mind? Why?

**10.** What have you observed throughout this book study that will help you follow God more closely?

**11.** We don't have a pillar of cloud or fire to give us guidance, but we do have God's Word and the Holy Spirit to guide us. Israel's problem throughout their history was not discerning what God wanted, but rather their own willingness to obey. What steps can you take now to obey what you believe God wants you to do?

Praise the Lord for always being with you. Pray that you will consistently live in ways that honor his presence.

# LEADER'S NOTES

**Question 5.** The setting was isolated, a good 250 difficult desert miles from the Nile River. Mt. Horeb (Mt. Sinai) would later be the place where God gave the Ten Commandments. It was a rocky, lonely area.

Midian, the home of Jethro, is the far northwest corner of modern Saudi Arabia. (See map on page 11). Moses was tending the family flocks in the southern part of the Sinai Peninsula. "The Midianites were descendants of Abraham through his second wife, Keturah. They were desert-dwellers, so Moses could scarcely have had better preparation for the wilderness journeys with Israel than these years of nomadic life" (*Eerdmans Handbook to the Bible,* pp. 155-156. Grand Rapids, Mich.: Eerdmans, 1973).

**Question 6.** Notice how the Lord took the initiative to help his people: "I have indeed seen . . .; I have heard them . . .; I have come down to rescue them . . . and to bring them up . . .; I am sending you . . ."

**Question 9.** "I Am Who I Am" is the divine Name which came to be regarded as so holy that devout Jews would not pronounce it. "It expresses the eternity and immutability of the divine nature, and the faithfulness of God to all his purposes and promises" (William Wilson, *Wilson's Old Testament Word Studies,* p. 259. Peabody, Mass.: Hendrickson Publishers, n.d.).

**Question 10.** To respond to this question, your situation does not have to be as dramatic as that of the Israelites in slavery. It can be anything which has you "crying out" or "suffering."

## ▉ Study 2/The Lord Overcomes Doubts

**Question 7.** God makes use of the Israelites' history to assure them of his faithfulness. The previous covenants God had made were with Noah (Genesis 9:8-17) and Abraham (Genesis 15:17-20).

**Question 11.** Draw on what you know of Christian history in general, the history of your own denomination, the history of your own local church, and the history of your family. Think about how the Lord made use of persecution as well as delivering his people from it. Recall famous and not-so-famous people who stood fast as examples of faith because they found God faithful.

## ▉ Study 3/The Lord of Power

**Question 4.** See Joshua 2:8-11 for a comparable example of how God's name was proclaimed in other nations as a result of miracles.

**Question 5.** "Clearly the abilities of several Egyptian gods were again being challenged. Nut, the sky goddess, was not able to forestall the storm; and Osiris, the god of crop fertility, could not maintain the crops in this hailstorm; nor could Set, the storm god,

. ; they [probably] avoided it because of the many
...ions and fortresses along the way. Migdol and Baal-
...ntioned at the start of the Exodus (Ex. 14:2; Num.
...nown from Egyptian sources as fortresses at the north-
...ge of the Delta, and it is thus clear that the Exodus
...the north" (Yohanan Aharoni and Michael Avi-Yonah, *The*
...*an Bible Atlas*, rev. ed., p. 40. New York: Macmillan, 1977).

...**ion 3.** It appears that this particular type of direct, continu-
... ..... guidance was only for the time of the Exodus, since
...is never repeated in Scripture.

**Question 8.** Compare two similar but later statements of Scripture
in Psalm 46:10 and 2 Chronicles 20:17.

## Study 6/Yielding Control

**Question 5.** The word *manna* means in Hebrew "What is it?"
(Exodus 16:15, 31).

**Question 8.** "Jethro's solution to this lengthy process, which was
wearing out both people and leader (v.18), was to give Moses that
portion of the work that involved a twofold office: (1) an advocate
on behalf of the people (v.19) and (2) an interpreter on behalf of
God to teach the people (v. 20). Jethro warned that his plan needed
to be executed only if God was pleased with this advice. . . .
...Moses' work was to be supplemented with additional help"
...*Expositor's Bible Commentary*, p. 413).

...**estion 10.** Without the burden of deciding all of the disputes,
...ses would have more time to devote to the more difficult cases.
... ...haring his leadership, Moses was preparing others for lead-
... ...o roles in the community.

hold back this storm" (John D. Ha[...]
*Knowledge Commentary: Old [...]*
Victor Books, 1985).

**Question 7.** Notice that some of t[...]
protect their possessions (Exodus 9:[...]
expect that if Moses said something wo[...]
pen.

## ■ Study 4/The Passover

**Question 6.** "The lamb was to be a year-old male bec[...]
taking the place of Israel's firstborn males who were y[...]
fresh with the vigor of life. The bitter herbs (lettuce and [...]
are indigenous to Egypt) were to recall the bitter years of servit[...]
(Exodus 1:14), and the unleavened bread was to reflect this event[...]
haste on that first night" (Walter C. Kaiser, Jr., "Exodus," p. 372.
*The Expositor's Bible Commentary,* vol. 2, Grand Rapids, Mich.:
Zondervan, 1990).

**Question 8.** In the spreading of the blood of the lamb on th[...]
doorpost to save from death, Christians see a foreshadowing [...]
the cross and the blood of Christ which saves us from spir[...]
death. Peter wrote that we are redeemed "with the precious [...]
of Christ, a lamb without blemish or defect" (1 Peter 1:19[...]
John the Baptist saw Jesus, he called out, "Look, the [...]
God, who takes away the sin of the world!" (John 1:2[...]

## ■ Study 5/The Lord Liberates His People

**Question 2.** The actual route of the Exodus is [...]
Israelites did not pass along the short sectio[...]
from Egypt, called in the Bible the 'way of [...]

74

Philistines' [...]
Egyptian sta[...]
zephon, m[...]
33:7) are [...]
eastern e[...]
stated i[...]
*Maill[...]*

## ■ Study 7/God's Perfect Law

**Question 3.** "The necessary process of ritual purification, or setting apart for God, included the washing of garments . . . and temporary abstention from sexual intercourse. . . . This was not because the latter was considered as wrong in any way, but because, by Mosaic law, it required ceremonial bathing for religious purification as an aftermath. . . . Nevertheless we may compare Paul's words, allowing temporary abstention that Christians may devote themselves to prayer (1 Cor. 7:5)" (R. Alan Cole, *Tyndale Old Testament Commentaries,* p. 146. Downers Grove, Ill.: Inter-Varsity Press, 1973).

**Question 6.** Compare the group's responses to questions 5 and 7 with Jesus' summary of the Law in Mark 12:28-31.

## ■ Study 8/Lord of Every Part of Life

**Question 6.** Allowing fields to rest or lie fallow is an accepted farming practice used in many parts of the world. Today the use of fertilizers and pesticides has largely replaced this practice.

**Question 9.** For further information on the feasts, compare with Deuteronomy 16:1-17.

**Question 10.** Though many of us don't live in an agricultural society working directly with land, we still are recipients of God's blessings and totally dependent on his generosity for all we have.

## ■ Study 9/Time with God

**Question 3.** Note that Exodus 24 continues the narrative from Exodus 20:21. The story "was temporarily interrupted for the contents of the 'Book of the Covenant' (20:22–23:33). . . . Moses and his aides were to ascend . . . the mountain after the actions mentioned in vv. 3-8 were completed" (*Expositor's Bible Commentary,* p. 448).

**Question 5.** The early sacrificial system which God set up for the Israelites was a foreshadowing of the coming eternal covenant through Christ's blood. Compare Hebrews 9:11-22.

### ■ Study 10/"Holy to the Lord"

**Question 8.** They were consecrated by God (Exodus 29:1, 44). The sacred garments symbolized the fact that they were set apart by God's choice (verses 5-8). They had to be washed (verse 4). They were anointed with oil (verse 7). Sacrifices were made for them (verses 10-14).

**Question 9.** The Hebrew word for *atonement* means "to cover, to cover sin, or to secure the sinner from guilt and punishment. . . . This word conveys the idea both of pacification of wrath, and of the covering of transgression, but does not seem to express of itself the idea of full and adequate satisfaction for sin" *(Wilson's Old Testament Word Studies,* p. 24). For further insight on the incompleteness of the Old Testament sacrifices and their fulfillment in Christ's sacrifice, refer to Hebrews 10:1-18.

### ■ Study 11/Rebellion, Intercession, and Restoration

**Question 3.** The civilizations surrounding the Israelites were polytheistic, worshiping multiple gods. Israel had been chosen by God to become a monotheistic people worshiping one God—a radical departure from other cultures. Obviously, temptations to polytheism were everywhere.

Regarding the golden calf, it's interesting to note that a silver calf idol was discovered in the summer of 1990 during an archeological dig at the Canaanite city of Ashkelon. "The bull or calf symbolism expressed in metal and other media was associated with El or Baal, leading deities in the Canaanite pantheon" (Lawrence E. Stager, "When Canaanites and Philistines Ruled Ashkelon," *Biblical Archaeology Review,* p. 28. March/April 1991).

■ **Study 12/A Lasting Covenant**

**Question 3.** A human analogy, though an imperfect one, of God's declaration of his character here is that of parents both praising and disciplining their children. Both are expressions of the parents' love.

**Question 4.** In Genesis 15, God had made a covenant with Abraham (Abram), promising to give this land to his descendants. In that covenant there were no requirements on Abraham's behavior. Now, at Sinai, God commanded obedience in order for the other peoples to be defeated and for Israel to possess the land.

**Question 5.** Compare this incident with Gideon's pulling down of the altar to Baal and the Asherah pole in Judges 6:25-27. The Lord was asking for the destruction of anything which competed with him as an object of worship. He had already warned the Israelites at Sinai that he was "a jealous God" (Exodus 20:5).

**Question 8.** The feasts would remind the people of their miraculous escape from Egypt and the Lord's provision for them in the harvest. They would serve as an annual reminder that they were dependent on the Lord for their freedom, their destiny as a nation, and their daily food.

## ■ Study 13/Giving Back to the Lord

**Question 5.** It's interesting to note that in Exodus 32 the people had freely given their gold to Aaron for an idol. Now, with changed hearts, they willingly brought their gold again to honor God.

Exodus 35:22 mentions that they presented their gold as a "wave offering." This was part of the larger ritual of a "fellowship offering" which expressed gratitude and symbolized peace with God (see Leviticus 7:28-34).

**Question 6.** Refer to Exodus 31:1-6 for God's earlier stamp of approval on these craftsmen.

**Question 9.** Exodus 36–39 give further details about the items the craftsmen built for the tabernacle. These chapters are similar to the descriptions we read previously in Exodus 25–30. While chapters 25–30 give God's instructions through Moses for constructing the items, chapters 36–39 relate how the Israelites carried through and obeyed, making each item as directed.

# WHAT SHOULD WE STUDY NEXT?

To help your group answer that question, we've listed the Fisherman Guides by category so you can choose your next study.

## TOPICAL STUDIES

**Angels,** Wright

**Becoming Women of Purpose,** Barton

**Building Your House on the Lord,** Brestin

**The Creative Heart of God,** Goring

**Discipleship,** Reapsome

**Doing Justice, Showing Mercy,** Wright

**Encouraging Others,** Johnson

**The End Times,** Rusten

**Examining the Claims of Jesus,** Brestin

**Friendship,** Brestin

**The Fruit of the Spirit,** Briscoe

**Great Doctrines of the Bible,** Board

**Great Passages of the Bible,** Plueddemann

**Great Prayers of the Bible,** Plueddemann

**Growing Through Life's Challenges,** Reapsome

**Guidance & God's Will,** Stark

**Heart Renewal,** Goring

**Higher Ground,** Brestin

**Integrity,** Engstrom & Larson

**Lifestyle Priorities,** White

**Marriage,** Stevens

**Miracles,** Castleman

**One Body, One Spirit,** Larson

**The Parables of Jesus,** Hunt

**Prayer,** Jones

**The Prophets,** Wright

**Proverbs & Parables,** Brestin

**Satisfying Work,** Stevens & Schoberg

**Senior Saints,** Reapsome

**Sermon on the Mount,** Hunt

**A Spiritual Legacy,** Christensen

**Spiritual Warfare,** Moreau

**The Ten Commandments,** Briscoe

**Who Is God?** Seemuth

**Who Is Jesus?** Van Reken

**Who Is the Holy Spirit?** Knuckles & Van Reken

**Wisdom for Today's Woman: Insights from Esther,** Smith

**Witnesses to All the World,** Plueddemann

**Worship,** Sibley

## BIBLE BOOK STUDIES

**Genesis,** Fromer & Keyes
**Exodus,** Larsen
**Job,** Klug
**Psalms,** Klug
**Proverbs: Wisdom That Works,**
   Wright
**Jeremiah,** Reapsome
**Jonah, Habakkuk, & Malachi,**
   Fromer & Keyes
**Matthew,** Sibley
**Mark,** Christensen
**Luke,** Keyes
**John: Living Word,** Kuniholm
**Acts 1-12,** Christensen
**Paul (Acts 13-28),** Christiansen
**Romans: The Christian
   Story,** Reapsome
**1 Corinthians,** Hummel

**Strengthened to Serve
   (2 Corinthians),**
   Plueddemann
**Galatians, Titus & Philemon,**
   Kuniholm
**Ephesians,** Baylis
**Philippians,** Klug
**Colossians,** Shaw
**Letters to the Thessalonians,**
   Fromer & Keyes
**Letters to Timothy,** Fromer &
   Keyes
**Hebrews,** Hunt
**James,** Christensen
**1 & 2 Peter, Jude,** Brestin
**How Should a Christian Live?
   (1, 2 & 3 John),** Brestin
**Revelation,** Hunt

## BIBLE CHARACTER STUDIES

**David: Man after God's Own
   Heart,** Castleman
**Elijah,** Castleman
**Great People of the Bible,**
   Plueddemann
**King David: Trusting God for
   a Lifetime,** Castleman
**Men Like Us,** Heidebrecht &
   Scheuermann

**Moses,** Asimakoupoulos
**Paul (Acts 13-28),** Christensen
**Ruth & Daniel,** Stokes
**Women Like Us,** Barton
**Women Who Achieved for
   God,** Christensen
**Women Who Believed God,**
   Christensen

# The Rose Rent

## The Thirteenth Chronicle
## of Brother Cadfael

# ELLIS PETERS

# THE ROSE RENT

## The Thirteenth Chronicle
of Brother Cadfael

Futura

A Futura Book

First published in Great Britain in 1986
by Macmillan London Limited

This Futura edition published in 1987

Copyright © Ellis Peters 1986

ISBN 0 7088 3610 0

Reproduced, printed and bound in Great Britain by
Hazell Watson & Viney Limited,
Member of the BPCC Group,
Aylesbury, Bucks


Futura Publications
A Division of
Macdonald & Co (Publishers) Ltd
Greater London House
Hampstead Road
London NW1 7QX
A BPCC plc Company

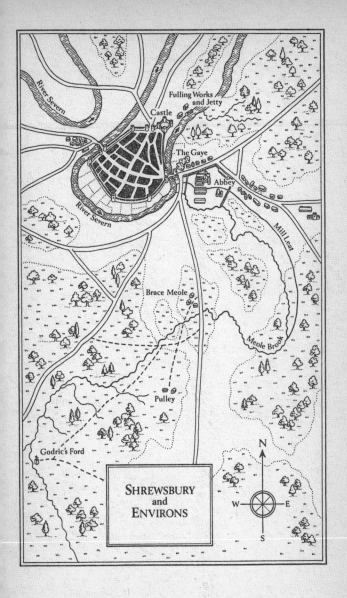

**River Severn**

Fulling Works
and Jetty

Castle

The Gaye

Abbey

River Severn

Mill Leat

Brace Meole

Meole Brook

Pulley

Godric's Ford

SHREWSBURY
and
ENVIRONS

N

W · E

S

# Chapter One

By reason of the prolonged cold, which lingered far into April, and had scarcely mellowed when the month of May began, everything came laggard and reluctant that spring of 1142. The birds kept close about the roofs, finding warmer places to roost. The bees slept late, depleted their stores, and had to be fed, but neither was there any early burst of blossom for them to make fruitful. In the gardens there was no point in planting seed that would rot or be eaten in soil too chilly to engender life.

The affairs of men, stricken with the same petrifying chill, seemed to have subsided into hibernation. Faction held its breath. King Stephen, after the first exhilaration of liberation from his prison, and the Easter journey north to draw together the frayed strings of his influence, had fallen ill in the south, so ill that the rumour of his death had spread throughout England, and his cousin and rival, the Empress Maud, had cautiously moved her headquarters to Oxford, and settled down there to wait patiently and vainly for him to make truth of rumour, which he stubbornly declined to do. He had still business to settle with the lady, and his constitution was more than a match for even this virulent fever. By the end of May he was on his way manfully back to health. By the early days of June the long sub-frost broke. The biting wind changed to a temperate breeze, the sun came out over the earth like a warm hand stroking, the seed stirred in the ground and put forth green blades, and a foam of flowers, all the more exuberant for having been so long restrained, burst forth in gold and purple and white over garden and meadow. The belated sowing began in jubilant haste. And King Stephen, like a giant breaking loose from some crippling enchantment, surged out of his convalescence into vigorous action, and bearing down on the port of Wareham, the most easterly still available to his enemies, seized both town and castle with hardly a graze to show for it.

'And is making north again now towards Cirencester,' reported Hugh Beringar, elated by the news, 'to pick off the empress's outposts one by one, if only he can keep up this storm of energy.' It was the one fatal flaw in the king's military make-up that he could not sustain action for long if he failed to get instant results, but would abandon a siege after three days, and go off to start another elsewhere, squandering for no gain the energy devoted to both. 'We may see a tidy end to it yet!'

Brother Cadfael, preoccupied with his own narrower concerns, continued to survey the vegetable patch outside the wall of his herb-garden, digging an experimental toe into soil grown darker and kinder after a mild morning shower. 'By rights,' he said thoughtfully, 'carrots should have been in more than a month ago, and the first radishes will be fibrous and shrunken as old leather, but we might get something with more juices in it from now on. Lucky the fruit-blossom held back until the bees began to wake up, but even so it will be a thin crop this year. Everything's four weeks behind, but the seasons have a way of catching up, somehow. Wareham, you were saying? What of Wareham?'

'Why, that Stephen has taken it, town and castle and harbour and all. So Robert of Gloucester, who went out by that gate barely ten days earlier, has it slammed in his face now. Did I not tell you? The word came three days since. It seems there was a meeting back in April, in Devizes, between the empress and her brother, and they made it up between them that it was high time the lady's husband should pay a little heed to her affairs, and come over in person to help her get her hands on Stephen's crown. They sent envoys over to Normandy to meet with Geoffrey, but he sent back to say he was well disposed, no question, but the men sent out to him were unknown to him, name or reputation, and he would be uneasy in dealing with any but the Earl of Gloucester himself. If Robert will not come, says Geoffrey, no use sending me any other.'

Cadfael was momentarily distracted from his laggard crops. 'And Robert let himself be persuaded?' he said, marvelling.

'Very reluctantly. He feared to leave his sister to the loyalties of some who were all but ready to desert her after the Westminster shambles, and I doubt if he has any great hopes of getting anything out of the Count of Anjou. But yes, he let himself be persuaded. And he's sailed from Wareham, with less trouble than he'll have sailing back into the same port, now the king holds it. A good, fast move, that was. If he can but maintain it now!'

'We said a Mass in thanksgiving for his recovery,' said Cadfael absently, and plucked out a leggy sow-thistle from among his mint. 'How is it that weeds grow three times faster than the plants we nurse so tenderly? Three days ago that was not even there. If the kale shot up like that I should be pricking the plants out by tomorrow.'

'No doubt your prayers will stiffen Stephen's resolution,' Hugh said, though with less than complete conviction. 'Have they not given you a helper yet, here in the garden? It's high time, there's more than one's work here in this season.'

'So I urged at chapter this morning. What they'll offer me there's no knowing. Prior Robert has one or two among the younger ones he'd be glad to shuffle off his hands and into mine. Happily the ones he least approves tend to be those with more wit and spirit than the rest, not less. I may yet be lucky in my apprentice.'

He straightened his back, and stood looking out over the newly turned beds, and the pease-fields that sloped down to the Meole Brook, mentally casting an indulgent eye back over the most recent of his helpers here in the herbarium. Big, jaunty, comely Brother John, who had blundered into the cloister by mistake, and backed out of it, not without the connivance of friends, in Wales, to exchange the role of brother for that of husband and father; Brother Mark, entering here as an undersized and maltreated sixteen-year-old, shy and quiet, and grown into a clear, serene maturity of spirit that drew him away inevitably towards the priesthood. Cadfael still missed Brother Mark, attached now to the household chapel of the Bishop of Lichfield, and already a deacon. And after Mark, Brother Oswin, cheerful, confident and ham-fisted, gone now to do his year's service at the lazarhouse of Saint Giles at the edge of the town. What next, wondered Cadfael? Put a dozen young men into the same rusty black habits, shave their heads, fit them into a single horarium day after day and year after year, and still they will all be irremediably different, every one unique. Thank God!

'Whatever they send you,' said Hugh, keeping pace with him along the broad green path that circled the fish-ponds, 'you'll have transformed by the time he leaves you. Why should they waste a simple, sweet saint like Rhun on you? He's made already, he came into the world made. You'll get the rough, the obdurate, the unstable to lick into shape. Not that it ever comes out the shape that was expected,' he added, with a flashing grin and a slanted glance along his shoulder at his friend.

'Rhun has taken upon himself the custody of Saint Winifred's altar,' said Cadfael. 'He has a proprietorial interest in the little lady. He makes the candles for her himself, and borrows essences from me to scent them for her. No, Rhun will find his own duties, and no one will stand in his way. He and she between them will see to that.'

They crossed the little foot-bridge over the leat that fed the pools and the mill, and emerged into the rose-garden. The trimmed bushes had made little growth as yet, but the first buds were swelling at last, the green sheaths parting to show a sliver of red or white. 'They'll open fast now,' said Cadfael contentedly. 'All they needed was warmth. I'd begun to wonder whether the Widow Perle would get her rent on time this year, but if these are making up for lost time, so will her white ones be. A sad year, if there were no roses by the twenty-second day of June!'

'The Widow Perle? Oh, yes, the Vestier girl!' said Hugh. 'I remember! So it's due on the day of Saint Winifred's translation, is it? How many years is it now since she made the gift?'

'This will be the fourth time we've paid her her annual rent. One white rose from that bush in her old garden, to be delivered to her on the day of Saint Winifred's translation—'

'Supposed translation,' said Hugh, grinning. 'And you

should blush when you name it.'

'So I do, but with my complexion who notices?' And he was indeed of a rosy russet colouring, confirmed by long years of outdoor living in both east and west, so engrained now that winters merely tarnished it a little, and summers regularly renewed the gloss.

'She made modest demands,' observed Hugh thoughtfully, as they came to the second plank-bridge that spanned the channel drawn off to service the guest-hall. 'Most of our solid merchants up in the town value property a good deal higher than roses.'

'She had already lost what she most valued,' said Cadfael. 'Husband and child both, within twenty days. He died, and she miscarried. She could not bear to go on living, alone, in the house where they had been happy together. But it was because she valued it that she wanted it spent for God, not hoarded up with the rest of a property large enough to provide handsomely even without it for herself and all her kinsfolk and workfolk. It pays for the lighting and draping of Our Lady's altar the whole year round. It's what she chose. But just the one link she kept – one rose a year. He was a very comely man, Edred Perle,' said Cadfael, shaking his head mildly over the vulnerability of beauty, 'I saw him pared away to the bone in a searing fever, and had no art to cool him. A man remembers that.'

'You've seen many such,' said Hugh reasonably, 'here and on the fields of Syria, long ago.'

'So I have! So I have! Did ever you hear me say I'd forgotten any one of them? But a young, handsome man, shrivelled away before his time, before even his prime, and his girl left without even his child to keep him in mind . . . A sad enough case, you'll allow.'

'She's young,' said Hugh with indifferent practicality, his mind being on other things. 'She should marry again.'

'So think a good many of our merchant fathers in the town,' agreed Cadfael with a wry smile, 'the lady being as wealthy as she is, and sole mistress of the Vestiers' clothier business. But after what she lost, I doubt if she'll look at a grey old skinflint like Godfrey Fuller, who's buried two wives already and made a profit out of both of them, and has his eye on a third fortune with the next. Or a fancy young fellow in search of an easy living!'

'Such as?' invited Hugh, amused.

'Two or three I could name. William Hynde's youngster, for one, if my gossips tell me truth. And the lad who's foreman of her own weavers is a very well-looking young man, and fancies his chance with her. Even her neighbour the saddler is looking for a wife, I'm told, and thinks she might very well do.'

Hugh burst into affectionate laughter, and clapped him boisterously on the shoulders as they emerged into the great court, and the quiet, purposeful bustle before Mass. 'How many eyes and ears have you in every street in Shrewsbury? I wish my own intelligencers knew half as much of what goes on. A pity your influence falls short of Normandy. I might get some inkling then of what Robert and Geoffrey are up to there. Though I think,' he said, growing grave again as he turned back to his own preoccupations, 'Geoffrey is far more concerned with getting possession of Normandy than with wasting his time on England. From all accounts he's making fast inroads there, he's not likely to draw off now. Far more like to inveigle Robert into helping him than offering much help to Robert.

'He certainly shows very little interest in his wife,' agreed Cadfael drily, 'or her ambitions. Well, we shall see if Robert can sway him. Are you coming in to Mass this morning?'

'No, I'm away to Maesbury tomorrow for a week or two. They should have been shearing before this, but they put it off for a while because of the cold. They'll be hard at it now. I'll leave Aline and Giles there for the summer. But I'll be back and forth, in case of need.'

'A summer without Aline, and without my godson,' said Cadfael reprovingly, 'is no prospect to spring on me without preamble, like this. Are you not ashamed?'

'Not a whit! For I came, among other errands, to bid you to supper with us tonight, before we leave early in the morning. Abbot Radulfus has given his leave and blessing. Go, pray for fair weather and a smooth ride for us,' said Hugh heartily, and gave his friend a vigorous shove towards the corner of the cloister and the south door of the church.

It was purely by chance, or a symbol of that strange compulsion that brings the substance hard on the heels of the recollection, that the sparse company of worshippers in the parish part of the church at the monastic Mass that day should include the Widow Perle. There were always a few of the laity there on their knees beyond the parish altar, some who had missed their parish Mass for varying reasons, some who were old and solitary and filled up their lonely time with supererogatory worship, some who had special pleas to make, and sought an extra opportunity of approaching grace. Some, even, who had other business in the Foregate, and welcomed a haven meantime for thought and quietness, which was the case of the Widow Perle.

From his stall in the choir Brother Cadfael could just see the suave line of her head, shoulder and arm, beyond the bulk of the parish altar. It was strange that so quiet and unobtrusive a woman should nevertheless be so instantly recognisable even in this fragmentary glimpse. It might have been the way she carried her straight and slender shoulders, or the great mass of her brown hair weighing down the head so reverently inclined over clasped hands, hidden from his sight by the altar. She was barely twenty-five years old, and had enjoyed only three years of a happy marriage, but she went about her deprived and solitary life without fuss or complaint, cared scrupulously for a business which gave her no personal pleasure, and faced the prospect of perpetual loneliness with a calm countenance and a surprising supply of practical energy. In happiness or unhappiness, living is a duty, and must be done thoroughly.

A blessing, at any rate, thought Cadfael, that she is not utterly alone, she has her mother's sister to keep the house for her now she lives, as it were, over her shop, and her cousin for a conscientious foreman and manager, to take the weight of the business off her shoulders. And one rose every year for the rent of the house and garden in the Foregate, where her man died. The only gesture of passion and grief and loss she ever made, to give away voluntarily her most valuable property, the house where she had been happy, and yet ask for that one reminder, and nothing more.

She was not a beautiful woman, Judith Perle, born Judith Vestier, and sole heiress to the biggest clothiers' business in the town. But she had a bodily dignity that would draw the eye even in a market crowd, above the common height for a woman, slender and erect, and with a carriage and walk of notable grace. The great coils of her shining light-brown hair, the colour of seasoned oak timber, crowned a pale face that tapered from wide and lofty brow to pointed chin, by way of strong cheekbones and hollow cheeks, and an eloquent, mobile mouth too wide for beauty, but elegantly shaped. Her eyes were of a deep grey, and very clear and wide, neither confiding nor hiding anything. Cadfael had been eye to eye with her, four years ago now, across her husband's death-bed, and she had neither lowered her lids nor turned her glance aside, but stared unwaveringly as her life's happiness slipped irresistibly away through her fingers. Two weeks later she had miscarried, and lost even her child. Edred had left her nothing.

Hugh is right, thought Cadfael, forcing his mind back to the liturgy. She is young, she should marry again.

The June light, now approaching the middle hours of the day, and radiant with sunshine, fell in long golden shafts across the body of the choir and into the ranks of the brothers and obedientiaries opposite, gilding half a face here and throwing its other half into exaggerated shade, there causing dazzled eyes in a blanched face to blink away the brightness. The vault above received the diffused reflections in a soft, muted glow, plucking into relief the curved leaves of the stone bosses. Music and light seemed to mate only there in the zenith. Summer trod hesitantly into the church at last, after prolonged hibernation.

It seemed that brother Cadfael was not the only one whose mind was wandering when it should have been fixed. Brother Anselm the precentor, absorbed into his singing, lifted a rapt face into the sun, his eyes closed, since he knew every note without study or thought. But beside him Brother Eluric, custodian of Saint Mary's altar in the Lady Chapel, responded only absently, his head turned aside, towards the parish altar and the soft murmur of responses from beyond.

Brother Eluric was a child of the cloister, not long a full brother, and entrusted with his particular charge by reason of his undoubted deserving, tempered by the reserve that was felt about admitting child oblates to full office, at least until they had been mature for a number of years. An unreasonable reserve, Cadfael had always felt, seeing that the child oblates were regarded as the perfect innocents, equivalent to the angels, while the *conversi*, those who came voluntarily and in maturity to the monastic life, were the fighting saints, those who had endured and mastered their imperfections. So Saint Anselm had classified them, and ordered them never to attempt reciprocal reproaches, never to feel envy. But still the *conversi* were preferred for the responsible offices, perhaps as having experience of the deceits and complexities and temptations of the world around them. But the care of an altar, its light, its draperies, the special prayers belonging to it, this could well be the charge of an innocent.

Brother Eluric was past twenty now, the most learned and devout of his contemporaries, a tall, well-made young man, black-haired and black-eyed. He had been in the cloister since he was three years old, and knew nothing outside it. Unacquainted with sin, he was all the more haunted by it, as by some unknown monster, and assiduous in confession, he picked to pieces his own infinitesimal failings, with the mortal penitence due to deadly sins. A curious thing, that so over-conscientious a youth should be paying so little heed to the holy office. His chin was on his shoulder, his lips still, forgetting the words of the psalm. He was gazing, in fact, precisely where Cadfael had been gazing only moments earlier. But from Eluric's stall there would be more of her to see, Cadfael reflected, the averted face, the linked hands, the folds of linen over her breast.

The contemplation, it seemed, gave him no joy, but only a brittle, quivering tension, taut as a drawn bow. When he recollected himself and tore his gaze away, it was with a wrench that shook him from head to foot.

Well, well! said Cadfael to himself, enlightened. And in eight days more he has to carry the rose rent to her. That task they should have allotted to some old hardened sinner like me, who would view and enjoy, and return untroubled and untroubling, not this vulnerable boy who surely can never else have been alone in a room with a woman since his mother let him be taken out of her arms. And a pity she ever did!

And this poor girl, the very image to wring him most painfully, grave, sad, with a piteous past and yet composed and calm like the Blessed Virgin herself. And he coming to her bearing a white rose, their hands perhaps touching as he delivers it. And now I recall that Anselm says he's something of a poet. Well, what follies we commit without evil intent!

It was far too late now to devote his mind to its proper business of prayer and praise. He contented himself with hoping that by the time the brothers emerged from the choir after service the lady would be gone.

By the mercy of God, she was.

But she was gone, it seemed, no further than Cadfael's workshop in the herb-garden, where he found her waiting patiently outside the open door when he came to decant the lotion he had left cooling before Mass. Her brow was smooth and her voice mild, and everything about her practical and sensible. The fire that burned Eluric was unknown to her. At Cadfael's invitation she followed him in, under the gently swaying bunches of herbs that rustled overhead from the beams.

'You once made me an ointment, Brother Cadfael, if you remember. For a rash on the hands. There's one of my carders breaks out in little pustules, handling the new fleeces. But not every season – that's strange too. This year she has trouble with it again.'

'I remember it,' said Cadfael. 'It was three years ago. Yes, I know the receipt. I can make some fresh for you in a matter of minutes, if you've leisure to wait?'

It seemed that she had. She sat down on the wooden bench against the timber wall, and drew her dark skirts close about her feet, very erect and still in the corner of the hut, as Cadfael reached for pestle and mortar, and the little scale with its brass weights.

'And how are you faring now?' he asked, busy with hog's fat and herbal oils. 'Up there in the town?'

'Well enough,' she said composedly. 'The business gives

me plenty to do, and the wool clip has turned out better than I feared. I can't complain. Isn't it strange,' she went on, warming, 'that wool should bring up this rash for Branwen, when you use the fat from wool to doctor skin diseases for many people?'

'Such contrary cases do happen,' he said. 'There are plants some people cannot handle without coming to grief. No one knows the reason. We learn by observing. You had good results with this salve, I remember.'

'Oh, yes, her hands healed very quickly. But I think perhaps I should keep her from carding, and teach her weaving. When the wool is washed and dyed and spun, perhaps she could handle it more safely. She's a good girl, she would soon learn.'

It seemed to Cadfael, working away with his back turned to her, that she was talking to fill the silence while she thought, and thought of something far removed from what she was saying. It was no great surprise when she said suddenly, and in a very different voice, abrupt and resolute: 'Brother Cadfael, I have thoughts of taking the veil. Serious thoughts! The world is not so desirable that I should hesitate to leave it, nor my condition so hopeful that I dare look for a better time to come. The business can do very well without me; Cousin Miles runs it very profitably, and values it more than I do. Oh, I do my duty well enough, as I was always taught to do, but he could do it every bit as well without me. Why should I hesitate?'

Cadfael turned to face her, the mortar balanced on his palm. 'Have you said as much to your aunt and your cousin?'

'I have mentioned it.'

'And what do they say to it?'

'Nothing. It's left to me. Miles will neither commend nor advise, he brushes it aside. I think he doesn't take me seriously. My aunt – you know her a little? She's widowed like me, and for ever lamenting it, even after years. She talks of the peace of the cloister, and release from the cares of the world. But she always talks so, though I know she's well content with her comfortable life if the truth were told. I live, Brother Cadfael, I do my work, but I am not content. It would be something settled and stable, to take to the cloister.'

'And wrong,' said Cadfael firmly. 'Wrong, at least, for you.'

'Why would it be so wrong?' she challenged. The hood had slipped back from her head, the great braid of light-brown hair, silver-lit like veined oak, glowed faintly in the subdued light.

'No one should take to the cloistered life as a second-best, and that is what you would be doing. It must be embraced out of genuine desire, or not at all. It is not enough to wish to escape from the world without, you must be on fire for the world within.'

'Was it so with you?' she asked, and suddenly she smiled, and her austere face kindled into warmth for a moment.

He considered that in silence for a brief, cautious while. 'I came late to it, and it may be that my fire burned somewhat dully,' he said honestly at length, 'but it gave light enough to show me the road to what I wanted. I was running towards, not away.'

She looked him full in the face with her daunting, direct eyes, and said with abrupt, bleak deliberation: 'Have you never thought, Brother Cadfael, that a woman may have more cause to run away than ever you had? More perils to run from, and fewer alternatives than flight?'

'That is truth,' admitted Cadfael, stirring vigorously. 'But you, as I know, are better placed than many to hold your own, as well as having more courage than a good many of us men. You are your own mistress, your kin depend on you, and not you on them. There is no overlord to claim the right to order your future, no one can force you into another marriage – yes, I have heard there are many would be only too pleased if they could, but they have no power over you. No father living, no elder kinsman to influence you. No matter how men may pester you or affairs weary you, you know you are more than equal to them. And as for what you have lost,' he said, after a moment's hesitation as to whether he should tread so near, 'it is lost only to this world. Waiting is not easy, but no harder, believe me, among the vexations and distractions of the world than in the solitude and silence of the cloister. I have seen men make that mistake, for as reasonable cause, and suffer all the more with the double deprivation. Do not you take that risk. Never unless you are sure of what you want, and want it with all your heart and soul.'

It was as much as he dared say, as much as and perhaps more than he had any right to say. She heard him out without turning her eyes away. He felt their clear stare heavy upon him all the time he was smoothing his ointment into its jar for her, and tying down the lid of the pot for safe carriage.

'Sister Magdalen, from the Benedictine cell at Godric's Ford,' he said, 'is coming to Shrewsbury in two days' time, to fetch away Brother Edmund's niece, who wants to join the sisterhood there. As for the girl's motives, I know nothing of them, but if Sister Magdalen is accepting her as a novice it must be from conviction, and moreover, the child will be carefully watched, and get no further than her novitiate unless Magdalen is satisfied of her vocation. Will you speak with her about this? I think you already know something of her.'

'I do.' Judith's voice was soft, and yet there was a shade of quiet amusement in the tone. 'Her own motives, I think, when she entered Godric's Ford, were scarcely what you are demanding.'

That was something he could not well deny. Sister Magdalen had formerly been, for many years, the constant mistress of a certain nobleman, and on his death had looked about her with single-minded resolution for another field in which to employ her undoubted talents. No question but the choice of the cloister had been coolly and practically made. What redeemed it was the vigour and loyalty she had devoted to it since the day of her entry, and would maintain, without question, until the day of her death.

'In no way that I know of,' admitted Cadfael, 'is Sister Magdalen anything but unique. You are right, she entered the cell seeking not a vocation, but a career, and a career she is making, and a notable one, too. Mother Mariana is old and bedridden now; the weight of the cell falls all on Magdalen, and I know no shoulders better fitted to carry it. And I do not think she would say to you, as I said, that there is but one good reason for taking the veil, true longing for the life of the spirit. The more reason you could and should listen to her

19

advice and weigh it carefully, before you take so grave a step. And bear in mind, you are young, she had said goodbye to her prime.'

'And I have buried mine,' said Judith very firmly, and as one stating truth, without self-pity.

'Well, if it comes to second-bests,' said Cadfael, 'they can be found outside the cloister as well as within. Managing the business your fathers built up, providing employment for so many people, is itself a sufficient justification for a life, for want of better.'

'It does not put me to any great test,' she said indifferently. 'Ah, well, I said only that I had been thinking of quitting the world. Nothing is done, as yet. And whether or no, I shall be glad to talk with Sister Magdalen, for I do value her wit, and know better than to discard unconsidered whatever she may say. Let me know when she comes, and I will send and bid her to my house, or go to her wherever she is lodged.'

She rose to take the jar of ointment from him. Standing, she was the breadth of two fingers taller than he, but thin and slender-boned. The coils of her hair would have seemed over-heavy if she had not carried her head so nobly.

'Your roses are budding well,' she said, as he went out with her along the gravel path from the workshop. 'However late they come, they always bloom equally in the end.'

It could have been a metaphor for the quality of a life, he thought, as they had been discussing it. But he did not say so. Better leave her to the shrewd and penetrating wisdom of Sister Magdalen. 'And yours?' he said. 'There'll be a choice of blooms when Saint Winifred's feast comes round. You should have the best and freshest for your fee.'

The most fleeting of smiles crossed her face, and left her sombre again, her eyes on the path. 'Yes,' she said, and nothing more, though it seemed there should have been more. Was it possible that she had noted and been troubled by the same trouble that haunted Eluric? Three times he had carried the rose rent to her, a matter of ... how long ... in her presence? Two minutes annually? Three, perhaps? But no man's shadow clouded Judith Perle's eyes, no living man's. She might, none the less, have become somehow aware, thought Cadfael, not of a young man's physical entrance into her house and presence, but of the nearness of pain.

'I'm going there now,' she said, stirring out of her preoccupation. 'I've lost the buckle of a good girdle, I should like to have a new one made, to match the rosettes that decorate the leather, and the end-tag. Enamel inlay on the bronze. It was a present Edred once made to me. Niall Bronzesmith will be able to copy the design. He's a fine craftsman. I'm glad the abbey has such a good tenant for the house.'

'A decent, quiet man,' agreed Cadfael, 'and keeps the garden well tended. You'll find your rose-bush in very good heart.'

To that she made no reply, only thanked him simply for his services as they entered the great court together, and there separated, she to continue along the Foregate to the large house beyond the abbey forge, where she had spent the few years of her married life, he to the lavatorium to wash his hands before dinner. But he turned at the corner of the cloister to look after her, and watched until she passed through the arch of the gatehouse and vanished from his sight. She had a walk that might be very becoming in an abbess, but to his mind it looked just as well on the capable heiress of the chief clothier in the town. He went on to the refectory convinced that he was right in dissuading her from the conventual life. If she looked upon it as a refuge now, the time might come when it would seem to her a prison, and none the less constricting because she would have entered it willingly.

# Chapter Two

The house in the Foregate stood well along towards the grassy triangle of the horse-fair ground, where the high road turned the corner of the abbey wall. A lower wall on the opposite side of the road closed in the yard where Niall the bronzesmith had his shop and workshop, and beyond lay the substantial and well-built house with its large garden, and a small field of grazing land behind. Niall did a good trade in everything from brooches and buttons, small weights and pins, to metal cooking pots, ewers and dishes, and paid the abbey a suitable rent for his premises. He had even worked occasionally with others of his trade in the founding of bells, but that was a very rare commission, and demanded travel to the site itself, rather than having to transport the heavy bells after casting.

The smith was working in a corner of his shop, on the rim of a dish beaten out in sheet metal, pecking away with punch and mallet at an incised decoration of leaves, when Judith came in to his counter. From the unshuttered window above the work-bench the light fell softly sidewise upon her face and figure, and Niall, turning to see who had entered, stood for a moment at gaze with his tools dangling in either hand, before he laid them down and came to wait upon her.

'Your servant, mistress! What can I do for you?'

They were barely acquaintances, merely shopkeeper-craftsman and customer, and yet the very fact that he now did his work in the house which she had given to the abbey made them study each other with a special intensity. She had been in his shop perhaps five times in the few years since he had rented it; he had supplied her with pins, points for the laces of bodices, small utensils for her kitchen, the matrix for the seal of the Vestier household. He knew her history, the gift of the house had made it public. She knew little of him beyond the fact that he had come to her erstwhile property as the abbey's tenant, and that the man and his work were well regarded in town and Foregate.

Judith laid her damaged girdle upon the long counter, a strip of fine, soft leather, excellently worked and ornamented with a series of small bronze rosettes round the holes for the tongue, and a bronze sheath protecting the end of the belt. The bright enamel inlays within the raised outlines were clear and fresh, but the stitching at the other end had worn through, and the buckle was gone.

'I lost it somewhere in the town,' she said, 'one night after dark, and never noticed under my cloak that girdle and all had slipped down and were gone. When I went back to look for it I could find only the belt, not the buckle. It was muddy weather, and the kennel running with the thaw. My own fault, I knew it was fraying, I should have made it secure.'

'Delicate work,' said the smith, fingering the end-tag with interest. 'That was not bought here, surely?'

'Yes, it was, but at the abbey fair, from a Flemish merchant. I wore it much,' she said, 'in earlier days, but it's been laid by since the winter, when I lost the buckle. Can you make me a new one, to match these colours and designs? It was a long shape – thus!' She drew it on the counter with a fingertip. 'But it need not be so, you could make it oval, or whatever you think suits best.'

Their heads were close together over the counter. She looked up into his face, mildly startled by its nearness, but he was intent upon the detail of the bronzework and inlay, and unaware of her sharp scrutiny. A decent, quiet man, Cadfael had called him, and coming from Cadfael there was nothing dismissive in that description. Decent, quiet men were the backbone of any community, to be respected and valued beyond those who made the biggest commotion and the most noise in the world. Niall the bronzesmith could have provided the portrait for them all. He was of the middle height and the middle years, and even of the middle brown colouring, and his voice was pitched pleasantly low. His age, she thought, might be forty years. When he straightened up they stood virtually eye to eye, and the movements of his large, capable hands were smooth, firm and deft.

Everything about him fitted into the picture of the ordinary, worthy soul almost indistinguishable from his neighbour, and yet the sum of the parts was very simply and positively himself and no other man. He had thick brown brows in a wide-boned face, and wide-set eyes of a deep, sunny hazel. There were a few grizzled hairs in his thick brown thatch, and a solid, peaceful jut to his shaven chin.

'Are you in haste for it?' he asked. 'I should like to make a good job of it. If I may take two or three days over it.'

'There's no hurry,' she said readily. 'I've neglected it long enough, another week is no great matter.'

'Then shall I bring it up to you in the town? I know the place, I could save you the walk.' He made the offer civilly but hesitantly, as though it might be taken as presumption rather than simply meant as a courtesy.

She cast a rapid glance about his shop, and saw evidences enough that he had in hand a great deal of work, more than enough to keep him busy all through the labouring day. 'But I think your time is very well filled. If you have a boy, perhaps – but I can as well come for it.'

'I work alone,' said Niall. 'But I'd willingly bring it up to you in the evening, when the light's going. I've no other calls on my time, it's no hardship to work the clock round.'

'You live alone here?' she asked, confirmed in her assumptions about him. 'No wife? No family?'

'I lost my wife, five years ago. I'm used to being alone, it's a simple enough matter to take care of my few needs. But I have a little girl. Her mother died bearing her.' He saw the sudden tension in her face, the faint spark in her eyes as she reared her head and glanced round, half expecting to see some evidence of a child's presence. 'Oh, not here! I should have been hard put to it to care for a newborn babe, and there's my sister, out at Pulley, no great distance, married to Mortimer's steward at the demesne there, and with two boys and a girl of her own, not very much older. My little lass stays there with them, where she has other children for playmates, and a woman's care. I walk over to see her every Sunday, and sometimes in the evenings, too, but she's better with Cecily and John and the youngsters than here solitary with me, leastways while she's still so young.'

Judith drew breath long and deeply. Widower he might be, and his loss there as bitter as hers, but he had one priceless pledge left to him, while she was barren. 'You don't know,' she said abruptly, 'how I envy you. My child I lost.' She had not meant to say so much, but it came out of her naturally and bluntly, and naturally and bluntly he received it.

'I heard of your trouble, mistress. I was mortally sorry then, having known the like myself not so long before. But the little one at least was spared to me. I thank God for that. When a man suffers such a wound, he also finds out how to value such a mercy.'

'Yes,' she said, and turned away sharply. 'Well . . . I trust your daughter thrives,' she said, recovering, 'and will always be a joy to you. I'll come for the girdle in three days' time, if that's enough for you. No need to bring it.'

She was in the doorway of the shop before he could speak, and then there seemed nothing of any significance to say. But he watched her cross the yard and turn into the Foregate, and turned back to his work at the bench only when she had vanished from his sight.

It was late in the afternoon, but still an hour short of Vespers at this season of the year, when Brother Eluric, custodian of Saint Mary's altar, slipped almost furtively away from his work in the scriptorium, crossed the great court to the abbot's lodging in its small fenced garden, and asked for audience. His manner was so taut and brittle that Brother Vitalis, chaplain and secretary to Abbot Radulfus, raised questioning eyebrows, and hesitated before announcing him. But Radulfus was absolute that every son of the house in trouble or need of advice must have ready access to him. Vitalis shrugged, and went in to ask leave, which was readily given.

In the panelled parlour the bright sunlight softened into a mellow haze. Eluric halted just within the doorway, and heard the door gently closed at his back. Radulfus was sitting at his desk near the open window, quill in hand, and did not look up for a moment from his writing. Against the light his aquiline profile showed dark and calm, an outline of gold shaping lofty brow and lean cheek. Eluric went in great awe of him, and yet was drawn gratefully to that composure and certainty, so far out of his own scope.

Radulfus put a period to his well-shaped sentence, and laid down his quill in the bronze tray before him. 'Yes, my son? I am here. I am listening.' He looked up. 'If you have need of me, ask freely.'

'Father,' said Eluric, from a throat constricted and dry, and in a voice so low it was barely audible across the room, 'I have a great trouble. I hardly know how to tell it, or how far it must be seen as shame and guilt to me, though God knows I have struggled with it, and been constant in prayer to keep myself from evil. I am both petitioner and penitent, and yet I have not sinned, and by your grace and understanding may still be saved from offence.'

Radulfus eyed him more sharply, and saw the tension that stiffened the young man's body, and set him quivering like a drawn bowstring. An over-intense boy, always racked by remorse for faults as often as not imaginary, or so venial that to inflate them into sins was itself an offence, being a distortion of truth.

'Child,' said the abbot tolerantly, 'from all I know of you, you are too forward to take to your charge as great sins such small matters as a wise man would think unworthy of mention. Beware of inverted pride! Moderation in all things is not the most spectacular path to perfection, but it is the safest and the most modest. Now speak up plainly, and let's see what between us we can do to end your trouble.' And he added briskly: 'Come closer! Let me see you clearly, and hear you make good sense.'

Eluric crept closer, linked his hands before him in a nervous convulsion that whitened the knuckles perceptibly, and moistened his dry lips. 'Father, in eight days' time it will be the day of Saint Winifred's translation, and the rose rent must be paid for the property in the Foregate . . . to Mistress Perle, who gave the house by charter on those terms . . .'

'Yes,' said Radulfus, 'I know it. Well?'

'Father, I came to beg you to release me from this duty. Three times I have carried the rose to her, according to the charter, and with every year it grows harder for me. Do not send me there again! Lift this burden from me, before I founder! It is more than I can bear.' He was shaking violently, and had difficulty in continuing to speak, so that the words came in painful bursts, like gouts of blood from a wound. 'Father, the very sight and sound of her are torment to me, to be in the same room with her is the pain of death. I have prayed, I have kept vigil, I have implored God and the saints for deliverance from sin, but not all my prayers and austerities could keep me from this uninvited love.'

Radulfus sat silent for a while after the last word had been said, and his face had not changed, beyond a certain sharpening of his attention, a steady gleam in his deep-set eyes.

'Love, of itself,' he said at last with deliberation, 'is not sin, cannot be sin, though it may lead into sin. Has any word of this inordinate affection ever been said between you and the woman, any act or look that would blemish your vows or her purity?'

'No! No, Father, never! Never word of any sort but in civil greeting and farewell, and a blessing, due to such a benefactress. Nothing wrong has been done or said, only my heart is the offender. She knows nothing of my torment, she never has nor never will give one thought to me but as the messenger of this house. God forbid she should ever come to know, for she is blameless. It is for her sake, as well as mine, that I pray to be excused from ever seeing her again, for such pain as I feel might well disturb and distress her, even without understanding. The last thing I wish is for her to suffer.'

Radulfus rose abruptly from his seat, and Eluric, drained with the effort of confession and convinced of guilt, sank to his knees and bowed his head into his hands, expecting condemnation. But the abbot merely turned away to the window, and stood for a while looking out into the sunlit afternoon, where his own roses were coming into lavish bud.

No more oblates, the abbot was reflecting ruefully, and thanking God for it. No more taking these babes out of their cradles and severing them from the very sight and sound of women, half the creation stolen out of their world. How can they be expected to deal capably at last with something as

27

strange and daunting to them as dragons? Sooner or later a woman must cross their path, terrible as an army with banners, and these wretched children without arms or armour to withstand the onslaught! We wrong women, and we wrong these boys, to send them unprepared into maturity, whole men, defenceless against the first pricking of the flesh. In defending them from perils we have deprived them of the means to defend themselves. Well, no more now! Those who enter here henceforward will be of manhood's years, enter of their own will, bear their own burdens. But this one's burden falls upon me.

He turned back into the room. Eluric knelt brokenly, his smooth young hands spread painfully to cover his face, and slow tears sliding between the fingers.

'Look up!' said Radulfus firmly, and as the young, tortured face was turned up to him fearfully: 'Now answer me truly, and don't be afraid. You have never spoken word of love to this lady?'

'No, Father!'

'Nor she ever offered such a word to you, nor such a look as could inflame or invite love?'

'No, Father, never, never! She is utterly untouched. I am nothing to her.' And he added with despairing tears: 'It is I who have in some way besmirched her, to my shame, by loving her, though she knows nothing of it.'

'Indeed? In what way has your unhappy affection befouled the lady? Tell me this, did ever you let your fancy dwell on touching her? On embracing her? On possessing her?'

'No!' cried Eluric in a great howl of pain and dismay. 'God forbid! How could I so profane her? I revere her, I think of her as of the company of the saints. When I trim the candles her goodness provides, I see her face as a brightness. I am no more than her pilgrim. But ah, it hurts . . .' he said, and bowed himself into the skirts of the abbot's gown and clung there.

'Hush!' said the abbot peremptorily, and laid his hand on the bowed head. 'You use extravagant terms for what is wholly human and natural. Excess is blameworthy, and in that field you do indeed offend. But it is plain that in the matter of this unhappy temptation you have not done ill, but

28

in truth rather well. Nor need you fear any reproach to the lady, whose virtue you do well to extol. You have not harmed her. I know you for one unfailingly truthful, insofar as you see and understand truth. For truth is no simple matter, my son, and the mind of man is stumbling and imperfect in wisdom. I blame myself that I submitted you to this trial. I should have foreseen its severity for one as young and unpractised as you. Get up now! You have what you came to ask. You are excused from this duty henceforth.'

He took Eluric by the wrists, and hoisted him firmly to his feet, for he was so drained and trembling with weakness that it seemed doubtful if he could have risen unaided. The boy began to utter stumbling thanks, his tongue lame now even upon ordinary words. The calm of exhaustion and relief came back gradually to his face. But still he found something to fret him even in his release.

'Father . . . the charter . . . It will be void if the rose is not delivered and the rent paid.'

'The rose will be delivered,' said Radulfus forcibly. 'The rent will be paid. This task I lift here and now from your shoulders. Tend your altar, and give no further thought to how or by whom the duty is undertaken from this day.'

'Father, what more should I do for the cleansing of my soul?' ventured Eluric, quivering to the last subsiding tremors of guilt.

'Penance may well be salutary for you,' admitted the abbot somewhat wearily. 'But beware of making extravagant claims even upon punishment. You are far from a saint – so are we all – but neither are you a notable sinner; nor, my child, will you ever be.'

'God forbid!' whispered Eluric, appalled.

'God does indeed forbid,' said Radulfus drily, 'that we should make more of our virtues or our failings than is due. More than your due you shall not have of, neither praise nor blame. For your soul's ease, go and make your confession as I have ordered, with moderation, but say to your confessor that you have also been with me, and have my countenance and blessing, and are by me delivered from the duty which was too heavy for you. Then perform whatever penance he may give you, and beware of asking or expecting more.'

Brother Eluric went out from the presence on shaky legs, emptied of all feeling, and dreading that this emptiness could not last. It was not pleasure, but at least it was not pain. He had been dealt with kindly, he who had come to this interview looking upon success and release from the ordeal of the woman's nearness as the end of all his troubles, yet now this void within him was like the house swept clean in the Bible, ready for residence, aching to be filled, and as apt for devils as for angels.

He did as he had been bidden. Until the end of his novitiate his confessor had been Brother Jerome, ear and shadow of Prior Robert, and from Jerome he could have counted on all the chastisement his over-anxious soul desired. But now it was to the sub-prior, Richard, that he must turn, and Richard was known to be easy and consoling to his penitents, as much out of laziness as kindliness. Eluric did his best to obey the abbot's injunction, not to spare himself but not to accuse himself of what he had not committed, even in his secret mind. When it was done, penance allotted and absolution given, still he knelt, with closed eyes and brows painfully drawn together.

'Is there more?' asked Richard.

'No, Father . . . No more to tell of what is done. Only I am afraid . . .' The numbness was beginning to melt, a small ache had begun in his guts, the empty house would not long be uninhabited. 'I will do all I may to put away even the memory of this illicit affection, but I am not sure . . . I am not sure! How if I fail? I go in dread of my own heart . . .'

'My son, whenever that heart fails you, you must go to the source of all strength and compassion, and pray to be aided, and grace will not fail you. You serve the altar of Our Lady, who is perfect purity. Where better could you turn for grace?'

Where, indeed! But grace is not a river into which a man can dip his pail at will, but a fountain that plays when it lists, and when it lists is dry and still. Eluric performed his penance before the altar he had newly trimmed, kneeling on the chill tiles of the floor, his whispering voice half-choked with passion, and kneeled still when he was done, with every nerve and sinew of his body imploring plenitude and peace.

Surely he should have been happy, for he was vindicated, delivered from the weight of mortal guilt, saved from ever having to see the face of Judith Perle again, or hear her voice, or breathe the faint sweetness that distilled out of her clothing as she moved. Free of that torment and temptation, he had believed his troubles were at an end. Now he knew better.

He knotted his hands into pain, and burst into a fury of passionate, silent prayers to the Virgin whose faithful servant he was, and who could and must stand by him now. But when he opened his eyes and looked up into the mellow golden cones of the candle-flames, there was the woman's face radiant before him, a dazzling, insistent brightness.

He had escaped nothing, all he had done was to cast away with the unbearable pain the transcendent bliss, and now all he had left was his barren virgin honour, this grim necessity to keep his vows at all costs. He was a man of his word, he would keep his word.

But he would never see her again.


Cadfael came back from the town in good time for Compline, well fed and well wined, and content with his evening's entertainment, though regretful that he would see no more of Aline and his godson Giles for three or four months. Doubtless Hugh would bring them back to the town house for the winter, by which time the boy would be grown out of all knowledge, and approaching his third birthday. Well, better they should spend the warm months up there in the north, at Maesbury, in the healthy caput of Hugh's modest honour, rather than in the congested streets of Shrewsbury, where disease had easier entry and exaggerated power. He ought not to grudge their going, however he was bound to miss them.

It was a warm early twilight as he crossed the bridge, matching his mood of content with its mild and pleasant melancholy. He passed the spot where trees and bushes bordered the path down to the lush riverside level of the Gaye, the abbey's main gardens, and the still silver gleam of the mill-pond on his right, and turned in at the gatehouse. The porter was sitting in the doorway of his lodge in the mild sweet air, taking the cool of the evening very pleasurably, but he also had an eye to his duties and the errand he had been given.

'So there you are!' he said comfortably, as Cadfael entered through the open wicket. 'Gallivanting again! I wish I had a godson up in the town.'

'I had leave,' said Cadfael complacently.

'I've known times when you couldn't have said that so smugly! But yes, I know you had leave tonight, and are back in good time for the office. But that's all one for tonight – Father Abbot wants you in his parlour. As soon as he returns, he said.'

'Does he so, indeed?' Cadfael echoed, brows aloft. 'What's afoot, then, at this hour? Has something wild been happening?'

'Not that I know of, there's been no stir about the place at all, everything as quiet as the night. Just the simple summons. Brother Anselm is sent for, too,' he added placidly. 'No mention of the occasion. Better go now and see.'

So Cadfael thought, too, and betook himself briskly down the length of the great court to the abbot's lodging. Brother Anselm the precentor was there before him, already ensconced on a carved bench against the panelled wall, and it appeared that nothing of too disturbing a nature was towards, for abbot and obedientiary were provided with wine-cups, and the like was offered to Cadfael as soon as he had reported himself in response to the abbot's summons. Anselm moved up on the bench to make room for his friend. The precentor, who also presided over the library, was ten years younger than Cadfael, a vague, unworldly man except where his personal enthusiasms were concerned, but alert and subtle enough in anything that concerned books, music or the instruments that make music, best of all the most perfect, the human voice. The blue eyes that peered out beneath his bushy brown eyebrows and shock of shaggy brown hair might be short-sighted, but they missed very little that went on, and had a tolerant twinkle for fallible human creatures and their failings, especially among the young.

'I have sent for you two,' said Radulfus, when the door

was firmly closed, and there was no fourth to overhear, 'because a thing has arisen that I would as lief not bring up in chapter tomorrow. It will certainly be known to one other, but through the confessional, which is secret enough. But else I want it kept within here, between us three. You have both long experience of the world and its pitfalls before you entered the cloister, you will comprehend my reasons. What is fortunate is that you were also the abbey witnesses to the charter by which we acquired the Widow Perle's house here in the Foregate. I have asked Anselm to bring with him a copy of the charter from the lieger-book.'

'I have it here,' said Brother Anselm, half-unfolding the leaf of vellum on his knee.

'Good! Presently! Now the matter is this. This afternoon Brother Eluric, who as custodian of the Lady Chapel altar, which benefits from the gift, seemed the natural person to pay the stipulated rent to the lady each year, came to me and requested to be excused from this duty. For reasons which I should have foreseen. For there is no denying that Mistress Perle is an attractive woman, and Brother Eluric is quite unpractised, young and vulnerable. He says, and I am sure truly, that no ill word or look has ever passed between them, nor has he ever entertained a single lustful thought concerning her. But he wished to be relieved of any further meeting, since he suffers and is tempted.'

It was a carefully temperate description, Cadfael thought, of what ailed Brother Eluric, but mercifully it seemed the disaster had been averted in time. The boy had got his asking, that was plain.

'And you have granted his wish,' said Anselm, rather stating than asking.

'I have. It is our work to teach the young how to deal with the temptations of the world and the flesh, but certainly not our duty to subject them to such temptations. I blame myself that I did not pay sufficient attention to what was arranged, or foresee the consequences. Eluric has behaved emotionally, but I believe him absolutely when he says he has not sinned, even in thought. I have therefore relieved him of his task. And I do not wish anything of his ordeal to be known among the other brothers. At best it will not be easy for him, let it at least be private, or confined to the few of us. He need not even know that I have confided in you.'

'He shall not,' said Cadfael firmly.

'So, then,' said Radulfus, 'having rescued one fallible child from the fire, I am all the more resolved not to subject another equally unprepared to the same danger. I cannot appoint another boy of Eluric's years to carry the rose. And if I nominate an elder, such as yourself, Cadfael, or Anselm here, it will be known all too well what the change means, and Brother Eluric's trouble will become matter for gossip and scandal. Oh, be sure I know that no rule of silence keeps news from spreading like bindweed. No, this must be seen as a change of policy for good and canonical reasons. Which is why I asked for the charter. Its purport I know, but its exact wording I cannot recall. Let us see what the possibilities are. Will you read it aloud, Anselm?'

Anselm unrolled his leaf and read, in the mellifluous voice that rejoiced in swaying hearers in the liturgy:

'"Be it known to all, present and future, that I, Judith, daughter of Richard Vestier and widow of Edred Perle, being in full health of mind, give and bestow, and by this present charter confirm to God and to the altar of Saint Mary in the church of the monks of Shrewsbury, my house in the Monks' Foregate, between the abbey forge and the messuage of Thomas the farrier, together with the garden and field pertaining to it, for an annual rent, during my lifetime, of one rose from the white rose-bush growing beside the north wall, to be delivered to me, Judith, upon the day of the translation of Saint Winifred. By these witnesses recorded: as to the abbey, Brother Anselm, precentor, Brother Cadfael; as to the town, John Ruddock, Nicholas of Meole, Henry Wyle."'

'Good!' said the abbot with a deep, satisfied breath, as Anselm lowered the leaf into the lap of his habit. 'So there is no mention of who is to deliver the rent, merely that it must be paid on the fixed day, and into the donor's own hand. So we may excuse Brother Eluric without infringing the terms, and as freely appoint another to bear the rose. There is no restriction, any man appointed may act for the abbey in this matter.'

'That's certain,' agreed Anselm heartily. 'But if you purpose to exclude all the young, Father, for fear of bringing them into temptation, and all of us elders for fear of exposing Brother Eluric to suspicion of, at least, weakness, and at worst, misconduct, are we to look to a lay servant? One of the stewards, perhaps?'

'It would be perfectly permissible,' said Radulfus practically, 'but perhaps might lose something of relevance. I would not wish to diminish the gratitude we feel, and should feel, for the lady's generous gift, nor the respect with which we regard the gesture of her choice of rent. It means much to her, it should and must be dealt with by us with equal gravity. I would welcome your thoughts on the matter.'

'The rose,' said Cadfael, slowly and consideringly, 'comes from the garden and the particular bush which the widow cherished during the years of her marriage, and tended along with her husband. The house has a tenant now, a decent widower and a good craftsman, who has cared for the bush, pruned and fed it ever since he took up household there. Why should not he be asked to deliver the rose? Not roundabout, through a third and by order, but direct from bush to lady? This house is his landlord, as it is her beneficiary, and its blessing goes with the rose without further word said.'

He was not sure himself what had moved him to make the suggestion. It may have been that the evening's wine, rewarmed in him now by the abbot's wine, rekindled with it the memory of the close and happy family he had left up in the town, where the marital warmth as sacred in its way as any monastic vows gave witness to heaven of a beneficent purpose for mankind. Whatever it was that had moved him to speak, surely they were here dealing with a confrontation of special significance between man and woman, as Eluric had all too clearly shown, and the champion sent into the lists might as well be a mature man who already knew about women, and about love, marriage and loss.

'It's a good thought,' said Anselm, having considered it dispassionately. 'If it's to be a layman, who better than the tenant? He also benefits from the gift, the premises suit him very well, his former quarters were too distant from the town and too cramped.'

'And you think he would be willing?' asked the abbot.

'We can but ask. He's already done work for the lady,' said Cadfael, 'they're acquainted. And the better his contacts with the townsfolk, the better for trade. I think he'd have no objection.'

'Then tomorrow,' decided the abbot with satisfaction, 'I will send Vitalis to put the matter to him. And our problem, small though it is, will be happily solved.'

# Chapter Three

Brother Vitalis had lived so long with documents and accounts and legal points that nothing surprised him, and about nothing that was not written down on vellum did he retain any curiosity. The errands that fell to his lot he discharged punctiliously but without personal interest. He delivered the abbot's message to Niall the bronzesmith word for word, expecting and receiving instant agreement, carried the satisfactory answer back, and promptly forgot the tenant's face. Not one word of one parchment that ever passed through his hands did he forget, those were immutable, even years would only slightly fade them, but the faces of laymen whom he might well never see again, and whom he could not recall ever noticing before, these vanished from his mind far more completely than words erased deliberately from a leaf of vellum to make way for a new text.

'The smith is quite willing,' he reported to Abbot Radulfus on his return, 'and promises faithful delivery.' He had not even wondered why the duty should have been transferred from a brother to a secular agent. It was in any case more seemly, since the donor was a woman.

'That's well,' said the abbot, content, and as promptly dismissed the matter from his mind as finished.

Niall, when he was left alone, stood for some minutes gazing after his departed visitor, leaving the all but completed dish with its incised border neglected on his workbench, the punch and mallet idle beside it. A small sector of the rim left to do, and then he could turn his hand to the supple leather girdle rolled up on a shelf and waiting for his attention. There would be a small mould to make, the body of the buckle to cast, and then the hammering out of the fine pattern and the mixing of the bright enamels to fill the incisions. Three times since she had brought it in he had unrolled it and run it caressingly through his fingers, dwelling on the delicate precision of the bronze rosettes. For her he would make a thing of beauty, however small and insignificant, and even if she never noticed it but as an article of apparel, a thing of use, at least she would wear it, it would encircle that body of hers that was so slender, too slender, and the buckle would rest close against the womb that had conceived but once and miscarried, leaving her so lasting and bitter a grief.

Not this night, but the night following, when the light began to fade and made fine work impossible, he would close the house and set out on the walk down through Brace Meole to the hamlet of Pulley, a minor manor of the Mortimers, where his sister's husband John Stury farmed the demesne as steward, and Cecily's boisterous children kept his own little girl company, made much of her, and ran wild with her among the chickens and the piglets. He was not utterly bereft, like Judith Perle. There was great consolation in a little daughter. He pitied those who had no children, and most of all such as had carried a child half the long, hard way into this world, only to lose it at last, and too late to conceive again. Judith's child had gone in haste after its father. The wife was left to make her way slowly, and alone.

He had no illusions about her. She knew little of him, desired no more, and thought of him not at all. Her composed courtesy was for every man, her closer regard for none. That he acknowledged without complaint or question. But fate and the lord abbot, and certain monastic scruples about encountering women, no doubt, had so decreed that on one day in the year, at least, he was to see her, to go to her house, to stand in her presence and pay her what was due, exchange a few civil words with her, see her face clearly, even be seen clearly by her, if only for a moment.

He left his work and went out by the house door into the garden. Within the high wall there were fruit trees bedded in grass, and a patch of vegetables, and to one side a narrow, tangled bed of flowers, overcrowded but spangled with bright colour. The white rose-bush grew against the north wall, tall as a man, and clutching the stonework with a dozen long, spiny arms. He had cut it back only seven weeks before, but it made rapid and lengthy growth every year. It was old; dead wood had been cut away from its stem several times, so that it had a thick, knotty bole at the base, and a sinewy stalk that was almost worthy of being called a trunk. A snow of white, half-open buds sprinkled it richly. The blooms were never very large, but of the purest white and very fragrant. There would be no lack of them at their best to choose from, when the day of Saint Winifred's translation came.

She should have the finest to be found on the tree. And even before that day he would see her again, when she came to fetch her girdle. Niall went back to his work with goodwill, shaping the new buckle in his mind while he completed the decoration of the dish for the provost's kitchen.

The burgage of the Vestier family occupied a prominent place at the head of the street called Maerdol, which led downhill to the western bridge. A right-angled house, with wide shop-front on the street, and the long stem of the hall and chambers running well back behind, with a spacious yard and stables. There was room enough in all that elongated building, besides the living rooms of the family, to house ample stores in a good dry undercroft, and provide space for all the girls who carded and combed the newly dyed wool, besides three horizontal looms set up in their own outbuilding, and plenty of room in the long hall for half a dozen spinsters at once. Others worked in their own homes, and so did five other weavers about the town. The Vestiers were the biggest and best-known clothiers in Shrewsbury.

Only the dyeing of the fleeces and fulling of the cloth were put out into the experienced hands of Godfrey Fuller, who had his dye-house and fulling-works and tenterground just down-river, under the wall of the castle.

At this time of year the first fleeces of the clip had already been purchased and sorted, and sent to be dyed, and on this same day had been duly delivered in person by Godfrey. Nor did he seem to be in any hurry to be off about his business, though he was known for a man to whom time was money, and money very dear. So was power. He enjoyed being one of the wealthiest of the town's guildsmen, and was always on the look-out for an extension to his realm and influence. He had his eye, so the common gossip said, on the almost comparable wealth of the Widow Perle, and never neglected an opportunity of urging the benefits of bringing the two together by a match.

Judith had sighed at his staying, but dutifully offered refreshment, and listened patiently to his dogged persuasions, which at least had the decency to avoid any semblance of loving courtship. He spoke solid sense, not dalliance, and all he said was true. His business and hers, put together, and run as well as they were being run now, would become a power in the shire, let alone the town. She would be the gainer, in terms of wealth at least, as well as he. Nor would he make too repulsive a husband, for if he was turned fifty he was still a presentable figure of a man, tall, vigorous, with a long stride on him, and a thick crop of steel-grey hair capping sharp features, and if he valued money, he also valued appearances and refinements, and would see to it, if only for his own prestige, that his wife went decked out as handsomely as any in the county.

'Well, well!' he said, recognising his dismissal and accepting it without resentment, 'I know how to bide my time, mistress, and I'm not one to give up short of the victory, nor one to change my mind, neither. You'll come to see the rights of what I've said, and I'm not afraid to stand my ground against any of these young fly-by-nights that have nothing to offer you but their pretty faces. Mine has seen long service, but I'll back it against theirs any day. You have too much good sense, girl, to choose a lad for his dainty seat on a horse, or his pink and yellow beauty. And think well on all we could do between us, if we had the whole of the trade brought together in our hands, from the ewe's back to the cloth on the counter and the gown on the customer's back.'

'I have thought of it,' she said simply, 'but the truth is, Master Fuller, I do not purpose to marry again.'

'Purposes can change,' said Godfrey firmly, and rose to take his leave. The hand she gave him resignedly he raised to his lips.

'Yours, too?' she said with a faint smile.

'My mind won't change. If yours does, here am I waiting.' And with that he did leave her, as briskly as he had come. Certainly there seemed to be no end to his persistence and patience, but fifty can ill afford to wait too long. Very soon she might have to do something decisive about Godfrey Fuller, and against that massive assurance it was hard to see what she could do but what she had been doing all along, fend him off and be as constant in denial as he was in demanding. She had been brought up to take good care of her business and her labourers, no less than he, she could ill afford to take her dyeing and fulling to another master.

Aunt Agatha Coliar, who had sat a little apart, sewing, bit off her thread, and said in the sweet, indulgent voice she affected sometimes towards the niece who kept her in comfort: 'You'll never rid yourself of him by being too civil. He takes it for encouragement.'

'He has a right to speak his mind,' said Judith indifferently, 'and he's in no doubt about mine. As often as he asks, I can refuse.'

'Oh, my dear soul, I trust you can. He's not the man for you. Nor none of those youngsters he spoke of, neither. You well know there's no second in the world for one who's known joy with the first. Better by far go the leave of the way alone! I still grieve for my own man, after all these years. I could never look at any other, after him.' So she had said, sighing and shaking her head and wiping away a facile tear, a thousand times since she had kept the storehouse and the linen here, and brought her son to help manage the business. 'If it had not been for my boy, who was young then to fend for himself, I would have taken the veil that same year that Will died. There'd be no fortune-hunting lads pestering a woman in the cloister. Peace of mind there'd be, there.' She was off upon her best theme, and sometimes seemed almost to forget that she was talking to anyone but herself.

She had been a pretty woman in youth, and still had a round, rosy, comfortable freshness, somewhat contradicted by the alert sharpness of her blue eyes, and the taut smile that visited her mouth very often when it should have been relaxed and easy in repose, as if shrewd thoughts within wore her soft outward seeming like a disguise. Judith could not remember her own mother, and often wondered if there had been much resemblance between the sisters. But these, mother and son, were the only kin she had, and she had taken them in without hesitation. Miles more than earned his keep, for he had shown himself an excellent manager during the long decline of Edred's health, when Judith had had no thought to spare for anything but her husband and the child to come. She had not had the heart, when she returned to the shop, to take back the reins into her own hands. Though she did her share, and kept a dutiful eye upon everything, she let him continue as master-clothier. So influential a house fared better with a man in the forefront.

'But there,' sighed Agatha, folding her sewing on her spacious lap and dropping a tear on the hem, 'I had my duty to do in the world, there was to be no such calm and quiet for me. But you have no chick nor child to cling to you, my poor dear, and nothing now to tie you to the world, if it should please you to leave it. You did speak of it once. Oh, take good thought, do nothing in haste. But should it come to that, there's nothing to hold you back.'

No, nothing! And sometimes the world did seem to Judith a waste, a tedium, hardly worth keeping. And in a day or two, perhaps tomorrow, Sister Magdalen would be coming from Godric's Ford, from the forest cell of the abbey of Polesworth, to fetch away Brother Edmund's niece as a postulant. She could as well take back with her two aspiring novices as one.

Judith was in the spinning room with the women when Sister Magdalen arrived, early the following afternoon. As heiress to the clothier's business for want of a brother, she had learned all the skills involved, from teasing and carding to the loom and the final cutting of garments, though she found herself much out of practice now at the distaff. The sheaf of carded wool before her was russet-red. Even the dye-stuffs came seasonally, and last summer's crop of woad for the blues was generally used up by April or May, to be followed by these variations on reds and browns and yellows, which Godfrey Fuller produced from the lichens and madders. He knew his craft. The lengths of cloth he would finally get back for fulling had a clear, fast colour, and fetched good prices.

It was Miles who came looking for her. 'You have a visitor,' he said, reaching over Judith's shoulder to rub a strand of wool from the distaff between finger and thumb, with cautious approval. 'There's a nun from Godric's Ford sitting in your small chamber, waiting for you. She says they told her at the abbey you'd be glad of a word with her. You're not still playing with the notion of quitting the world, are you? I thought that nonsense was over.'

'I did tell Brother Cadfael I should like to see her,' said Judith, stilling her spindle. 'No more than that. She's here to fetch a new novice away – the infirmarer's sister's girl.'

'Then don't you be fool enough to offer her a second. Though you do have your follies, as I know,' he said lightly, and clapped her affectionately on the shoulder. 'Like giving away for a rose-leaf the best property in the Foregate. Do you intend to cap that by giving away yourself?'

He was two years older than his cousin, and given to playing the elder, full of sage advice, though with a lightness that tempered the image. A young man very neatly and compactly made, strong and lissome, and as good at riding and wrestling and shooting at the butts by the riverside as he was at managing a clothier's business. He had his mother's blue, alert eyes and light-brown hair, but none of her blurred complacency. All that was, or seemed, vague and shallow in the mother became clear and decisive in the son. Judith had had good cause to be glad of him, and to rely on his solid good sense in all matters concerning commerce.

'I may do as I please with myself,' she said, rising and laying her spindle down in safety with its cone of russet yarn, 'if only I knew what *does* best please me! But truth to tell, I'm utterly in the dark. All I've done is to say I should be glad to talk to her. So I shall. I like Sister Magdalen.'

'So do I,' agreed Miles heartily. 'But I should grudge *you* to her. This house would founder without you.'

'Folly!' said Judith sharply. 'You know well enough it could fare as well without me as with me. It's you who hold up the roof, not I.'

If he disclaimed that, she did not wait to hear, but gave

him a sudden reassuring smile and a touch of her hand on his sleeve as she passed, and went to join her guest. Miles had a ruthless honesty, he knew that what she had said was no more than truth, he could have run everything here without her. The sharp reminder pricked her. She was indeed expendable, a woman without purpose here in this world, she might well consider whether there was not a better use for her out of the world. In urging her against it, he had reopened the hollow in her heart, and turned her thoughts again towards the cloister.

Sister Magdalen was sitting on a cushioned bench beside the unshuttered window in Judith's small private chamber, broad, composed and placid in her black habit. Agatha had brought her fruit and wine, and left her to herself, for she went in some awe of her. Judith sat down beside her visitor.

'Cadfael has told me,' said the nun simply, 'what ails you, and what you have confided to him. God forbid I should press you one way or the other, for in the end the decision is yours to make, and no other can make it for you. I am taking into account how grievous your losses have been.'

'I envy you,' said Judith, looking down into her linked hands. 'You are kind, and I am sure you are wise and strong. I do not believe I am now any of these things, and it is tempting to lean upon someone who is. Oh, I do live, I do work, I have not abandoned house, or kinsfolk, or duties. Yet all this could as well go on without me. My cousin has just shown me as much by denying it. It would be a most welcome refuge, to have a vocation elsewhere.'

'Which you have not,' said Sister Magdalen shrewdly, 'or you could not have said that.' Her sudden smile was like a ray of warmth, and the dimple that darted in and out of her cheek sparkled and was gone.

'No. Brother Cadfael said as much. He said the religious life should not be embraced as a second-best, but only as the best – not a hiding-place, but a passion.'

'He would be hard put to it to apply that to me,' said Sister Magdalen bluntly. 'But neither do I recommend to others what I myself do. If truth be told, I am no example to any woman. I took what I chose, I have still some years of life in which to pay for it. And if the debt is not discharged by then,

44

I'll pay the balance after, ungrudging. But you have incurred no such debt, and I do not think you should. The price comes high. You, I judge, will do better to wait, and spend your substance for something different.'

'I know of nothing,' said Judith bleakly, after a long moment of thought, 'that I find worth buying in this world now. But you and Brother Cadfael are right, if I took the veil I should be hiding behind a lie. All I covet in the cloister is the quiet, and the wall around me, keeping the world out.'

'Bear in mind, then,' said the nun emphatically, 'that our doors are not closed against any woman in need, and the quiet is not reserved for those who have taken vows. The time may come when you truly need a place to be apart, time for thought and rest, even time to recover lost courage, though of that I think you have enough. I said I would not advise, and I am advising. Wait, bear with things as they are. But if ever you need a place to hide, for a little while or a long while, come to Godric's Ford and bring all your frets in with you, and you shall find a refuge for as long as you need, with no vows taken, never unless you come to it with a whole heart. And I will keep the door against the world until you see fit to go forth again.'

Late after supper that night, in the small manor-house of Pulley, in the open scrubland fringes of the Long Forest, Niall opened the outer door of his brother-in-law's timber hall, and looked out into the twilight that was just deepening into night. He had a walk of three miles or so before him, back to his house in the Foregate of the town, but it was a familiar and pleasant walk in fair weather, and he was accustomed to making the trip two or three times in the week after work, and home in the early dark, to be up and at work again betimes in the morning. But on this night he saw with some surprise that there was a steady rain falling, so quietly and straightly that within the house they had been quite unaware of it.

'Bide overnight,' said his sister at his shoulder. 'No need to get wet through, and this won't last the night out.'

'I don't mind it,' said Niall simply. 'I shan't hurt.'

'With all that way to go? Get some sense,' advised Cecily

comfortably, 'and stay here in the dry, there's room enough, and you know you're welcome. You can be up and away in good time tomorrow, no fear of oversleeping, these early dawns.'

'Shut the door on it,' urged John from the table, 'and come and have another sup. Better wet inside than out. It's not often we have time for a talk among the three of us, after the children are all abed and asleep.'

With four of them about the place, and all lively as squirrels, that was true enough; the grown folk were at the beck and call of their young for all manner of services, mending toys, joining in games, telling stories, singing rhymes. Cecily's two boys and a girl ranged from ten years old down to six, and Niall's own chick was the youngest and the pet. Now all four were curled up like a litter of puppies on their hay mattresses in the little loft, fast asleep, and round the trestle table in the hall the elders could talk freely without disturbing them.

It had been a good day for Niall. He had cast and decorated and polished the new buckle for Judith's girdle, and was not displeased with his work. Tomorrow she might come to fetch it, and if he saw pleasure in her eyes when she took it, he would be well rewarded. Meantime, why not settle here cosily for the night, and get up with the dawn to a newly washed world, and a sweet green walk home?

He slept well, and was roused at first light by the usual wild, waking rapture of the birds, at once sweet and strident. Cecily was up and busy, and had small ale and bread ready for him. She was younger than he, fair and benign, happy in her husband and a born hand with children, no wonder the motherless child thrived here. Stury would take nothing for her keep. What was one more little bird, he said, in a full nest? And indeed the family was well provided here, keeping Mortimer's little manor prosperous and in good repair, the cleared fields productive, the forest well managed, the small coppice ditched against the invading deer. A good place for children. And yet it was always an effort to set out for the town, and leave her behind, and he visited often for fear she should begin to forget that she was his, and not the youngest of the Stury brood, fathered and mothered here from birth.

Niall set out through an early morning moist and sweet, the rain over, seemingly, for some hours, for though the grass sparkled, the open soil had swallowed up the fall, and was beginning to dry. The first long, low beams of the rising sun lanced through the trees and drew patterns of light and dark along the ground. The first passion of bird-song gradually softened and lost its belligerence, grew busy and sweet and at ease. Here also the nests were full of fledgelings, hard work day-long to feed them all.

The first mile was through the edges of the forest, the ground opening gradually into heath and scrub, dotted with small groves of trees. Then he came to the hamlet of Brace Meole, and from there it was a beaten road, widening as it neared the town into a cart-track, which crossed the Meole Brook by a narrow bridge, and brought him into the Foregate between the stone bridge into the town and the mill and mill-pond at the edge of the abbey enclave. He had set off early and walked briskly, and the Foregate was still barely awake; only a few cottagers and labourers were up and about their business, and gave him good day as he passed. The monks were not yet down for Prime, there was no sound in the church as Niall went by, but faintly from the dortoir the waking bell was ringing. The high road had dried after the rain, but the soil of the gardens showed richly dark, promising grateful growth.

He came to the gate in his own burgage wall, and let himself through into the yard, set the door of his shop open, and made ready for the day's work. Judith's girdle lay coiled on a shelf. He held his hand from taking it down to caress yet again, for he had no rights in her, and never would have. But this very day he might at least see her again and hear her voice, and in five days' time he surely would, and that in her own house. Their hands might touch on the stem of the rose. He would choose carefully, wary of offering her thorns, who had been pierced by too many and too sharp thorns already in her brief life.

The thought drove him out into the garden, which lay behind the yard, entered by a door from the house and a wicket in the wall from the yard. After the indoor chill left from the night, the bright sunlight embraced him in the doorway, a scarf of warmth, and gleamed moistly through the branches of the fruit trees and over the tangled flower-bed. He took one step over the threshold and halted, stricken and appalled.

Against the north wall the white rose-bush sagged sidelong, its thorny arms dragged from the stone, its thickened bole hacked in a long, downward gash that split away a third of its weight and growth dangling into the grass. Beneath it the soil of the bed was stirred and churned as if dogs had battled there, and beside the battlefield lay huddled a still heap of rusty black, half sunk in the grass. Niall took no more than three hasty steps towards the wreckage when he saw the pale gleam of a naked ankle jutting from the heap, an arm in a wide black sleeve flung out, a hand convulsively clenched into the soil, and the pallid circle of a tonsure startlingly white in all the blackness. A monk of Shrewsbury, young and slight, almost more habit than body within it, and what, in God's name, was he doing here, dead or wounded under the wounded tree?

Niall went close and kneeled beside him, in too much awe, at first, to touch. Then he saw the knife, lying close beside the outstretched hand, its blade glazed with drying blood. There was a thick dark moisture that was not rain, sodden into the soil under the body. The forearm exposed by the wide black sleeve was smooth and fair. This was no more than a boy. Niall reached a hand to touch at last, and the flesh was chill but not yet cold. Nevertheless, he knew death. With careful dread he eased a hand under the head, and turned to the morning light the soiled young face of Brother Eluric.

# Chapter Four

Brother Jerome, who counted heads and censored behaviour in all the brothers, young and old, and whether within his province or no, had marked the silence within one dormitory cell when all the rest were rising dutifully for Prime, and made it his business to look within, somewhat surprised in this case, for Brother Eluric rated normally as a model of virtue. But even the virtuous may backslide now and then, and the opportunity to reprove so exemplary a brother came rarely, and was certainly not to be missed. This time Jerome's zeal was wasted, and the pious words of reproach died unspoken, for the cell was empty, the cot immaculately neat, the breviary open on the narrow desk. Brother Eluric had surely risen ahead of his kin, and was already on his knees somewhere in the church, engaged in supererogatory prayer. Jerome felt cheated, and snapped with more than his usual acidity at any who looked blear-eyed with sleep, or came yawning to the night-stairs. He was equally at odds with those who exceeded him in devotion and those who fell short. One way or another, Eluric would pay for this check.

Once they were all in their stalls in the choir, and Brother Anselm was launched into the liturgy – how could a man past fifty, who spoke in a round, human voice deeper than most, sing at will in that upper register, like the most perfect of boy cantors? And how dared he! – Jerome again began to count heads, and grew even happier in his self-vindication, for there was one missing, and that one was Brother Eluric. The fallen paragon, who had actually won his way into Prior Robert's dignified and influential favour, to Jerome's jealous concern! Let him look to his laurels now! The prior would never demean himself to count or search for defections, but he would listen when they were brought to his notice.

Prime came to its end, and the brothers began to file back to the night-stairs, to complete their toilets and make ready for breakfast. Jerome lingered to sidle confidentially to Prior Robert's elbow, and whisper into his ear, with righteous disapproval: 'Father, we have a truant this morning. Brother Eluric was not present in church. Nor is he in his cell. All is left in order there, I thought surely he was before us into the church. Now I cannot think where he may be, nor what he is about, to neglect his duties so.'

Prior Robert in his turn paused and frowned. 'Strange! He of all people! Have you looked in the Lady Chapel? If he rose very early to tend the altar and has lingered long in prayer he may have fallen asleep. The best of us may do so.'

But Brother Eluric was not in the Lady Chapel. Prior Robert hurried to detain the abbot on his way across the great court towards his lodging.

'Father Abbot, we are in some concern over Brother Eluric.'

The name produced instant and sharp attention. Abbot Radulfus turned a fixed and guarded countenance. 'Brother Eluric? Why, what of him?'

'He was not in attendance at Prime, and he is nowhere to be found. Nowhere, at least, that he should be at this hour. It is not like him to absent himself from the office,' said the prior fairly.

'It is not. He is a devoted soul.' The abbot spoke almost absently, for his mind was back in the privacy of his parlour, facing that all too brittle devotee as he poured out his illicit and bravely resisted love. This reminder came all too aptly. How if confession and absolution and the release from temptation had not been enough? Radulfus, not a hesitant man, was still hesitating how to act now, when they were interrupted by the sight of the porter coming down from the gatehouse at a scurrying run, skirts and sleeves flying.

'Father Abbot, there's one here at the gate, the bronze-smith who rents the Widow Perle's old house, says he has dire news that won't wait. He asks for you – would not give me the message—'

'I'll come,' said Radulfus instantly. And to the prior, who would have made to follow him: 'Robert, do you have

50

someone search further, the gardens, the grange court . . . If you do not find him, come back to me.' And he was off at a long, raking stride towards the gate, and the authority of his voice and the vehemence of his going forbade pursuit. There were too many interwoven threads here – the lady of the rose, the house of the rose, the tenant who had willingly undertaken the errand Eluric dreaded, and now Eluric lost from within, and dire news entering from without. A woven pattern began to appear, and its colours were sombre.

Niall was waiting at the door of the porter's lodge, his broad, strongly boned face very still and blanched with shock under its summer brown.

'You asked for me,' said Radulfus quietly, viewing him with a steady, measuring stare. 'I am here. What is this news you bring?'

'My lord,' said Niall, 'I thought best you should know it first alone, and then dispose as you see fit. Last night I lay at my sister's house overnight because of the rain. When I came back this morning I went into the garden. My lord, Mistress Perle's rose-bush has been hacked and broken, and one of your brothers lies dead there under it.'

After a brief, profound silence Radulfus said: 'If you know him, name him.'

'I do know him. For three years he came to the garden to cut the rose for Mistress Perle. He is Brother Eluric, the custodian of Saint Mary's altar.'

This time the silence was longer and deeper. Then the abbot asked simply: 'How long since you discovered him there?'

'About the length of Prime, my lord, for it was nearly the hour when I passed the church on my way home. I came at once, but the porter would not disturb you during the office.'

'And you left all as you found it? Touched nothing?'

'I lifted his head to see his face. Nothing else. He lies just as I found him.'

'Good!' said Radulfus, and winced at using the word even for one right act, where everything else went grimly awry. 'Then wait but a moment, while I send for certain others, and we will go back with you to that garden.'

* * *

Those he took with him, saying nothing as yet to any other, even the prior, were Brother Anselm and Brother Cadfael, witnesses for the abbey to the charter drawn up with Judith Perle. They alone had been told of Brother Eluric's trouble, and shared the sorry knowledge that might be relevant here. The young man's confessor was silenced by his office, and in any case Sub-Prior Richard was not the man Radulfus would have chosen as a wise counsellor in such dark matters.

The four of them stood in silence round the body of Brother Eluric, taking in the pitiful heap of black folds, the outflung hand, the mangled tree and the bloody knife. Niall had withdrawn a few paces to leave them alone, but stood watchful in attendance, to answer whatever they might ask.

'Poor, tormented child,' said Radulfus heavily. 'I doubt I failed him fatally, his disease was worse than I knew. He begged to be relieved of his task, but surely he grudged it to any other, and has tried here to destroy the bush. And himself with it.'

Cadfael was silent, his eyes roving thoughtfully over the trampled ground. They had all refrained from treading too close, nothing had been disturbed since Niall went on his knees to turn the pallid face up to the light.

'Is that how you read it?' asked Anselm. 'Are we to condemn him as a suicide? However we may pity?'

'What else can it be? Surely this involuntary love had so eaten into him that he could not bear another should take his place with the woman. Why else should he steal out by night and come here to this garden, why else should he hack at the roots of the tree? And from that it would be but a step, in his despair, to the unholy temptation to destroy himself with the roses. What could fix his image more terribly and for ever in her memory than such a death? For you know – you two do know – the measure of his desperation. And there lies the knife beside his hand.'

It was not a dagger, but a good, long-hafted knife, sharp and thin, such as any practical man might carry on him for a dozen lawful purposes, from carving his meat at the table to scaring off footpads on a journey, or the occasional wild boar in the forest.

'Beside it,' said Cadfael shortly, 'not in it.'

They turned their eyes on him cautiously, even hopefully.

'You see how his hand is clenched into the soil,' he went on slowly, 'and there is no blood upon it, though the knife is bloodied to the hilt. Touch his hand – I think you'll find it is already stiffening as it lies, clutching the earth. He never held this knife. And if he had, would not the sheath be on his girdle? No man in his senses would carry such a knife about him unsheathed.'

'A man not in his right senses might, however,' said Radulfus ruefully. 'He needed it, did he not, for what he has done to the rose-bush.'

'What was done to the rose-bush,' said Cadfael firmly, 'was not done with that knife. Could not be! A man would have to saw away for half an hour or more, even with a sharp knife, at such a thick bole. That was done with a heavier weapon, meant for such work, a broom-hook or a hatchet. Moreover, you see the gash begins higher, where a single blow, or two at the most, should have severed the stem, but it swerves downwards into the thick of the bole, where dead wood has been cut away for years, and left this woody encrustation.'

'I fear,' said Brother Anselm wryly, 'that Brother Eluric would hardly be expert with such a tool.'

'And there was no second blow,' said Cadfael, undeterred. 'If there had been, the bush would be severed utterly. And the first blow, I think, the only blow – even that was deflected. Someone interrupted the act. Someone clutched at the arm that was swinging the hatchet, and sent the blade down into the thick of the bole. I think – I *think* – it stuck fast there, and the man who held it had not time to get both hands to the haft and pull it out. Why else should he draw his knife?'

'You are saying,' said Radulfus intently, 'that there were two men here in the night, not one? One who tried to destroy, and one who tried to prevent?'

'Yes, that is what I see here.'

'And that the one who tried to protect the tree, who caught at the attacker's arm and caused his weapon to lodge fast – and who was struck down instead with the knife . . .'

'Is Brother Eluric. Yes. How else can it have been?

Certainly he came here secretly in the night of his own will, but not to destroy, rather to take a last farewell of this wild dream of his, to look for one last time on the roses, and then never no more. But he came just in time to see another man here, one who had other thoughts, and for other motives, one who had come to destroy the rose-bush. Would Eluric endure to see that done? Surely he leaped to protect the tree, clutched at the arm wielding the hatchet, drove the blade down to stick fast in the bole. If there was a struggle, as the ground shows, I do not think it lasted long. Eluric was unarmed. The other, if he could not then make use of his hatchet, carried a knife. And used it.'

There was a long silence, while they all stared at him and thought out slowly the implications of what he was saying. And gradually something of conviction came easefully into their faces, even something of relief and gratitude. For if Eluric was not a suicide, but had gone to his end faithfully bearing his burden and seeking to prevent an evil act, then his resting-place in the cemetery was assured, and his passage through death, however his account might stand for little sins needing purging, as safe as a prodigal son re-entering his father's house.

'If it were not as I've said,' Cadfael pointed out, 'then the hatchet would still be here in the garden. It is not. And certainly it was not our brother here who carried it away. And neither did he bring it here, I pledge my word on that.'

'Yet if this is true,' said Anselm consideringly, 'the other did not stay to complete his work.'

'No, he lugged out his hatchet and made off as fast as he could, away from the place where he had made himself a murderer. A thing I daresay he never intended, done in a moment of alarm and terror, when this poor lad in his outrage lunged at him. He would run from Eluric dead in far greater horror than he ever need have done from Eluric living.'

'Nevertheless,' said Abbot Radulfus strongly, 'this is murder.'

'It is.'

'Then I must send word to the castle. It is for the secular authorities to pursue murderers. A pity,' he said, 'that Hugh

Beringar is gone north, we shall have to wait for his return, though no doubt Alan Herbard will send to him at once, and let him know what has happened. Is there more that we here must do, before we have Brother Eluric carried home?'

'We can at least observe whatever is here to be seen, Father. One thing I can tell you, indeed you yourself will see it, what happened here happened after the rain stopped. The ground was soft when they came together here, see how they've marked it. And back and shoulder of the boy's habit are dry. May we now move him? There are witnesses enough here as to how he was found.'

They stooped in all reverence and lifted the stiffening but not yet rigid body, and laid him out on the grass, stretched on his back. From throat to toes the front of his habit was dark with the moisture from the earth, and the great dark stain of his blood clotted the cloth over his left breast. His face, if it had borne the stamp of sudden anger, dread and pain, had now lost that tension, and eased into the smoothness of youth and innocence. Only his eyes, half-open, retained the frowning anxiety of a troubled soul. Radulfus stooped and closed them gently, and wiped the mud from the pale cheeks.

'You take a load from my heart, Cadfael. Surely you are right, he did not take his own life, it was rapt from him cruelly and unjustly, and there must be a price to pay for it. But as for this child here, he is safe enough. I would I had known better how to deal with him, he might still have been living.' He drew the two smooth hands together, and folded them on the bloodied breast.

'I sleep too well,' said Cadfael wryly, 'I never heard when the rain ceased. Did anyone mark the end of it?'

Niall had drawn a little nearer, waiting patiently in case anything further should be required of him.

'It was over by about midnight,' he said, 'for before we went to our beds, there at Pulley, my sister opened the door and looked out, and said that the sky had cleared and it was bidding to be a fine night. But it was too late to start out then.' He added, putting his own interpretation on the way they turned to look at him, after so long of forgetting his presence: 'My sister and her man and the children will tell you I stayed the night over, and left in the dawn. It might be said a family will hold together, however. But I can tell you the names of two or three I said good day to, coming back along the Foregate this morning. They'll bear me out.'

The abbot gave him a startled and preoccupied look, and understood. 'Such checks and counter-checks are for the sheriff's men,' he said. 'But I make no doubt you've told us simple truth. And the rain was over by midnight, you say?'

'It was, my lord. There's but three miles between, it would surely be much the same here.'

'It fits well,' said Cadfael, kneeling over the body. 'He must surely have died about six or seven hours ago. And since he came after the rain stopped, when the ground was soft and moist to tread, there should be traces they've left after them. Here they've stamped the ground raw between them, there's nothing clear, but by one way or another they walked in here in the night, and one walked out again.'

He rose from his knees and rubbed his moist palms together. 'Hold your places where you stand, and look about you. We may have trampled out something of value ourselves, but at least all of us here but one wear sandals, and so did Eluric. Master Bronzesmith, how did you enter here this morning, when you found him?'

'Through the house-door,' said Niall, nodding in that direction.

'And when Brother Eluric came each year to fetch the rose, how did he enter?'

'Through the wicket from the front yard, as we did now. And was very quiet and modest about it.'

'Then this night past, coming with no ill intent, though so secretly, surely he would come as he always came. Let us see,' said Cadfael, treading carefully along the grass to the wicket gate in the wall, 'if any but sandalled feet came that way.'

The earth path, watered into mud by the rain, and again dried into a smooth, soft surface, had taken all their entering footprints and held them clear to view, three pairs of flat soles, here and there overlaid one on another. Or were there four pairs? With these common sandals size meant nothing very helpful, but Cadfael thought he could detect, among all those prints entering and none leaving, one which had trodden deeper than the rest, having entered here while the ground was wetter than now, and by lucky chance escaped being trodden out of shape with their morning invasion. There was also a broad, sturdy shoe-sole, recent like the sandals, which Niall claimed for his, and showed as much by fitting his foot to it.

'Whoever the second was,' said Cadfael, 'I fancy he did not come by the front way, as innocent men do. Nor leave by it, either, having left a dead man behind here. Let us look elsewhere.'

On the eastward side the garden was hemmed in by the wall of the house belonging to Thomas the farrier, on the west by Niall's workshop and dwelling; there was no way out there. But to the rear, on the other side of the north wall, lay a paddock, very easily entered from the fields, and no way overlooked by any building. A few paces along the wall from the mutilated rose-bush there was a vine growing, crabbed and old and seldom fruitful. A part of its twisted trunk had been pulled away from the wall, and when Niall approached it closely he saw that where the trunk turned sidelong and afforded a foothold, a foot had indeed scored it, mounting in panic haste.

'Here! Here he climbed. The ground is higher outside in the paddock, but leaving he needed a holt on the way.'

They drew close, peering. The climber's boot had scratched the bark and left soil in the scratches. And below, in the exposed earth of the bed, the other foot, the left, had stamped a deep and perfect print as he lunged upward, for he had had to reach high. A booted foot, with a raised heel that had dug deep, but less deep on the outer edge at the back, where the wearer habitually trod his boot down. By the shape his footgear had been well made, but well worn also. There was a fine ridge of earth that crossed from below the great toe diagonally half across the sole, narrowing to vanishing point as it went, left by a crack in the leather. Opposite the downtrodden heel, the toe also had left an imprint shallowing slightly. Whoever the man was, he trod from the left of the heel clean to the right of the toe with this left foot. His spring from the ground had forced the print in deep, but his foot had left the soil cleanly, and the wet earth, gradually drying, had preserved the perfect mould.

'A little warm wax,' said Cadfael, half to himself, intently staring, 'a little warm wax and a steady hand, and we have him by the heel!'

They were so intent upon that single spot, the last remaining trace of Brother Eluric's murderer, that none of them heard the light footsteps approaching the open house-door from within, or caught in the corner of an eye the slight gleam of the sun upon movement and colour, as Judith came into the doorway. She had found the workshop empty, and waited some minutes for Niall to appear. But since the door into his living quarters was wide open as he had left it, and the shifting green and gold of sunlit branches stirring showed in reflection across the room within, and since she knew the house so well, she had ventured to pass through to find him in the garden, where she judged he must be.

'I ask pardon,' she was saying as she stepped into the doorway, 'but the doors were open. I did call—'

She broke off there, startled and bewildered to see the whole group of them swing about and stare in consternation at her. Three black Benedictine habits gathered beside the old, barren vine, and one of them the lord abbot himself. What errand could they possibly have here?

'Oh, forgive me,' she began haltingly. 'I didn't know . . .'

Niall sprang out of his shocked stillness and came running, putting himself between her and what else she might see if once she took her eyes off the abbot. He spread an arm protectively to urge her back into the house.

'Come within, mistress, here's nothing to trouble you. I have the girdle ready. You're early, I hadn't expected you. . .'

He was not good at providing a flood of reassuring words. She held her ground, and over his shoulder she swept the enclosed space of the garden with dilated eyes blanched into the chill grey of glass, and found the still body lying aloof and indifferent in the grass. She saw the pale oval of the face, the pale cross of the hands on the breast of the habit, the hacked bole of the rose-bush, and its sagging branches torn from the wall. As yet she neither recognised the dead youth, nor understood at all what could have been happening here.

But all too well she understood that whatever befell in this place, between these walls which had once been hers, somehow lay heavy upon her, as if she had set in motion some terrible procession of events which she was powerless to stop, as if a gathering guilt had begun to fold round her, and mock her with her purity of intent and the corruption of its consequences.

She made no sound at all, she did not shrink, or yield to Niall's awkward, concerned pleading: 'Come, come within and sit you down quietly, and leave all here to the lord abbot. Come!' He had an arm about her, rather persuading than supporting, for she stood quite still and erect, not a quiver in her body. She laid her hands on his shoulders, resisting his urging with resigned determination.

'No, let me be. This has to do with me. I know it.'

They were all drawing anxiously about her by then. The abbot accepted necessity. 'Madam, there is here matter that must distress you, that we cannot deny. I will not hide anything from you. This house is your gift, and truth is your due. But you must not take to yourself more than is customary from any godly gentlewoman in compassion for a young life taken untimely. No part of this stems from you, and no part of what must be done about it falls to your duty. Go within, and all that we know – all that is of consequence – you shall be told. I promise it.'

She hesitated, her eyes still on the dead youth. 'Father, I will not further embitter what is surely hard enough for you,' she said slowly. 'But let me see him. I owe him that.'

Radulfus looked her in the eyes, and stood aside. Niall took away his arm from about her almost stealthily, for fear she should suddenly become aware of his touch in the instant when it was removed. She crossed the grass with a firm and steady step, and stood looking down at Brother Eluric. In death he looked even younger and more vulnerable than in life, for all his immovable calm. Judith reached over him to the dangling, wounded bush, plucked one of the half-open buds, and slipped it carefully into his folded hands.

'For all those you brought to me,' she said. And to the rest of those present, raising her head: 'Yes, it is he. I knew it must be he.'

'Brother Eluric,' said the abbot.

'I never knew his name. Is not that strange?' She looked round them all, from face to face, with drawn brows. 'I never asked, and he never told. So few words we ever had to say to each other, and too late now for more.' She fastened last and longest, and with the first returning warmth of pain in her eyes as the numbness passed, on Cadfael, whom she knew best here. 'How could this happen?' she said.

'Come within now,' said Cadfael, 'and you shall know.'

# Chapter Five

The abbot and Brother Anselm departed, back to the abbey to send men with a litter to bring Brother Eluric home, and a messenger to Hugh's young deputy at the castle, to warn him he had a murder on his hands. Very soon word would go forth through the Foregate that a brother was mysteriously dead, and many and strange rumours would be blown on the summer winds all through the town. Some carefully truncated version of Eluric's tragedy the abbot would surely make public, to silence the wildest tales. He would not lie, but he would judiciously omit what was eternally private between himself, the two brother witnesses, and the dead man. Cadfael could guess how it would read. It had been decided, on maturer reflection, that it would be more suitable for the rose rent to be paid direct by the tenant, rather than by the custodian of the altar of Saint Mary, and therefore Brother Eluric had been excused from the duty he had formerly fulfilled. That he had gone in secret to the garden was perhaps foolish, but not blameworthy. No doubt he had simply wished to verify that the bush was well cared for and in blossom, and finding a malefactor in the very act of destroying it, he had naturally tried to prevent the act, and had been struck down by the attacker. A creditable death, an honourable grave. What need to mention the conflict and suffering that lay behind it?

But in the meantime here was he, Cadfael, confronted with a woman who surely had the right to know everything. It would not, in any case, be easy to lie to this woman, or even to prevaricate. She would not be satisfied with anything less than truth.

Since the sun was now reaching the flower-bed under the north wall of the garden, and the edge of the deep print might become dry and friable before noon, and perhaps powder away, Cadfael had borrowed some ends of candle from Niall on the spot, melted them in one of the smith's small crucibles, and gone to fill in carefully the shape of the bootprint. With patient coaxing the congealed form came away intact. It would have to go into a cold place to preserve its sharpness, but for good measure he had also purloined a discarded offcut of thin leather, and made a careful outline of the print, marking where heel and toe were worn down, and the diagonal crack across the ball of the foot. Sooner or later boots come into the hands of the cobbler, they are far too precious to be discarded until they are completely worn out and can no longer be mended. Often they are handed down through three generations before finally being thrown away. So, reflected Cadfael, would this boot some day need attention from Provost Corviser or one of his trade. How soon there was no telling, but justice has to learn to wait, and not to forget.

Judith sat waiting for him now in Niall's neat, bare and austere living room, the room of a man living alone, orderly and clean, but with none of the small adornments a woman would have added. The doors still stood wide open, there were two unshuttered windows, green of foliage and gold of sun came quivering in, and filled the chamber with light. She was not afraid of light, she sat where it played over her, gilding and trembling as the breeze quickened. She was alone when Cadfael came back from the garden.

'The smith has a customer,' she said with the palest of smiles. 'I bade him go. A man must tend to his trade.'

'So must a woman,' said Cadfael, and laid his moulded waxen form carefully down on the stone floor, where the draught would play over it as the sunlight did over her.

'Yes, so I shall. You need not fear me, I have a respect for life. All the more,' she said gravely, 'now that I have seen death close to, yet again. Tell me! You said you would.'

He sat down with her on the uncushioned bench, and told her fully all that had happened that morning – the defection of Eluric, the coming of Niall with his story of finding the crumpled body and the broken bush, even the first grim suspicion of deliberate damage and self-murder, before sign after sign pointed another way. She heard him out with unwavering attention, those arresting grey eyes dauntingly wide and intelligent.

'But still,' she said, 'I do not understand. You speak as if there was nothing of note or consequence in his leaving the enclave by night as he did. But you know it is something utterly unknown, for a young brother so to dare. And he, I thought, so meek and dutiful, no breaker of rules. Why did he do so? What can have made it so important to him to visit the rose-bush? Secretly, illicitly, by night? What did it mean to him, to drive him so far out of his proper way?'

No question but she was asking honestly. She had never thought of herself as a disturber of any man's peace. And she meant to have an answer, and there was none to give her but the truth. The abbot might have hesitated at this point. Cadfael did not hesitate.

'It meant to him,' he said simply, 'the memory of you. It was no change of policy that removed him from being bearer of the rose. He had begged to be relieved of a task which had become torment to him, and his request was granted. He could no longer bear the pain of being in your presence and as far from you as the moon, of seeing you, and being within touch of you, and forbidden to love. But when he was released, it seems he could not bear absence, either. In a manner, he was saying his goodbye to you. He would have got over it,' said Cadfael with resigned regret, 'if he had lived. But it would have been a long, bleak sickness.'

Still her eyes had not wavered nor her face changed, except that the blood had drained from her cheeks and left her pale and translucent as ice. 'Oh, God!' she said in a whisper. 'And I never knew! There was never word said, never a look . . . And I so much his elder, and no beauty! It was like sending one of the singing boys from the school to me. Never a wrong thought, how could there be?'

'He was cloistered almost from his cradle,' said Cadfael gently, 'he had never had to do with a woman since he left his mother. He had no defence against a gentle face, a soft voice and a motion of grace. You cannot see yourself with his eyes, or you might find yourself dazzled.'

After a moment of silence she said: 'I did feel, somehow,

63

that he was not happy. No more than that. And how many in this world can boast of being happy?' And she asked, looking up again into Cadfael's face: 'How many know of this? Need it be spoken of?'

'No one but Father Abbot, Brother Richard his confessor, Brother Anselm and myself. And now you. No, it will never be spoken of to any other. And none of these can or will ever think one thought of blame for you. How could we?'

'But I can,' said Judith.

'Not if you are just. You must not take to yourself more than your due. That was Eluric's error.'

A man's voice was raised suddenly in the shop, young and agitated, and Niall's voice replying in hasty reassurance. Miles burst in through the open doorway, the sunlight behind him casting him into sharp silhouette, and shining through his ruffled fair hair, turning light brown into flaxen. He was flushed and out of breath, but he heaved a great, relieved sigh at the sight of Judith sitting composed and tearless and in calm company.

'Dear God, what has been happening here? The tales they're buzzing along the Foregate of murder and malice! Brother, is it true? My cousin ... I knew she was coming here this morning. Thank God, girl dear, I find you safe and well befriended. No harm has come to you? I came on the run as soon as I heard what they were saying, to take you home.'

His boisterous coming had blown away, like a March wind, the heavy solemnity that had pervaded the room, and his vigour had brought back some rising colour to Judith's frozen face. She rose to meet him, and let him embrace her in an impulsive hug, and kiss her cold cheek.

'I've taken no harm, no need to fret for me. Brother Cadfael has been kind enough to keep me company. He was here before I came, and Father Abbot also, there was never any threat or danger to me.'

'But there *has* been a death?' With his arms still protectively about her he looked from her face to Cadfael's, anxiously frowning. 'Or is it all a false tale? They were saying – a brother of the abbey was carried home from this place, and his face covered ...'

'It's all too true,' said Cadfael, rising somewhat wearily. 'Brother Eluric, the custodian of Saint Mary's altar, was found here this morning stabbed to death.'

'Here? What, within the house?' He sounded incredulous, as well he might. What would a brother of the abbey be doing invading a craftsman's house?

'In the garden. Under the rose-tree,' said Cadfael briefly, 'and that rose-tree hacked and damaged. Your cousin will tell you all. Better you should hear truth than the common rumours none of us will quite escape. But the lady should be taken home at once and allowed to rest. She has need of it.' He took up from the stone threshold the form of wax, on which the young man's eyes rested with wondering curiosity, and laid it carefully away in his linen scrip to avoid handling.

'Indeed!' agreed Miles, recalled to his duty and flushing boyishly. 'And thank you, Brother, for your kindness.'

Cadfael followed them out into the workshop. Niall was at his bench, but he rose to meet them as they took their leave, a modest man, who had had the delicacy to remove himself from any attendance on what should be private between comforter and comforted. Judith looked at him gravely, and suddenly recovered from some deep reserve of untouched innocence within her a pale but lovely smile. 'Master Niall, I grieve that I have caused you so much trouble and distress, and I do thank you for your goodness. And I have a thing to collect, and a debt to pay – have you forgotten?'

'No,' said Niall. 'But I would have brought it to you when the time was better suited.' He turned to the shelf behind him, and brought out to her the coiled girdle. She paid him what he asked, as simply as he asked it, and then she unrolled the buckle end in her hands, and looked long at her dead husband's mended gift, and for the first time her eyes moistened with a pearly sheen, though no tears fell.

'It is a time very well suited now,' she said, looking up into Niall's face, 'for a small, precious thing to provide me with a pure pleasure.'

It was the only pleasure she had that day, and even that carried with it a piercing undercurrent of pain. Agatha's flustered and voluble fussing and Miles's restrained but all too attentive concern were equally burdensome to her. The dead face of Brother Eluric remained with her every moment. How could she have failed to feel his anguish? Once, twice, three times she had received him and parted from him, with no deeper misgiving than a mild sense of his discomfort, which could well be merely shyness, and a conviction that here was a young man none too happy, which she had attributed to want of a true vocation in one cloistered from childhood. She had been so deeply sunk in her own griefs as to be insensitive to his. Even in death he did not reproach her. He had no need. She reproached herself.

She would have sought distraction at least in occupying her hands, but she could not face the awed whispers and heavy silences of the girls in the spinning room. She chose rather to sit in the shop, where, if the curious came to stare and exclaim, at least they were likely to come one at a time, and some at least might come honestly to buy cloth, not even having heard yet the news that was being blown round the alleys of Shrewsbury like thistledown, and taking root as blithely.

But even that was hard to bear. She would have been glad when evening came, and the shutters were put up, but that one late customer, coming to collect a length of cloth for his mother, elected to stay a while and commiserate with the lady in private, or at least as much privacy as he could contrive between the clucking forays of Agatha, who could not leave her niece unattended for many minutes together. Those brief intervals, however, Vivian Hynde knew how to use to the best advantage.

He was the only son of old William Hynde, who ran the biggest flocks of sheep in the central western uplands of the shire, and who for years had regularly sold the less select fleeces of his clip to the Vestiers, while the finest were reserved to be collected by the middlemen for shipping to the north of France and the wool towns of Flanders, from his warehouse and jetty downstream, beyond Godfrey Fuller's workshops. The partnership between the two families for business purposes had existed for two generations, and made close contact plausible even for this young sprig who was said to be at odds with his father, and highly unlikely to prove a third successful woolman, his talent being more highly developed in spending the money his father made. So much so that it was rumoured the old man had put his foot down heavily, and refused to pay any more debts for his son and heir, or allow him any more funds to squander on dice, and girls, and riotous living. William had bailed him out of trouble often enough already, but now, without his backing, Vivian's usual resources were far less likely to lend to him or give him extended credit. And easy friends fall off from an idol and patron who no longer has money to spend.

There was no sign of drooping as yet, however, in Vivian's bright crest when he came, with his considerable charm and grace, to console a dismayed widow. He was a very personable young man indeed, tall and athletic, with corn-yellow hair that curled becomingly, and dancing pebble-brown eyes in which a full light found surprising golden glints. He was invariably elegant in his gear and wear, and knew very well how pleasant a picture he made in most women's eyes. And if he had made no headway yet with the Widow Perle, neither had anyone else, and there was still hope.

He had the wit to approach delicately on this occasion, with a declaration of sympathy and concern that stopped short of probing too deeply. Excellent at keeping his feet on thin ice, indeed sensible enough to know himself a man for surfaces, not for depths, he also had the gall to rally and tease a little in the hope of raising a smile.

'And now if you shut yourself up here and grieve in private for someone you hardly knew, that aunt of yours will drive you ever more melancholy. She has you talked halfway to a nunnery already. And that,' said Vivian with emphatic pleading, 'you *must not do*.'

'Many another has,' she said, 'with no better cause. Why not I?'

'Because,' he said, glittering, and leaning closer to lower his voice for fear Agatha should choose that moment to enter yet again on some pretext or other, 'because you are young and beautiful, and have no real wish to bury yourself in a convent. You know it! And because I am your devoted worshipper, as well you know, and if you vanish from my life it will be the death of me.'

She took that as a well-intended if ill-judged flourish, and was even a little touched by his suddenly caught breath and stricken gaze as he realised what he had said, and how it must bite home on this of all days. He caught at her hand, voluble and honeyed in dismay. 'Oh, forgive me, forgive me! Fool that I am, I never meant ... There is no blame, none, can touch you. Let me in to your life closer, and I'll convince you. Marry me, and I'll shut out all vexations and doubts from you ...'

She did begin to wonder, afterwards, if it was all calculated, for he was a subtle and persuasive young man; but then she was disarmed and self-doubting, and could not bring herself to attribute deceit or self-interest to any other. Vivian had often enough pressed his attentions upon her and made no impression. Now what she saw in him was a boy no more than a year older than Brother Eluric, one who might, for all his flattery and exaggeration, be suffering something of what Brother Eluric had suffered. She had so lamentably failed to offer the slightest help to the one, the more reason she should deal considerately with the other. So she tolerated him, and made firm but gentle answers, longer than she would have done at any other time.

'It's foolish to talk so,' she said. 'You and I have known each other from childhood. I'm your elder, and a widow, by no means a match for you, and I do not intend to marry again with any man. You must accept that for an answer. Waste no more time here on me.'

'You are fretting now,' he said vehemently, 'over this monk who is dead, though God knows that's none of your fault. But it will not always be so, you'll see all very differently in a month or so. And for this charter that troubles you, it can be changed. You can, you should rid yourself of the bargain, and with it the reproach. You see now it was folly.'

'Yes,' she agreed resignedly, 'it was indeed folly to put a price, even a nominal price, upon a gift. I should never have done it. It has brought nothing but grief. But yes, it can be undone.'

It seemed to her that he was drawing encouragement from this lengthening colloquy, and that she certainly did not desire. So she rose, and pleaded her very real weariness to rid herself of his continuing assiduities as gently as possible. Vivian departed reluctantly but still gracefully, looking back from the doorway for a long, ingratiating moment before he swung about and went, lithe and long-legged and elegant, down the street called Maerdol towards the bridge.

But even when he was gone, the evening was full of echoes of the morning, reminders of disaster, reproaches of folly, as Agatha worried away at the past.

'You see now how foolish it was to make such a ballad-romance agreement, like any green girl. A rose, indeed! You should never have given away half your patrimony so rashly, how could you know when you and yours might have great need of it? And now see what it's come to! A death, and all at the door of that foolish charter.'

'You need not trouble any longer,' said Judith wearily. 'I do repent it. It is not too late to amend it. Let me alone now. There is nothing you could say to me that I have not already said to myself.'

She went early to her bed, and the girl Branwen, relieved of the carding that brought her out in a rash, and put to work for a time in the household, came to fetch and carry for her, fold away into the chest the gown her mistress discarded, and curtain the unshuttered window. Branwen was fond of Judith, but not sorry, on this occasion, to be dismissed early, for Vivian's serving-man, left behind to carry home the bolt of cloth for Mistress Hynde, was settled cosily in the kitchen, throwing dice with Bertred, the foreman of the weavers, and both of them were personable fellows with an eye for a pretty girl. Branwen was not at all averse to being the desirable bone between two handsome dogs. Sometimes she had felt that Bertred had ideas above his station, and was casting a greedy eye in the direction of his mistress, being vain of his sturdy, straight body and fresh, comely face, and a silver tongue to match. But nothing would ever come of that! And when he had Master Hynde's Gunnar across the table from him, plainly captivated, he might better appreciate more accessible meat.

'Go now,' said Judith, loosing the great sheaf of her hair about her shoulders. 'I shan't need you tonight. But call me very early in the morning,' she added with sudden resolution, 'for I'm going to the abbey. I'll not leave this matter lying one hour more than need be. Tomorrow I'll go to the abbot and have a new charter drawn up. No more roses! The gift I made for so foolish a fee I'll now make unconditional.'

Branwen was proud of her advancement into Judith's personal service, and fondly imagined herself closer in her mistress's confidence than in fact she was. And with two young men in the kitchen already interested in her and prepared to be impressed, what wonder if she boasted of being the first to be entrusted with Judith's plans for the morrow? It seemed a pity that Gunnar should so soon afterwards recall that he had to carry home Mistress Hynde's cloth, and might end with a flea in his ear if he delayed too long. And though that left her the attentions of Bertred, whom on the whole she preferred, his pricked sense of proprietorship in a woman of this household seemed to flag disappointingly once his rival was out of the house. It was not, after all, a satisfactory evening. Branwen went to her bed out of temper between disillusionment and dudgeon, and out of sorts with men.

Young Alan Herbard, Hugh's deputy, dutiful and determined though he was, drew the line at coping unaided with murder, and had had a courier on the road as soon as the news came to his ears. By noon of the next day, which was the eighteenth day of June, Hugh would surely be back in Shrewsbury, not in his own house, where only one elderly servant remained during the family's absence, but at the castle, where garrison, sergeant and all were at his disposal.

Meantime, Cadfael betook himself and his waxen footprint, with the abbot's blessing, into the town, and showed mould and drawing to Geoffrey Corviser, the provost, and his son Philip, the foremost shoemakers and leather workers in the town. 'For sooner or later every boot comes into the cobbler's hands,' he said simply, 'though it may be a year ahead or more. No harm, at least, in keeping a copy of such witness as you see there, and looking out for the like among any you repair.'

Philip handled the wax delicately, and nodded over the evidence it provided of its wearer's tread. 'I don't know it, but it will be easily seen if ever it does find its way in here. And I'll show it to the cobbler over the bridge, in Frankwell. Between us, who knows, we may run the fellow down in the end. But there's many a man patches his own,' said the good craftsman with professional disdain.

A thin chance enough, Cadfael admitted to himself on his way back over the bridge, but one that could not be neglected. What else had they to offer a lead? Little enough, except the inevitable and unanswerable question: Who could possibly have wanted to destroy the rose-bush? And for what conceivable reason? A question they had all voiced already, without profit, and one that would be posed all over again when Hugh arrived.

Instead of turning in at the gatehouse Cadfael passed by and walked the length of the Foregate, along the dusty highway, past the bakery, past the forge, exchanging greetings in at doorways and over hedges as he went, to turn in at the gate of Niall's yard, and cross to the wicket which led through into the garden. It was bolted fast on the inner side. Cadfael turned instead to the shop, where Niall was at work with a small ceramic crucible and a tiny clay mould for a brooch.

'I came to see if you'd had any further night visitors,' said Cadfael, 'but I see you've secured one way in, at least. A pity there's no wall ever built high enough to keep out a man determined to get in. But even stopping one hole is something. What of the bush? Will it live?'

'Come and see. One side may die off, but it's no more than two or three branches. It may leave the tree lopsided, but a year or so, and pruning and growth will balance all.'

In the green and sunlight and tangled colour of the garden the rose-bush spread its arms firmly against the north wall, the dangling trailers pegged back to the stone with strips of cloth. Niall had wound a length of stout canvas round and round the damaged bole, binding the severed wood together, and coated the covering with a thick layer of wax and grease.

'There's love been put into this,' said Cadfael approvingly, but wisely did not say whether for the bush or the woman. The leaves on the half-severed part had wilted, and a few had fallen, but the bulk of the tree stood green and glossy, and full of half-open buds. 'You've done well by it. I could use you inside the enclave, if ever you tire of bronze and the world.'

The quiet, decent man never opened his mouth to answer that. Whatever he felt for woman or rose was his business, no other man's. Cadfael respected that, and viewing the wide, wide-set, honest and yet reticent eyes, he took his leave and set off back to his proper duties feeling somewhat reproved, and curiously elated. One man at least in this sorry business kept his eyes on his own course, and would not easily be turned aside. And he, surely, looking for no gain. Somewhere in all this there was greed of gain more than enough, and little enough of love.

It was almost noon by this time, and the sun high and hot, a true June day. Saint Winifred must have been at work coaxing the heavens to do her honour for the festival of her translation. As so often happened in a late season, the summer had all but caught up with the laggard spring, flowers which had lingered shivering and reluctant to bloom suddenly sprang into fevered haste, bursting their buds overnight into a blazing prime. The crops, slower to take risks, might still be as much as a month late, but they would be lavish and clean, half their hereditary enemies chilled to death in April and May.

In the doorway of his lodge in the gatehouse Brother Porter was standing in earnest talk with an agitated young man. Cadfael, always vulnerable to curiosity, his prevalent sin, halted, wavered and turned aside, recognising Miles Coliar, that tidy, practical, trim young fellow a great deal less trim than usual, his hair blown and teased erect in disorder, his bright blue eyes dilated beneath drawn and anxious copper brows. Miles turned his head, hearing a new step approaching, and recognised, through a haze of worry, a brother he had seen only the previous day sitting amicably with his cousin. He swung about eagerly.

'Brother, I remember you – you were of some comfort and

help yesterday to Judith. You have not seen her today? She has not spoken again with you?'

'She has not,' said Cadfael, surprised. 'Why? What is new now? She went home with you yesterday. I trust she has met with no further grief?'

'No, none that I know of. I do know she went to her bed in good time, and I hoped she would sleep well. But now . . .' He cast a vague, distracted glance about him: 'They tell me at home she set out to come here. But . . .'

'She has not been here,' said the porter positively. 'I have not left my post, I should know if she had entered the gate. I know the lady from the time she came here making her gift to the house. I have not set eyes on her today. But Master Coliar here says she left home very early . . .'

'*Very* early,' Miles confirmed vehemently. 'Before I was waking.'

'And with intent to come here on some errand to the lord abbot,' concluded the porter.

'So her maid told me,' said Miles, sweating. 'Judith told her so last night, when the girl attended her to bed. I knew nothing of it until this morning. But it seems she has not been here. She never reached here. And she has not come home again. Midday, and she has not come home! I dread something ill has befallen her.'

## Chapter Six

There were five of them gathered in the abbot's parlour that
afternoon, in urgent conclave: Radulfus himself, Brothers
Anselm and Cadfael, witnesses to the charter which had
somehow precipitated these dire events, Miles Coliar,
restless and fevered with anxiety, and Hugh Beringar, who
had ridden south in haste from Maesbury with Eluric's
murder on his mind, to find on arrival that a second crisis had
followed hard on the heels of the first. He had already
deputed Alan Herbard to send men hunting through the
town and the Foregate for any sign or news of the missing
lady, with orders to send word if by any chance she should
have returned home. There could, after all, be legitimate
reasons for her absence, something unforeseen that had met
and deflected her on her way. But minute by minute it began
to look less likely. Branwen had told her tearful story, and
there was no question but Judith had indeed set out from
home to visit the abbey. None, either, that she had never
reached it.

'The girl never told me what my cousin had said, until this
morning,' said Miles, twisting frustrated hands. 'I knew
nothing of it, or I could have borne her company. So short a
walk, down here from the town! And the watchman at the
town gate said good day to her and saw her start across the
bridge, but after that he was busy, and had no call to watch
her go. And not a sign of her from that moment.'

'And she said her errand was to remit the rose rent,' said
Hugh intently, 'and make her gift to the abbey free of all
conditions?'

'So her maid says. So Judith told her. She was much
distressed,' said Miles, 'over the young brother's death. She
surely took it to heart that it was her whim brought about
that murder.'

'It has yet to be explained,' said Abbot Radulfus, 'why that should be. Truly it does appear that Brother Eluric interrupted the attack upon the rose-bush, and was killed for his pains, perhaps in mere panic, yet killed he was. What I do not understand is why anyone should wish to destroy the rose-bush in the first place. But for that inexplicable deed there would have been no interruption and no death. Who could want to hack down the bush? What possible motive could there be?'

'Ah, but, Father, there could!' Miles turned on him with feverish vehemence. 'There were some not best pleased when my cousin gave away so valuable a property, worth the half of all she has. If the bush was hacked down and all the roses dead by the day of Saint Winifred's translation, the rent could not be paid, and the terms of the charter would have been broken. The whole bargain could be repudiated.'

'Could,' Hugh pointed out briskly, 'but would not. The matter would still be in the lady's hands, she could remit the rent at will. And you see she had the will.'

'She *could* remit it,' Miles echoed with sharp intent, '*if she were here to do it.* But she is not here. Four days until the payment is due, and she has vanished. Time gained, time gained! Whoever failed to destroy the bush has now abducted my cousin. She is not here to grant or deny. What he did not accomplish by one way he now approaches by another.'

There was a brief, intent silence, and then the abbot said slowly: 'Do you indeed believe that? You speak as one believing.'

'I do, my lord. I see no other possibility. Yesterday she announced her intention of making her gift unconditional. Today that has been prevented. There was no time to be lost.'

'Yet you yourself did not know what she meant to do,' said Hugh, 'not until today. Did any other know of it?'

'Her maid owns she repeated it in the kitchen. Who knows how many heard it then, or got it from those who did? Such things come out through keyholes and the chinks of shutters. Moreover, Judith may have met with some acquaintance on the bridge or in the Foregate, and told them where she was bound. However lightly and thoughtlessly she had that provision written into the charter, the failure to observe it would render the bargain null and void. Father, you know that is true.'

'I do know it,' acknowledged Radulfus, and came at last to the unavoidable question: 'Who, then, could possibly stand to gain by breaking the agreement, by whatever means?'

'Father, my cousin is young, and a widow, and a rich prize in marriage, all the richer if her gift to you could be annulled. There are a bevy of suitors about the town pursuing her, and have been now for a year and more, and every one of them would rather marry the whole of her wealth than merely the half. Me, I manage the business for her, I'm very well content with what I have, and with the wife I'm to marry before the year's out, a good match. But even if we were not first cousins I should have no interest in Judith but as a loyal kinsman and craftsman should. But I cannot choose but know how she is pestered with wooers. Not that she encourages any of them, nor ever gives them grounds for hope, but they never cease their efforts. After three years and more of widowhood, they reason, her resolution must surely weaken, and she'll be worn down into taking a second husband at last. It may be that one of them is running out of patience.'

'To name names,' said Hugh mildly, 'may sometimes be dangerous, but to call a man a wooer is not necessarily to call him an abductor and murderer into the bargain. And I think you have gone so far, Master Coliar, that in this company you may as well go the rest of the way.'

Miles moistened his lips and brushed a sleeve across his beaded forehead. 'Business looks to business for a match, my lord. There are two guildsmen in the town, at least, who would be only too glad to get hold of Judith's trade, and both of them work in with us, and know well enough what she's worth. There's Godfrey Fuller does all the dyeing of our fleeces, and the fulling of the cloth at the end of it, and he'd dearly like to make himself the master of the spinning and weaving, too, and have all in one profitable basket. And then there's old William Hynde, he has a wife still, but by another road he could get his hands on the Vestier property, for he has a young spark of a son who comes courting her day in,

76

day out, and has the entry because they know each other from children. The father might be willing to use him as bait for a woman, though he's drawn his purse-strings tight from paying the young fellow's debts any longer. And the son – if he could win her I fancy he'd be set up for life, but not dance to his father's tune, more likely to laugh in his face. And that's not the whole of it, for our neighbour the saddler is just of an age to feel the want of a wife, and in his plodding way has settled on her as suitable. And our best weaver chances to be a very good craftsmen and a fine-looking man, and fancies himself even prettier than he is, and he's been casting sheep's eyes at her lately, though I doubt if she even noticed. There's more than one comely journeyman has caught his mistress's eye and done very well for himself.'

'Hard to imagine our solid guildsmen resorting to murder and abduction,' objected the abbot, unwilling to accept so readily a suggestion so outrageous.

'But the murder,' Hugh pointed out alertly, 'seems to have been done in alarm and terror, and probably never was intended. Yet having so far committed himself, why should a man stop at the second crime?'

'Still it seems to me a hazardous business, for from all I know or have heard about the lady, she would not easily give way to persuasion. Captive or free, she has thus far resisted all blandishments, she will not change now. I do understand,' said Radulfus ruefully, 'what force of compulsion the common report may bring to bear in such a case, how a woman might feel it better to yield and marry than endure the scandal of suspicion and the ill will between families that must follow. But this lady, it seems to me, might well survive even that pressure. Then her captor would have gained nothing.'

Miles drew deep breath, and ran a hand through his fair curls, dragging them wildly awry. 'Father, what you say is true, Judith is a strong spirit, and will not easily be broken. But, Father, there may be worse! Marriage by rape is no new thing. Once in a man's power, hidden away with no means of escape, if coaxing and persuasion have no effect, there remains force. It has been known time and time again. My lord Beringar here will witness it happens among the nobility, and I know it happens among the commonalty. Even a town tradesman might resort to it at last. And I know my cousin, if once her virtue was lost, she might well think it best to mend her sorry state by marriage. Wretched though that remedy must be.'

'Wretched indeed!' agreed Radulfus with detestation. 'Such a thing must not be. Hugh, this house is deeply committed here, the charter and the gift draw us in, and whatever aid we can lend you to recover this unhappy lady is at your disposal, men, funds, whatever you require. No need to ask – take! And as for our prayers, they shall not be wanting. There is still some frail chance that no harm has come to her, and she may yet return home of her own volition, and wonder at this fury and alarm. But now we must reckon with the worst, and hunt as for a soul in danger.'

'Then we'd best be about it,' said Hugh, and rose to take his leave. Miles was on his feet with a nervous spring, eager and anxious, and would have been first out at the door if Cadfael had not opened his mouth for the first time in this conference.

'I did hear, Master Coliar, indeed I know from Mistress Perle herself, that she has sometimes thought of leaving the world and taking the veil. Sister Magdalen talked with her about such a vocation a few days ago, I believe. Did you know of it?'

'I knew the sister came visiting,' said Miles, his blue eyes widening. 'What they said I was not told and did not ask. That was Judith's business. She has sometimes talked of it, but less of late.'

'Did you encourage such a step?' asked Cadfael.

'I never interfered, one way or the other. It would have been her decision. I would not urge it,' said Miles forcibly, 'but neither would I stand in her way if that was what she wanted. At least,' he said with sudden bitterness, 'that would have been a good and peaceful ending. Now only God knows what her dismay and despair must be.'

'There goes a most dutiful and loving cousin,' said Hugh, as Cadfael walked beside him across the great court. Miles was striding out at the gatehouse arch with hair on end, making for the town, and the house and shop at Maerdol-head, where there might by this time be news. A frail chance, but still possible.

'He has good cause,' said Cadfael reasonably. 'But for Mistress Perle and the Vestier business he and his mother would not be in the comfortable state they are. He has everything to lose, should she give in to force and agree to marriage. He owes his cousin much, and by all accounts he's requited her very well, with gratitude and good management. Works hard and to good effect, the business is flourishing. He may well be frantic about her now. Do I hear a certain sting in your voice, lad? Have you doubts about him?'

'No, none. He has no more idea where the girl is now than you or I, that's clear. A man may dissemble very well, up to a point, but I never knew a man who could sweat at will. No, Miles is telling the truth. He's off now to turn the town upside-down hunting for her. And so must I.'

'She had but so short a way to go,' said Cadfael, fretting at the fine detail, which left so little room for doubt that she was gone, that something untoward had indeed happened to her. 'The watch at the gate spoke to her, she had only to cross the bridge and walk this short piece of the Foregate to our gatehouse. A river to cross, a short walk along open road, and in those few minutes she's gone.'

'The river,' said Hugh honestly, 'has been on my mind. I won't deny it.'

'I doubt if it need be. Unless truly by some ill chance. No man is going to make himself rich or his business more prosperous by marriage with a dead woman. Only her heir would benefit by that, and her heir – I suppose that boy must be her nearest kin? – is going out of his mind worrying over what's happened to her, as you yourself have seen. There's nothing false about the state he's in. No, *if* some wooer has determined on drastic action, he'll have spirited her away into some safe place, not done her harm. We need not mourn for the lady, not yet, she'll be guarded like a miser's gold.'

* * *

Cadfael's mind was occupied with the problem until Vespers and beyond. From the bridge to the abbey gatehouse there were but three footpaths leaving the Foregate, two that branched off to the right, one on either side the mill-pond, to serve the six small houses there, the other descending on the left to the long riverside tract of the Gaye, the main abbey gardens. Cover was sparse along the high road, any act of violence would be risky there, and the paths that served the abbey houses suffered the disadvantage, from a conspirator's point of view, of being overlooked by the windows of all six cottages, and in this high summer there would be no shutters closed. The old woman in one cot was stone deaf, and would not have heard even the loudest screams, but generally old people sleep lightly and fitfully, and also, being no longer able to get about as actively as before, they have rather more than their share of curiosity, to fill up the tedium of their days. It would be a bold or a desperate man who attempted violence under their windows.

No trees drew close about the road on that, the southern side of the Foregate, only a few low bushes fringing the pond, and the scrub-covered slope down to the river. Only on the northern side were there well-grown trees, from the end of the bridge, where the path wound down to the Gaye, to a grove some little way short of the abbey gatehouse, where the houses of the Foregate began.

Now if a woman could be drawn aside there, even into the fringe of shadow, at that early hour and with few people abroad, it would not be so difficult to seize a moment when the road was empty and drag her further into the grove, or down among the bushes, with a cloak twisted about her head and arms. But in that case the person involved, man or woman, would have to be someone known to her, someone who could detain her plausibly in talk for a matter of minutes beside the road. Which fitted in well enough with the suggestion Miles had made, for even an unwelcome suitor who was also a town neighbour would be encountered in the ordinary meetings of the day with tolerance and civility. Life in a walled and crowded borough cannot be carried on otherwise.

There might, of course, be other reasons for removing the

girl from home and family, though they would have to have something to do with the matter of the charter and the rose-bush, for surely that could not be some lunatic accident, unconnected with her disappearance. There might! But with all the cudgelling of his brains Cadfael could think of none. And a rich merchant widow in a town where everyone knew everyone was inevitably besieged by suitors out to make their fortunes. Her only safe defence was the one Judith had contemplated, withdrawal into a convent. Or, of course, marriage to whichever of the contestants best pleased or least repelled her. And that, so far, she had not contemplated. It might well be true that the one who considered himself most likely to please had risked all on his chance of softening the lady's heart in a few days of secret courtship. And keeping her hidden until after the twenty-second day of June could break the bargain with the abbey just as surely as destroying the rose-bush and all its blossoms. However many roses survived now, unless Judith was found in time not one of them could be paid into her hand on the day the rent was due. So provided her captor prevailed at last, and drove her to marry him, her affairs would then be his, and he could refuse to renew and prevent her from renewing the broken agreement. And he would have won all, not the half. Yes, whichever way Cadfael viewed the affair, this notion propounded by Miles, who had everything to lose, looked ever more convincing.

He went to his cell with Judith still on his mind. Her well-being seemed to him very much the abbey's business, something that could not be left merely to the secular arm. Tomorrow, he thought, lying awake in the dim dortoir, to the regular bass music of Brother Richard's snores, I'll walk that stretch of road, and see what's there to be found. Who knows but there may be something left behind, more to the point than a single print of a worn boot-heel.

He asked no special leave, for had not the abbot already pledged Hugh whatever men or horses or gear he needed? It was but a small mental leap to establish in his own mind that if Hugh had not specifically demanded his help, he would have done so had he known how his friend's mind was working. Such small exercises in moral agility still came easily to him, where the need seemed to justify them.

He set out after chapter, sallying forth into a Foregate swept by the long, slanting rays of the climbing sun, brilliantly lit and darkly shadowed. In the shade there was dew still on the grass, and a glisten in the leaves as a faint, steady, silent breeze ruffled them unceasingly. The Foregate on which he turned his back was bustling with life, every shop-front and house-door opened wide to the summer, and a constant traffic of housewives, urchins, dogs, carters and pedlars on the move, or gathered in gossiping groups. In this belated but lovely burst of summer, life quitted the confines of walls and roof, and moved into the sunshine. Under the west front of the church and across the gateway the knife-edged shadow of the tower fell, but along the enclave boundary it lay close and narrow, huddled under the foot of the wall.

Cadfael went slowly, exchanging greetings with such acquaintances as he met, but unwilling to be sidetracked into lingering. This first stretch of the road she could not have reached, and the steps he was retracing on her behalf were those of a pious intent which had never come to fruit. On his left, the lofty stone wall continued for the length of the great court and the infirmary and school within, then turned away at a right-angle, and alongside it went the first pathway that led past three small grace houses to the mill, on this near side of the mill-pond. Then the wide expanse of the pool, fringed with a low hedge of bushes. He would not and could not believe that Judith Perle had vanished into either this water or the waves of the river. Whoever had taken her – if someone had indeed taken her – wanted and needed her alive and unharmed and ripe for conquest. Hugh had no choice but to draw his net wide and entertain every possibility. Cadfael preferred to follow one notion at a time. Hugh would almost certainly have enlisted the help of Madog of the Dead Boat by this time, to pursue the worst possibilities of death by water, while the king's sergeants scoured the streets and alleys and houses of Shrewsbury for a live and captive lady. Madog knew every wave of the Severn, every seasonal trick it had in its power to play, every bend or shoal where things swept away by its currents would be cast up again. If the river had taken her, Madog would find her. But Cadfael would not believe it.

And if Hugh also failed to find her within the walls of Shrewsbury? Then they would have to look beyond. It's no simple matter to transport an unwilling lady very far, and by daylight. Could it even be done at all, short of using a cart? A horseman carrying such a swathed burden would need a horse powerful enough to carry the extra weight, and worse, would certainly be conspicuous. Someone would surely remember him, or even question him on the spot, human curiosity being what it is. No, she could not, surely, be far away.

Cadfael passed by the pool, and came to the second pathway, on this further side, which served the other three little houses. Beyond, after their narrow gardens, there was an open field, and at the end of that, turning sharply left, a narrow high road going south along the riverside. By that track an abductor might certainly retreat within a mile or so into the forest, but on the other hand there was no cover here along the riverside, any attack perpetrated there could be seen even from the town walls across the water.

But on the right of the Foregate, once the houses ended, the thick grove of trees began, and after that the steep path dived down sidelong to the bank of the Severn, through bushes and trees, giving access to the long, lush level of the Gaye. Beyond that, she would still have been on the open bridge, and surely inviolable. Here, if anywhere in this short walk, there was room for a predator to strike and withdraw with his prey. She had to be prevented from reaching the abbey and doing what she intended to do. There would be no second chance. And the house of the rose was indeed a property well worth reclaiming.

With every moment the thing began to look more and more credible. Improbable, perhaps, in an ordinary tradesman, as law-abiding as his neighbours and respected by all; but a man who has tried one relatively harmless expedient, and inadvertently killed a man in consequence, is no longer ordinary.

Cadfael crossed the Foregate and went into the grove of

trees, stepping warily to avoid adding any tracks to those already all too plentiful. The imps of the Foregate played here, attended by their noisy camp-following of dogs, and tearfully trailed by those lesser imps as yet too small to be taken seriously and admitted to their games, and too short in the legs to keep up with them. In the more secluded clearings lovers met in the dark, their nests neatly coiled in the flattened grasses. Small hope of finding anything of use here.

He turned back to the road, and walked on the few paces to the path that descended to the Gaye. Before him the stone bridge extended, and beyond it the high town wall and the tower of the gate. Sunlight bathed the roadway and the walls, blanching the stone to a creamy pallor. The Severn, running a little higher than its usual summer level, shimmered and stirred with a deceptive appearance of placidity and languor, but Cadfael knew how fast those smooth currents were running, and what vehement undertows coursed beneath the blue, sky-mirroring surface. Most male children here learned to swim almost as soon as they learned to walk, and there were places where the Severn could be as gentle and safe as its smiling mask, but here where it coiled about the town, leaving only one approach by land, the narrow neck straddled by the castle, it was a perilous water. Could Judith Perle swim? It was no easy matter for girl-children to strip and caper along the grassy shores and flash in and out of the stream as the boys did, and for them it must be a more rare accomplishment.

At the town end of the bridge Judith had passed, unhindered and alone; the watchman had seen her begin to cross. Hard to believe that any man had dared to molest her here on the open crossing, where she had only to utter a single cry, and the watchman would have heard her, and looked out in instant alarm. So she had arrived at this spot where Cadfael was standing. And then? As far as present reports went, no one had seen her since.

Cadfael began the descent to the Gaye. This path was trodden regularly, and bare of grass, and the landward bushes that fringed it drew gradually back from its edge, leaving the level, cultivated ground open. On the river side they grew thickly, all down the slope to the water, and under the first arch of the bridge, where once a boat-mill had been moored to make use of the force of the current. Close to the waterside a footpath led off downstream, and beside it the abbey's gardens lay neatly arrayed all along the rich plain, and three or four brothers were pricking out plants of cabbage and colewort. Further along came the orchards, apple and pear and plum, the sweet cherry, and two big walnut trees, and the low bushes of little sour gooseberries that were only just beginning to flush into colour. There was another disused mill at the end of the level, and the final abbey ground was a field of corn. Then ridges of woodland came down and overhung the water, and the curling eddies ate away the bank beneath their roots.

Across the broad river the hill of Shrewsbury rose in a great sweep of green, that wore the town wall like a coronet. Two or three small wickets gave access through the wall to gardens and grass below. They could easily be barred and blocked in case of attack, and the clear outlook such a raised fortress commanded gave ample notice of any approach. The vulnerable neck unprotected by water was filled by the castle, completing the circle of the wall. A strong place, as well as a very fair one, yet King Stephen had taken it by storm, four years ago, and held it through his sheriffs ever since.

But all this stretch of our land, Cadfael thought, brooding over its prolific green, is overlooked by hundreds of houses and households there within the wall. How many moments can there be in the day when someone is not peering out from a window, this weather, or below by the riverside, fishing, or hanging out washing, or the children playing and bathing? Not, perhaps, so many of them, so early in the morning, but surely someone. And never a word said of struggle or flight, or of something heavy and human-shaped being carried. No, not this way. Our lands here are open and innocent. The only hidden reach is here, here beside the bridge or under it, where trees and bushes give cover.

He waded the bushes towards the arch, and the last of the dew darkened his sandals and the skirt of his habit, but sparsely now, surviving only here, in the deep green shade. Below the stone arch the water had sunk only a foot or so from its earlier fullness, leaving a bleaching fringe of grass and water-plants. A man could walk through dry-shod but for dew. Even the winter level or the flush of the spring thaw never came nearer than six feet of the crown of the arch. The green growth was fat and lavish and tangled, suckled on rich, moist earth.

Someone had been before him here, the grasses were parted and bent aside by the passage of at least one person, probably more. That was nothing very unusual, boys roam everywhere in their play, and in their mischief, too. What was less usual here was the deep groove driven into the moist soil uncovered by the recent lowering of the level, and prolonged into the grass above. A boat had been drawn aground there, and no long time ago, either. At the town end of the bridge there were always boats beached or moored, handy for their owners' use. But seldom here.

Cadfael squatted close to view the ground. The grass had absorbed any marks left by feet, except for the lowest lip of the land, and there certainly at least one man had trampled the moist ground, but the mud had slithered under him and obliterated any shape he had left behind. One man or two, for the spread of slippery mud showed both sides of the groove the skiff had made.

If he had not been sitting on his heels he would never have caught the single alien thing, for there under the arch there was no glint of sunlight to betray it. But there it was, trodden into the disturbed mud, a metallic thread like a wisp of reddish-gold straw, no longer than the top joint of his thumb. He prised it out and it lay in his palm, a tiny arrow-head without a shaft, bent a little out of shape by the foot that had trodden it in. He stooped to rinse it in the edge of the river, and carried it out into the sunshine.

And now he saw it for what it was, the bronze tag which had sealed the end of a leather girdle, a delicate piece of work, incised with punch and hammer after being attached to the belt, and surely not torn from its anchorage now without considerable violence and struggle.

Cadfael turned in his tracks, strode up the steep path to the road, and set off back along the Foregate at his fastest pace.

# Chapter Seven

'This is hers,' said Niall, looking up from the scrap of bronze with a fixed and formidable face. 'I know it, though I did not make it. It belongs to that girdle she took back with her, the morning Brother Eluric lay here dead. I made the new buckle to match this design, this and the rosettes round the tongue-holes. I should know it anywhere. It is hers. Where did you find it?'

'Under the first arch of the bridge, where a boat had been hauled up in hiding.'

'To carry her away! And this – trodden into the mud, you say. See, when this was set in place it was hammered home into the leather with the pattern, it would not come loose easily, even after years, and with the leather softening and thinning from use, and perhaps a little greasy with handling. Someone was rough with the girdle, to tear this away.'

'And with the lady also,' Cadfael agreed grimly. 'I could not be sure, myself, I hardly saw the girdle when she took it in her hands that day. But you could not be mistaken. Now I know. One step at least on the way. And a boat – a boat would be the simplest means of all of carrying her off. No neighbour passing close, to query such large freight, no one ashore to wonder at any passing skiff, they're common enough along the Severn. The girdle from which this came may well have been snatched to help to bind her.'

'And she to be used so foully!' Niall wiped his large, capable hands on the rag of woollen cloth on his bench, and began purposefully unfastening and laying by his leathern apron. 'What is to be done now? Tell me how best I can help – where first to look for her. I'll close my shop—'

'No,' said Cadfael, 'make no move, only keep watch still on the rose-bush, for I have this strange fancy the life of the

87

one is bound up fast with the life of the other. What is there you could do elsewhere that Hugh Beringar cannot? He has men enough, and trust me, they're all hard at it, he'll see to that. Stay here and be patient, and whatever I discover you shall know. Your business is bronze, not boats, you've done your part.'

'And you, what will you do now?' Niall hesitated, frowning, unwilling to be left with the passive part.

'I'm off to find Hugh Beringar as fast as I can, and after him Madog, who knows all there is to know about boats, from his own coracles to the freight barges that fetch the wool clips away. Madog may be able to tell what manner of boat it was from the very dent it left behind in the mud. You bide here and be as easy as you can. With God's help we'll find her.'

He looked back once from the doorway, impressed by the charged silence at his back. The man of few words remained quite still, staring into some invisible place where Judith Perle stood embattled and alone, captive to greed and brutality. Even her good works conspired against her, even her generosity turned venomous, to poison her life. The controlled and uncommunicative face was eloquent enough at that moment. And if those big, adroit hands, so precise on his tiny crucibles and moulds, could once get a hold on the throat of whoever has rapt away Judith Perle, thought Cadfael as he hurried back towards the town, I doubt if the king's justice would have any need of a hangman, or the trial cost the shire much money.

The porter at the town gate sent a boy hotfoot up to the castle in search of Hugh as soon as Cadfael came to report, somewhat breathlessly, that there was need of the sheriff down at the waterside. It took a little time to find him, however, and Cadfael made use of the interval by going in search of Madog of the Dead Boat. He knew well enough where to find him, provided he was not already out on the water somewhere, about some curious part of his varied business. He had a hut tucked under the lee of the western bridge that opened the road into his native Wales, and there he made coracles, or timber boats if required, fished in season, ferried fares on request, carried goods for a fee, anything to do with transport by water. The time being then past noon, Madog happened to be taking a brief rest and a solitary meal when Cadfael reached the bridge. A squat, muscular, hairy elderly Welshman, without kith or kin and in no need of either, for he was sufficient to himself and had been since childhood, he yet had an open welcome for his friends. He needed no one, but if others needed him he was at their disposal. Once summoned, he rose and came.

Hugh was at the gate before them. They crossed the bridge together, and came down to the waterside and under the dim, cool shadow of the arch.

'Here in the mud,' said Cadfael, 'I found this, torn off surely in a struggle. It comes from a girdle belonging to Mistress Perle, for Niall Bronzesmith made a new buckle to match the belt fittings only a few days ago, and this was the pattern he had to copy. That puts it past doubt, he knows his work. And here someone had a boat laid up ready.'

'As like as not stolen,' said Madog judicially, eyeing the deep mark in the soil. 'For such a cantrip, why use your own? Then if it's noted, and any man smells something amiss about where it's seen and what's within it, nothing leads towards you. And this was early in the morning, yesterday? Now I wonder if any fisherman or waterman from the town has mislaid his boat from its moorings? I know a dozen could have left this scar. And all you need do, when you'd done with the skiff, would be turn it adrift to fetch up where it would.'

'That could only be downstream,' said Hugh, looking up from the little arrow-head of bronze in his palm.

'So it could! Only downstream from wherever he had done with it. And even that would surely be downstream from here, if here he set out with such a cargo. Far easier and safer than heading upstream. Early in the morning it may have been, and few people yet abroad, but by the time one rower, or even a pair, had taken a boat all round the walls of the town against the stream, as they'd have to do to get clear, there'd be folks enough about the shore and the water. Even after turning away from the town they'd have Frankwell to face – a good hour's rowing before they'd be free of notice and curiosity. Downstream, once past this stretch of the wall and out from under the castle, they could breathe easily, they'd be between fields and woodland, clear of the town.'

'That's good sense,' said Hugh. 'I don't say upstream is impossible, but we'll follow the best chance first. God knows we've dragged every alley within the walls, and ransacked most of the houses, and are still hard at it in there finishing the work. Not a soul owns to having seen or heard anything of her since last she spoke with the watchman at the gate, and started across the bridge here. And if ever she went, or was taken, back into the town, it was not by the gate. The porter passed in no cart or load that could have been hiding her, so he swears. Still, there are wickets through here and there, though most of them into burgage gardens, and it would be no easy matter to get through to the streets without the household knowing of it. I begin to believe that she cannot be within the walls, but I've set men at every wicket that gives access to a street, and made entry to every house an order under the king's justice. What's the same for all cannot well be resisted or complained of.'

'And has not?' wondered Cadfael. 'Never once?'

'They grumble, but even that under their breath. No, not one has put up any objection, nor shuffled and contrived to keep anything closed. And all yesterday until dusk I had her cousin treading on my heels, probing here and there like a worried hound on an uncertain scent. He's set two or three of his weavers to help in the hunt for her. The foreman – Bertred they call him, a strapping young fellow all brawn and brag – he's been out and about with us again all day, nose-down. He's gone with a party of my men now, out along the Castle Foregate, searching the yards and gardens in the suburb, and round to the river again. All her household is biting its nails, frantic to find her. And no wonder, for it's she who provides a living for the lot of them – a matter of twenty families or more depend on her. And never a hair of her to be found, and never a shadow of suspicion against any other creature, so far.'

'How did you do with Godfrey Fuller?' asked Cadfael, recalling what rumour said of Judith's wooers.

Hugh laughed briefly. 'I remember, too! And truth is truth, he seems as concerned about her almost as her cousin. What does he do but hand me all his keys, and bid me make free. And I did.'

'His keys for the dye-works and the fulling sheds, too?'

'All, though I needed none, for all his men were at work, and every corner open to view, and as innocent as the day. I think he would even have lent me some men to join the hunt, but that he's too fond of money to let the work slacken.'

'And William Hynde?'

'The old woolman? He's been away sleeping the night over with his shepherds and flocks, so his household said, and came home only this morning. He knew nothing about the girl going astray until then. Alan was there yesterday, and Hynde's wife made no demur, but let him look where he would, but I went back there this morning and spoke with the man himself. He's off back to the hills before night. It seems he has some hoggets up there with a rot of the feet, he and his man came back only to get a supply of the wash to treat them. And more concerned about them than about Mistress Perle, though he did say he was sorry to hear such news of her. By this time I'm certain she's not within the town. So,' said Hugh briskly, 'we may well look elsewhere. Downstream, we're agreed. Madog, come back with us to the town gate and get us a boat, and we'll take a look at what offers, downstream.'

In midstream, running with the current, and with only a twitch of Madog's oars now and then to keep them on course, they had the whole expanse of Shrewsbury's eastern side unrolling past them, a steep bank of green under the wall, here and there a cluster of low bushes at the water's edge, here and there a trailing willow tree, but chiefly one long sweep of seeding summer grass, and then the lofty grey stone of the wall. Barely a single ridge of roof showed over the crest, only the top of Saint Mary's spire and tower, and a more distant glimpse of the tip of Saint Alkmund's. There were three wickets in the wall before they reached the mouth of Saint Mary's water-lane, which gave access to the river from town and castle at need, and in places the householders within had extended their gardens to the outer side, or made use of the ground, where it was level enough, for their stores of wood or other materials for their crafts. But the slope here made cultivation difficult except in favoured spots, and the best gardens outside the wall were on the south-west, within the great serpent-coil of the river.

They passed the narrow walled chute of the water-lane, and beyond was another steep slope of grass, more cloaked in bushes here, before the town wall drew closer to the river, flanking the level, cleared strip of green where the young men were accustomed to set up the butts and practise their archery on holidays and fair-days. At the end of this ground there was one last wicket, close under the first tower of the castle, and past that the ground levelled, a sweep of open field between the water and the high road that emerged under the castle gates. Here, as on the Welsh side, the town had spilled beyond the wall for a short way, and little houses, close-set, bordered the road, huddling under the shadow of the great hulk of stone towers and curtain wall that straddled the only dry-shod approach to Shrewsbury.

The open meadows stretched away, widening, into an undulating expanse of field and woodland, peaceful and serene. The only remaining reminders of the town were here close beside the river, Godfrey Fuller's sheds and fulling-troughs and tenterground, and a short way beyond, the substantial warehouse where William Hynde's best fleeces lay corded and ready, waiting for the middleman's barge to come and collect them, and the narrow, stout jetty where it would draw alongside to load.

There were men going busily in and out here about the fulling workshop, and two lengths of bright russet cloth stretched and drying on the frames. This was the season for the reds, browns and yellows. Cadfael looked back along the castle wall to the last wicket giving access to the town, and recalled that Fuller's house lay not far from the castle precinct. So, for that matter, though a little more distant, close to the high cross, did William Hynde's. This gate was convenient for both. Fuller kept a watchman here at night, living on the workshop premises.

'Small chance of ever hiding a captive lady here,' said

Hugh resignedly. 'By day it would be impossible, with so many busy about the place, and by night the fellow who sleeps here is paid to keep a close eye on Hynde's property, too, and keeps a mastiff into the bargain. I don't recall that there's anything but meadow and woodland beyond, but we'll go a little further.'

The green banks drifted by on either side, encroaching trees overhanging both shores, but there was no thick woodland, and no building, not even a hut for half a mile or more. They were about to give up the hunt and turn back, and Cadfael was preparing to tuck up his sleeves and take an oar to help Madog back upstream, when Madog checked and pointed.

'What did I say? No need to go beyond this, here's what marks the end of the chase.'

Close under the left bank, where a curving current had hollowed the ground and exposed the roots of a small hawthorn, causing it to lean at an angle over the water, its branches had snared a fish of their own. The empty boat lay unevenly, its bow held between two thorn-boughs, its oars shipped, rocking gently in the shallows.

'This one I know,' said Madog, drawing alongside and laying a hand to the thwart to hold them together. 'It belongs to Arnald the fishmonger, under the Wyle, he moors it there at the town end of the bridge. Your man had nothing to do but row it across and hide it. Arnald will be raging round Shrewsbury clouting every lad on suspicion. I'd best do him a good turn and get it back to him, before he twists off an ear or two. He's had this borrowed once before, but at least they brought it back that time. Well, my lord, here it ends. Are you satisfied?'

'Bitterly unsatisfied,' said Hugh ruefully, 'but I take your meaning. Downstream, we agreed! Well, somewhere downstream from the bridge and upstream from here, it seems, Mistress Perle was put ashore and laid in safe-keeping. Too safe by far! For still I have no notion where.'

With the aid of a trailing mooring rope, which had been frayed to suggest that it had parted of itself, they took the stolen boat in tow, and turned to the hard pull upstream,

Cadfael taking an oar, and settling himself solidly on the thwart to try and match Madog's experienced skill. But when they drew level with the fuller's workshop they were hailed from the bank, and down to the water's edge came two of Hugh's officers, dusty and tired, with three or four volunteers from among the townsmen holding off respectfully at a little distance. Among them, Cadfael observed, was that same weaver Bertred, all brawn and brag, as Hugh had called him, bestriding the greensward with the large confidence of a man who likes himself well, and by the look of him not at all downcast at fetching up empty-handed at the end of his voluntary search. Cadfael had seen him occasionally in attendance on Miles Coliar, though he knew little of him but his appearance. Which was eminently presentable, fresh-coloured and healthy and beautifully built, with the kind of open face which may be just what it seems, or may be well adapted to conceal the fact that there is an inner chamber which is very firmly closed. Something slightly knowing about the apparently candid eyes, and a smile just a little too ready. And what was there to smile about in failing to find Judith Perle, close to the end of this second day of searching for her?

'My lord,' said the older sergeant, laying a hand to hold the boat still and inshore, 'we've been over well-nigh every tuft of grass between these two reaches of the river, both sides, and nothing to be found, nor a soul who owns to knowing anything.'

'I've done no better,' said Hugh resignedly, 'except that this must be the boat that carried her off. It was caught in thorn-branches, a little way downstream from here, but it belongs at the bridge. No need to look beyond here, unless the poor woman's been moved and moved again, and that's unlikely.'

'Every house and garden along the road we've searched. We saw you making down-river, my lord, so we took yet another look round here, but you see everything's open as the day. Master Fuller made us free of all his holding.'

Hugh looked about him in a long, sweeping, none too hopeful glance. 'No, small chance of doing anything here unperceived, at least by daylight, and it was early in the day she vanished. Someone has looked in Master Hynde's warehouse there?'

'Yesterday, my lord. His wife gave us the key readily, I was there myself, so was my lord Herbard. Nothing within but his baled fleeces, the loft all but full of them, floor to roof. He had a good clip this year, seemingly.'

'Better than I did,' said Hugh. 'But I don't keep above three hundred sheep, small coin to him. Well, you've been at it all day, as well take a rest and be off home.' He set foot lightly to the thwart and stepped ashore. The boat rocked softly to the motion. 'There's nothing more we can do here. I'd best get back to the castle, and see if by chance someone else has had better luck. I'll go in here by the eastern gate, Madog, but we can lend you two rowers, if you like, and help you back upstream with both boats. Some of these lads who've been on the hunt with us could do with a voyage back to the bridge.' He cast a glance round the group that held off respectfully, watching and listening. 'Better than walking, lads, after all the walking you've done this day. Who's first?'

Two of the men came forward eagerly to uncouple the boats and settle themselves on the thwarts. They shoved gently off into the stream ahead of Madog, and set a practised pace. And it might well be, Cadfael thought, noting how Bertred the weaver hung well back from offering his own stout arms, that his walk home from the nearby castle gate into the town was barely longer than it would have been from the bridge gate after disembarking, so that he saw small gain in volunteering. It might even be that he was no expert with an oar. But that did not quite account for the small, bland smile and the look of glossy content on his comely young face as he withdrew himself discreetly from notice behind his companions. And it certainly did not account for the last glimpse Cadfael had of him, as he glanced back over his shoulder from midstream. For Bertred had lagged behind Hugh and his henchmen as they set off briskly towards the road and the eastern gate of the town, had halted a moment to watch them as they breasted the rise, and then had turned his back and made off at a purposeful but unhurried pace in the opposite direction, towards the nearest stand of woodland, as though he had important business there.

Bertred came home for his supper only with the early dusk, to a distracted household which had lost its routine and limped through the day forgetful of work, meal-times, and every other factor that served to mark the hours in an orderly and customary fashion. Miles fretted from workshop to street a dozen times an hour, and ran out to accost any passing soldier of the garrison for news, of which there was none. In two days he had grown so tense and brittle that even his mother, for once daunted into comparative silence, tended to slip aside out of his way. The girls in the spinning room whispered and wondered far more than they worked, and foregathered with the weavers to gossip as often as his back was turned.

'Who'd have thought he cared so much for his cousin!' Branwen marvelled, awed by his strained and anxious face. 'Of course a man feels for his own kin, but – you'd have thought it was his bride he'd lost, not his cousin, he goes so grieved.'

'He'd be a sight less concerned for his Isabel,' said a cynic among the weavers. 'She'll bring him a passable dowry, and he's well enough satisfied with his bargain, but there are as good fish in the sea if she slipped off the hook. Mistress Judith is his keep and future and all. Besides, the two get on well enough, for all I could ever see. He's got every call to worry.'

And worry he did, in a nail-biting, brow-furrowing frenzy of concern and anxiety that continued unbroken through the day, and at night, when search was perforce abandoned, subsided into a mute, resigned dejection, waiting for morning to renew the hunt. But by this second twilight it seemed every corner of the town had been ransacked, and every house and garden and pasture in the suburbs at least visited, and where were they to look next?

'She can't be far,' Dame Agatha insisted strenuously. 'They'll surely find her.'

'Far or near,' said Miles wretchedly, 'she's too well hidden.

And some villain holding her, for certain. And how if she's forced to give way and take him? Then what's to become of you and me, if she lets a master into the house?'

'She never would, and she so set against marrying. No, that she won't do. Why, if a man uses her so ill, more like by far, once she's free of him – as she will be! – to do what she's thought of doing so long, and go into a nunnery. And only two days now to the day of the rent!' Agatha pointed out. 'Then what's to be done, if that passes and she still lost?'

'Then the bargain's broken, and there's time to think again and think better, but only she can do it. Until she's found there's nothing to be done, and no comfort. Tomorrow I'll go out again myself,' Miles vowed, shaking an exasperated head over the failure of the king's sheriff and all his men.

'But where? Where is there left they haven't searched already?'

A hard question indeed, and one without an answer. And into this waiting and frustrated household Bertred came sidling in the dusk, discreetly quiet and solemn about the continuing failure to find any trace of his mistress, and yet looking so sleek and bright-eyed that Miles was brutally short with him, not at all his usual good-tempered self, and followed him with a long, glowering stare when Bertred wisely made off into the kitchen. On warm summer evenings it was pleasanter to be outdoors than there in the dim, smoky room with the heat of the fire, even when it was turfed down for the night or raked out until morning, and the rest of the household had gone out on their own ploys. Only Bertred's mother Alison, who cooked for the family and its workers, was waiting there none too patiently for her truant son, with a pot still warming over the naked fire.

'Where have you been till this time?' she wanted to know, turning on him with the ladle in her hand as he tramped briskly in at the door and went to his place at the long trestle table. He gave her a casual kiss in passing, brushing her round red cheek lightly. She was a plump, comfortable figure of a woman with some worn traces still of the good looks she had handed on to her son. 'All very well,' she said, setting the wooden bowl before him with a crash, 'after keeping me waiting here so late. And much good you must have done all day, or you'd be telling me now you've brought her home, and preening yourself like a peacock over it. There were some of the men came home two hours ago and more. Where have you been loitering since then?'

In the dim kitchen his small, self-satisfied smile could barely be seen, but the tone of his voice conveyed the same carefully contained elation. He took her by the arm and drew her down to the bench beside him.

'Never mind where, and leave it to me why! There was a thing I had to wait for, and it was worth the waiting. Mother ...' He leaned close, and sank his voice to a confidential whisper. '... how would you like to be more than a servant in this house? A gentlewoman, an honoured dowager! Wait a little while, and I mean to make my fortune and yours, too. What do you say to that?'

'Great notions you always had,' she said, none too impressed, but too fond to mock him. 'And how do you mean to do that?'

'I'm telling nothing yet, not till I can say it's done. There's not one of those busy hounds out hunting all this day knows what I know. That's all I'm saying, and not a word to any but you. And ... Mother, I must go out again tonight, when it's well dark. Never you worry, I know what I'm about, only wait, and you'll be glad of it. But tonight you mustn't say a word, not to anyone.'

She held him off doubtfully to get a better look at his smiling, teasing face. 'What are you up to? I can keep as close a mouth as any where there's need. But don't you go running your head into trouble. If there's ought you know, why haven't you told?'

'And spend the credit along with my breath? No, leave all to me, Mother, I know what I'm about. Tomorrow you'll see for yourself, but not a word tonight. Promise it!'

'Your sire was just such another,' she said, relaxing into smiles, 'always full of great plans. Well, if I spend the night wakeful out of pure curiosity, so be it. Would I ever stand in your way? Not a word out of me, I promise.' And instantly she added, with a brief blaze of unease and foreboding: 'Only take care! There may be more than you out about risky business in the night.'

Bertred laughed, and hugged her impulsively in long arms, and went away whistling into the dusk of the yard.

His bed was in the weaving-shed with the looms, and there he had no companion to wake and hear him rise and do on his clothes, more than an hour after midnight. Nor was it any problem to slip out from the yard by the narrow passage to the street, without so much as risking being seen by any other member of the household. He had chosen his time with care. It must not be too soon, or there would still be people stirring. It must not be too late, or the moon would be up, and darkness suited his purpose better. And it was dark indeed in the narrow lanes between the overhanging houses and shops, as he threaded the mass of streets between Maerdol-head and the castle. The town gate there on the eastern side was a part of the castle defences, and would be closed and guarded during the night hours. For the past few years Shrewsbury had been safe enough from any threat on the eastern approach, only the occasional brief Welsh raid from the west had troubled the peace of the shire, but Hugh Beringar maintained the routine watchfulness without a break. But the most easterly wicket, giving access to the river under the very towers of the fortress, was there to be used freely. Only in times of possible danger were all the wickets closed and barred, and sentries set on the walls. Horsemen, carts, market wagons, all must wait for the gates to be opened at dawn, but a solitary man might pass through at any hour.

Bertred knew his way in the dark as well as by day, and could tread as lightly and move as silently as a cat. He stepped through the wicket into the slope of grass and bushes above the river, and drew the wooden door closed after him. Below him the flow of the Severn made fleeting ribbons and glints of moving light, just perceptible as tremors in the darkness. The sky was lightly veiled and showed no stars, and was just sufficiently less dark than the solid masses of masonry, earth and trees to show their outlines in deeper black. When the moon came up, more than an hour later than this, the heavens would probably clear. He had time to stand for a moment and think out what he had to do. There was little wind, but he had better take it into consideration, it would not do to approach the watchman's mastiff at the fulling works downwind. He wet a finger and tested. The slight, steady breeze was blowing from the south-west, from upstream. He would have to move round the bulk of the castle virtually to the fringes of the gardens along the high road, and come about from downwind in a cautious circle to reach the back of the wool warehouse.

He had taken a good look at it in the afternoon. So had they all, the sheriff and his sergeants and the townsmen helping them in the search. But they had not, like Bertred, been in and out two or three times at that warehouse, when fetching away fleeces for Mistress Perle. Nor had they been present in Mistress Perle's kitchen on the night before her disappearance, to hear Branwen declare her mistress's intent to go to the abbey early in the morning and make a new charter, rendering her gift of property unconditional. So they had not seen, as Bertred had, Hynde's man Gunnar drink up his ale and pocket his dice shortly afterwards, and take himself off in some haste, though he had seemed to be comfortably rooted for the evening. That was one more creature besides Bertred who had known of that intent, and surely had slipped so promptly away to disclose it to yet one more. Which one, the old or the young, made no matter. The strange thing was that it had taken Bertred himself so long to grasp the possibilities. The sight of the old counting-house hatch, that afternoon, securely shuttered and barred on the outer side, and probably also made fast within, had been all that was needed to enlighten him. If he had then waited patiently in the cover of the trees until dusk, to see who slipped out from the wicket in the town wall, and exactly where he headed with his rush basket, it had been only a final precaution, to render certainty even more certain.

Heavy against his side, in the great pocket stitched inside his coat, he had a long chisel and a hammer, though he would have to avoid noise if he could. The outer bar across the hatch need only be drawn back out of the socket, but he suspected the shutter was also nailed fast to its frame. A year ago a bale of fleeces had been stolen by entry through this hatch, and as the small counting-house within was already disused, old Hynde had had the window sealed against any further attempt. That was one more thing the sheriff did not know.

Bertred came down softly along the meadow beyond the warehouse, with the gentle wind in his face. By then shapes of things showed clearly, black against faded black. The bulk of the building was between him and Godfrey Fuller's workshops, the very faint shimmer of the river a little way off on his left hand. And double his own height above him was the square of the shuttered hatch, just perceptible to his night eyes.

The climb presented no problems, he had made sure of that. The building was old, and due to this rear wall backing into the slope, the base of the wall of vertical planks had suffered wet damage over the years, and rotted, and old Hynde, never one to spend lavishly, had reinforced it with split logs fastened across horizontally on top of the massive sill-beam, affording easy toe-holds high enough for him to reach up and get a grip on the rough sill under the hatch, which was just wide enough to lend him a secure resting-place with an ear to the shutters.

He drew himself up carefully, got a hand firmly on the bar that sealed the hatch, and a thigh along the sill, and drew breath and cautiously held it, wary of the first strange and unexpected thing. The shutters fitted together well, but not quite perfectly. For about a hand's-length down the centre, where the two leaves met, a hairline of light showed, too fine to give a view of anything within, a mere quill-stroke of faint gold. Perhaps not so strange, after all. Perhaps they had had the grace at least to let her have a candle or a lamp in her prison. It would pay, surely, to accommodate her in as many harmless ways as possible, while trying to break down her resistance. Force need only be tried if all else failed. But two days without gain began to look very like failure.

The chisel inside his coat was jabbing him painfully in the ribs. He worked a hand cautiously into the pocket and drew out the tools, laying them beside him on the sill, so that he could ease himself a little nearer to the sliver of light, and lay his ear to the crack.

The sudden start he made all but toppled him from his perch. For a voice spoke up, firmly and clearly, quite close on the inner side of the shutters:

'No, you will not change me. You should have known it. I am your problem. You brought me here, now get me hence as best you can.'

The voice that answered was more distant, perhaps at the far side of the room, in hopeless retreat, and the words did not come over clearly, but the tone was of desperate complaining and abject pleading, and the speaker was a man, though so unrecognisable that Bertred could not be sure whether he was old or young, master or servant.

His own plan was already awry. At best he must wait, and if he had to wait too long the moon would be up, and the risks more than doubled. The place was right, his judgement confirmed, the woman was there. But the time was ill-guessed, for her gaoler was there with her.

# Chapter Eight

'You brought me here,' she said, 'now get me hence as best you can.'

In the narrow, bare room which had once been Hynde's counting-house, the small flame of the saucer lamp barely showed them to each other. He had flung away from her, and stood in the far corner, his back turned, his head bowed into the forearm he had braced against the wall, his other fist driving uselessly and painfully against the timber. His voice emerged muffled, its helpless rage degraded into a feeble wail: 'How can I? How can I? There is no way out now!'

'You could unlock the door,' she said simply, 'and let me go. Nothing could be easier.'

'For you!' he protested furiously, and swung about to glare at her with all the venom of which his nature was capable. It did not amount to much more than self-pity. He was not a venomous man, only a vain and foolish one. He wearied her, but he did not frighten her. 'All very well for you! And I should be finished, damned ... thrown into prison to rot. Once out, you'd denounce me and take your revenge.'

'You should have thought of that,' she said, 'before you snatched me away, you and your rogue servant. You brought me here to this sordid hole, locked in behind your wool bales, without comfort, without decency, subject to your man's rough handling and your insolent pestering, and do you expect gratitude? Or even mercy? Why should I not denounce you? You had best think hard and fast. You will have to release me or kill me at last, and the longer the delay, the worse will be your own plight. Mine,' she said bitterly, 'is already bad enough. What has become by now of my good name? What will my situation be when I go back to my own house and family?'

Vivian came back to her with a rush, flinging himself on his knees beside the rough bench where she had taken what rest she could, and where she sat now erect and pale, her hands gripped together in her lap, her skirts drawn close about her as though to avoid not only his touch, but the very dust and desolation of her prison. There was nothing else in the room but the broken desk where once the clerk had worked over his figures, and a stone ewer with a chipped lip, and a pile of dust and debris in the corner. The lamp stood on the end of the bench beside her, its light now full on Vivian's dishevelled hair and woeful face. He clutched at her hands imploringly, but she withdrew them so sharply that he sat back on his heels with a great gulp of despair.

'I never meant such mischief, I swear it! I thought you had a fondness for me, I thought I had only to get you to myself a while, and it would all be agreed between us ... Oh, God, I wish I'd never begun it! But indeed, indeed, I did believe you could love me ...'

'No! Never!' She had said it many times in these past two days, and always with the same irrevocable coldness. He should have recognised from the first utterance that his cause was hopeless. But he had not even been deceiving himself into the conviction that he loved her. What he coveted was the security and comfort she could bring him, the payment of his debts and the prospect of an easy life. Perhaps even the pleasure of cocking a snook at his parsimonious father – parsimonious at least in Vivian's eyes, because he had finally tired of bailing his heir out of debt and trouble. Oh, no doubt the young man had found the prospect of marriage with her pleasurable in itself, but that was not the reason he had chosen that particular morning for his bid. Why let half a fortune slip through your fingers, when with one bold stroke you might have the whole?

'How have they accounted for my vanishing?' she asked. 'Is the worst said of me already? Have they been looking for me at all? Am I thought dead?'

One faint spasm of defiance and spite passed over Vivian's face. 'Looking for you? The whole town's turned upside-down looking for you, the sheriff and all his men, your cousin and half your workmen. Not a house but they've visited, not a barn but they've searched. They were here yesterday, towards evening. Alan Herbard and three of the garrison with him. We opened the doors to them, and showed the baled fleeces, and they went away satisfied. Why did you not cry out to them then, if you wanted rescue from me?'

'They were here?' Judith stiffened, chilled by this spurt of malice. But it was the last, he had done his worst, and could not maintain it long. 'I never heard them!' she said with resigned bitterness.

'No.' He said it quite simply now, all his resistance spent. 'They were easily satisfied. The room is quite forgotten, and all those bales shut out sound. They never questioned. They were here again this afternoon, but not asking for the keys. They'd found the boat ... No, you might not hear them. Would you have cried out to them if you had?'

It was a meaningless question, and she did not answer it, but she gave it some thought. Would she have wished to be heard calling for help, and haled out of this mean prison, unprepared, dusty and stained, compromised, piteous? Might it not have been better to be silent, and make her own way out of this predicament? For the truth was that after the first confusion, indignation and alarm she had never been afraid of Vivian, nor in any danger of giving way to him, and now she would welcome as much as he would a solution which would smooth out of sight all that had happened, and leave her her dignity and integrity independent of any other soul. In the end he would have to release her. She was the stronger of the two.

He ventured a hand to clutch at a fold of her skirt. The face he lifted to her, seen clearly thus close and lit by the yellow flame of the wick, was strangely vulnerable and young, like a guilty boy pleading in extenuation of some heinous fault and not yet resigned to punishment. The brow he had braced against the wall was smeared with dust, and with the back of his hand, sweeping away tears or sweat or both, he had made a long black stain down his cheek. There was a trail of cobweb in the bright, fair, tangled hair. The wide brown eyes, dilated with stress, glinted gold from the spark of the lamp, and hung in desperate appeal upon her face.

105

'Judith, Judith, do me right! I could have used you worse . . . I could have taken you by force—'

She shook her head scornfully. 'No, you could not. You have not the hardihood. You are too cautious – or perhaps too decent – both, it may be! Nor would it have benefited you if you had,' she said starkly, and turned herself away to evade the desperate and desolate youth of his face, with its piercing reflections of Brother Eluric, who had agonised in silence and without hope or appeal. 'And now here we are, you and I both, and you know as well as I know that this must end. You have no choice but to let me go.'

'And you'll destroy me!' he said in a whisper, and sank his corn-gold head into his hands.

'I wish you no harm,' she said wearily. 'But it was you brought us to this, not I.'

'I know it, I own it, God knows I wish it undone! Oh, Judith, help me, help me!'

It had come to that, the bleak acknowledgement that he had lost, that he was now her prisoner, not she his, even that he was dependent upon her to save him from the trap he himself had set. He laid his head in her lap and shook as though with cold. And she was so tired and so astray that she had lifted a resigned hand to lay upon his head and quiet him, when the sudden tearing, rushing slither of sound outside the shutters at her back caused them both to start and freeze in alarm. Not a loud sound, merely like some not very heavy weight sliding down and ending in a dull fall into grass. Vivian started to his feet, quivering.

'For God's sake, what was that?'

They held their breath, straining into a silence as sudden as the sound, and as brief. Then, more distant from the direction of the riverside fulling-works, came the loud, savage alarm-baying of the chained mastiff; and after a few moments this changed abruptly into the deeper, more purposeful note of the chase, as he was loosed from his chain.

Bertred had trusted too confidently to old, worn, neglected wood, left too long uncared for on the weather side of the warehouse. The sill on which he was perched had been fixed in position with long nails, but at the more exposed end the nails had rusted in many rains, and the wood round them had rotted. When he shifted his weight further forward to ease an uncomfortable cramp, and get an ear more avidly to the crack, the wood splintered and parted, and the sill swung down before him, scraping the planks of the wall, and sent him slithering and clawing to the ground. Not a great fall nor a very loud sound, but loud enough in that depth of the night to carry to the fulling-works.

He was on his feet as he reached the ground, and leaned for a moment against the wall to get his breath back and steady his legs under him after the shock of the fall. The next moment he heard the mastiff give tongue.

Bertred's instinct was to run uphill towards the houses along the high road, and he set off in that direction, alerted to terror, only to check a moment later in the despairing knowledge that the hound was far faster than he could be, and would overhaul him long before he reached any shelter. The river was nearer. Better by far make for that, and swim across to the open spur of woodland at the end of the Gaye. In the water he could more than match the hound, and surely the watchman would call the dog off rather than let it pursue further.

He turned, and began to run in wild hare-leaps downhill across the tussocky grass, full tilt towards the river-bank. But both dog and man were out after him now, roused to a thief-hunt in the small hours, when all honest folk should be in their beds, and only malefactors could be abroad. They had traced the sound of his fall only too accurately; they knew someone had been clambering round the warehouse, and surely with no good intent. A detached part of Bertred's mind somehow had time to wonder, even as his legs and lungs strained for the speed of terror, how young Hynde managed to go back and forth by night without raising the same alarm. But of course the mastiff knew him, he was one of the guarded, an ally in the protection of property here, not an enemy and a threat.

Flight and pursuit made strangely little noise in the night, or disturbance in the darkness, and yet he felt, rather than saw, man and hound converging upon his path, and heard the rush of movement and the purposeful in-and-out of breath drawing close from his right flank. The watchman lunged at him with a long staff, and caught him a glancing blow on the head that half-stunned him, and sent him hurtling forward out of balance to the very edge of the river-bank. But he was past the man now, and could leave him behind, it was the dog, close on his heels, that terrified him, and gave him the strength for the last great leap that carried him out from the grass spur overhanging the water.

The bank was higher than he had realised, and the water somewhat lower, exposing shelving faces of rock. Instead of clearing these into deep water, he fell with a crash among the tilted stones, though his outflung arm raised a splash from the shallows between. His head, already ringing from the watchman's blow, struck hard against a sharp edge of stone. He lay stunned where he had fallen, half-concealed beneath the bushy overhang, wholly shrouded in the darkness. The mastiff, no lover of water, padded uneasily along the grassy shelf and whined, but went no further.

The watchman, left well behind and out of breath, heard the splash, caught even a brief shimmer in the fitful pallor of the river's surface, and halted well short of the bank to whistle and call off his dog. The would-be thief must be half across the river by now, no use troubling further. He was reasonably sure that the felon had not succeeded in making an entry anywhere, or the dog would have raised the alarm earlier. But he did walk round the warehouse and the dye-sheds to make sure all was in order. The dangling sill under the dark shutters hung vertically, like the planks against which it rested, and the watchman did not observe it. In the morning he would have a thorough look round, but it seemed no harm had been done. He went back contentedly to his hut, with the dog padding at his heels.

Vivian stood rigid, listening, until the dog's baying grew more distant, and finally ceased. He stirred almost painfully out of his stillness.

'Someone was prowling! Someone guesses – or knows!' He wiped sweat from his forehead with a dirty hand, prolonging the smears already there. 'Oh, God, what am I to do? I can't let you go free, and I can't keep you here any longer, not another day. If someone suspects . . .'

Judith sat silent, steadily watching him. His soiled and disillusioned beauty moved her against her will, as he could never have moved her at his most decorative and elated, the finest cock on the midden. Afraid to go on with his over-bold scheme, unable to retreat from it, frenziedly wishing he had never embarked upon it, he was like a fly in a cobweb, tangling himself ever more inextricably.

'Judith . . .' He was on his knees again at her feet, clinging to her hands, pleading, cajoling, but passionately, like a child, quite forgetful of his charm and stripped naked of his vanity. 'Judith, help me! Help me out of this! If there is a way, help me to find it. If they come and find you, I'm ruined, disgraced . . . If I let you go, you'll destroy me just the same—'

'Hush!' she said wearily. 'I don't wish you harm, I want no revenge, only to be free of you on the best terms I may.'

'How does that help me? Do you think they'll let you reappear, and ask no questions? Even if you hold your peace, how am I helped? There'll be no respite until you tell them all, and that's my undoing. Oh, if I knew which way to turn!'

'It would suit me no less than you,' said Judith, 'if we could smooth away this scandal peacably, but it needs a miracle to account for these two lost days. And I must protect myself, if that's possible. You must fend for yourself, but I'd as lief you went unharmed, too, if that may be. What now? What ails you?'

He had started and stiffened, quick to alarm, and was listening with stretched sinews. 'Someone outside,' he said in a whisper. 'Again – didn't you hear? Someone is spying . . . Listen!'

She fell silent, though she was not convinced. He was so tense and frightened by this time that he could have conjured enemies out of the air. Through a long, hushed moment she heard no sound at all, even the very slight sigh of the breeze in the shutters had ceased.

'There's no one; you imagined it. Nothing!' She gripped his hands suddenly, asserting her mastery, where hitherto she had merely suffered his touch without response. 'Listen to me! There might be a way! When Sister Magdalen visited me, she offered me a place of retreat at Godric's Ford with her, if ever I reached the end of my tether and needed a refuge and a pause for breath. As God knows I have needed both, and still do. If you will take me there by night, secretly, then I can return later and say where I have been, and why, and how this turmoil and hunt for me never came to our ears there. As I hope may be true. I will say that I fled from my life for a while, to get courage to take it up again to better purpose. And I hope to God that may also be true. I will not name you, nor betray what you have done to me.'

He was staring up at her wide-eyed, hesitant to hope but unable to resist, glowing only to doubt again the possibility of salvation. 'They'll press you hard, they'll ask why did you say no word, why go away and leave everyone to fear for you. And the boat – they know about the boat, they must know—'

'When they ask,' she said starkly, 'I'll answer, or refuse them an answer. Fret as you may, you must needs leave all that to me. I am offering you a way of escape. Take it or leave it.'

'I daren't go all the way with you,' he said, writhing. 'If I were seen it would all come out in spite of you.'

'You need not come all the way. You may leave me to go the last piece of the way alone, I am not afraid. No one need see you.'

He was flushing into hope with every word. 'My father is gone back to his flocks today, he'll stay two nights or more up there with the shepherds, and there's one good horse still in the stable, stout enough to carry two, if you'll ride pillion with me. I could bring him out of the town before the gate's closed. Best not pass through the town together, but set out this way. There's a ford a little way downstream from here, we can make our way south on the other side and get to the road to Beistan. At dusk – if we start at dusk tomorrow . . . Oh, Judith, and I've done you such wrong, and can you so far forgive me? I have not deserved!'

It was something new, she thought wryly, for Vivian Hynde to suppose that his deserts were small, or that there was anything to which he was not entitled. He might yet be all the better for this one salutary fright which he had brought upon himself. He was no great villain, only a weak and self-indulgent boy. But she did not answer his question. There was one thing at least she found it hard to forgive him, and that was that he had exposed her to the rough handling of Gunnar, who had taken palpable delight in the close embrace of her body and the strength which had held her helpless. She had no fear of Vivian, but of Gunnar, if ever she encountered him without Vivian, she might be very much afraid.

'I do this for myself as much as for you,' she said. 'I've given my word and I'll keep it. Tomorrow at dusk. Agreed, it's too late to move tonight.'

He had recoiled again into doubt and fear, recalling the noises without, and the baying of the mastiff. 'But how if someone has suspicions of this place? How if they come again tomorrow demanding the keys? Judith, come back with me now, come to our house, it's not far from the wicket, no one will see us now. My mother will hide you and help us, and be grateful to you for sparing me. And my father's away in the hills, he'll never know. And there you may have rest and a bed, and water for washing, and all you need for your comfort . . .'

'Your mother knows of what you've done?' she demanded, aghast.

'No, no, nothing! But she'll help us now, for my sake.' He was at the narrow door which had lain hidden behind the baled fleeces, turning the key, drawing her after him, feverish in his haste to be out of here and safe in his own home. 'I'll send Gunnar to make all innocent here. If they come they must find the place bare and deserted.'

She blew out the wick of the lamp and went with him, backwards down the ladder from the loft, out through the lower door and into the night. The moon was just rising, bathing the slope in pale-green light. The air was sweet and cool on her face after the close, musty smell of dust and the smoke of the lamp in the enclosed space. It was no very long walk to the shadows of the castle towers, and the wicket in the wall.

A darker shadow made its way round the spreading plane of moonlight, by the shortest route from behind the warehouse to the cover of trees, and so roundabout to the river-bank, rapid and silent. The overhang where Bertred had made his leap to evade the mastiff was still in shadow. He lay as he had fallen, still out of his senses, though he was beginning to stir and groan, and draw the laborious breath of one quickening to the consciousness of pain. The deeper shadow that fell across his body just as the edge of the moonlight reached the river did not penetrate his dazed mind or trouble his closed eyes. A hand reached down and took him by the hair, turning his face up to view it closely. He lived, he breathed, a little patching and a few hours to recover, and he would be able to account for himself and confess everything he knew.

The shadow stooping over him straightened and stood a moment looking down at him dispassionately. Then he thrust a booted toe into Bertred's side, levered him towards the edge of the stones on which he lay, and heaved him out into deep water, where the current curled fast, bearing the body out across midstream towards the further shore.

The twentieth of June dawned in a series of sparkling showers, settling by mid-morning into a fine, warm day. There was plenty of work waiting to be done in the orchards of the Gaye, but because of the morning rain it was necessary to wait for the midday heat before tackling them. The sweet cherries were ready for picking, but needed to be gathered dry, and there were also the first strawberries to pick, and there it was equally desirable to let the sun dry off the early moisture. On the open, sunlit expanse of the vegetable plots the ground dried out earlier, and the brothers on duty were busy sowing lettuces for succession, and hoeing and weeding, before noon, but it was after dinner that the orchard party began work at the extreme end of the abbey grounds.

There was no particular need for Brother Cadfael to go out with them, but neither was there anything urgently needing his attention in the herbarium, and the mounting uneasiness of the three-day vain hunt for Judith Perle would not let him rest or settle to any routine occupation. There had been no further word from Hugh, and nothing to tell Niall when he came anxiously enquiring. The entire affair stood still, the very hours of the day held their breath, making time endless.

To fill it at least with some physical movement, Cadfael went out to the orchards with the rest. As so often in a late season, nature had set out to make good the weeks that had been lost to the spring cold, and contrived to bring on, almost at the usual time, both strawberries and the first of the little hard gooseberries on their thorny bushes. But Cadfael's mind was not on fruit-picking. The orchards lay just opposite the level where the young archers shot at the butts on fair-days, under the sweep of the town wall and in the lee of the castle towers. Only a little way beyond, through the first belt of woodland, and he would be gazing straight across the water at the fulling-works, and just downstream at William Hynde's jetty.

Cadfael worked for a while, so distractedly that he collected more than his share of scratches. But after a while he straightened his back, sucked out of his finger the latest of many thorns, and walked on along the riverside into the belt of trees. Through their leaning branches the sweeping coronal of the town wall unrolled beside him across the water, and the steep green slope beneath the wall. Then the first jutting bastion of the castle, with the narrower level of meadow under it. Cadfael walked on, through the trees and out to a broad greensward beyond, dotted with low bushes close to the bank, and here and there a bed of reeds where the shallows ran gently and the fast current sped out into midstream. Now he was opposite the tenterground, where Godfrey Fuller's men were working, and a length of brown cloth was stretched taut between the frames to dry.

He reached a spot directly opposite the overhanging bushes where they had found the stolen boat abandoned. Along the bank beyond, a small boy was pasturing goats. Sunlit and peaceful, the Severn landscape lay somnolent in the afternoon light, denying the existence of murder, malice and abduction in so lovely a world.

Cadfael had gone but a hundred or so paces further, and was about to turn back, when he reached a curve where the bank opposite was undercut and the water beneath it deep, while on his side it shallowed into a sandy shoal, and subsided into soft, innocent ripples, barely moving. One of those places Madog knew well, where whatever had gone

113

into the river upstream might fetch up again on land.

And something had indeed fetched up here in the night just past. It lay almost submerged, at rest on the sand but barely breaking the surface, a mass of darker colour washed over by the silvery shimmer of water, and lodged in the dull gold of the sand beneath. It was the small, languid pallor, which swung lightly with the flow but was no fish, that first caught Cadfael's eye. A man's hand, at the end of a dark sleeve that buoyed it up just enough to set it swaying. A man's brown head, the back of it just dimpling the surface, all its curling locks stretching out with the ripples and stirring like drowsy living things.

Cadfael slid down the shelving bank in haste, and waded into the shallow water to get a double grip on the sodden clothing under the trailing arms, and drag the body ashore. Dead beyond doubt, probably several hours dead. He lay on his face in the sand just clear of the water, and tiny rivulets ran out of him from every fold of clothing and every tangled curl of hair. A young man, very well made and shapely. Far too late to do anything for him but carry him home and provide him a decent burial. It would need more than one man to get him up the bank and bear him back along the Gaye, and Cadfael had better be about getting help as fast as possible.

The build, the common dun-coloured coat and chausses, might have belonged to a hundred young fellows from Shrewsbury, being the common working wear, and the body was not immediately recognisable to Cadfael. He stooped to resume a careful hold under the lax arms, and turned the dead man over to lie on his back, revealing to the indifferent sunlight the smeared, pallid but still comely face of Bertred, Judith Perle's foreman weaver.

# Chapter Nine

They came in haste at his call, fluttered and dismayed, though a drowned man cast up by the Severn was no such rare matter, and these young brothers knew no more of the affair than that. No doubt whispers of the outer world's crises made their way in among the elders, but by and large the novices lived in innocence. Cadfael chose the strongest and the least likely to be distressed by the contemplation of death, and sent the others back to their work. With their hoes and rope girdles and scapulars they rigged a makeshift litter, and carried it down the riverside path to where the dead man lay.

In awed silence they took up their sodden burden, and bore him back in dripping procession through the belt of woodland and all along the lush level of the Gaye, to the path that climbed to the Foregate.

'We'd best take him to the abbey,' said Cadfael, halting a moment to consider. 'That's the quickest means of getting him decently out of the public view, and we can send for his master or his kin from there.' There were other reasons for the decision, too, but he did not think fit to mention them at this point. The dead man came from Judith Perle's household, and what had befallen him surely could not be entirely disconnected from all the other disasters which seemed to be haunting the house and the heiress of the Vestier business. In which case Abbot Radulfus had a direct interest and a right to be informed, and even more surely, so had Hugh Beringar. Not only a right, but a need. Two deaths and a disappearance, all circling round the same lady and her dealings with the abbey, demanded very close attention. Even young, strong men in the most exuberant of health can drown. But Cadfael had already seen the broken bruise on the dead man's

115

right temple, washed white and bleached of blood by the water of the river. 'Run on ahead, lad,' he said to Brother Rhun, the youngest of the novices, 'and let Father Prior know what manner of guest we're bringing.'

The boy bowed his flaxen head in the small gesture of respect with which he received any order from an elder, and was off in an instant, willing and eager. To bid Rhun run was a kindness rather than an imposition, for there was nothing in which he took greater delight than making use of the fleetness and grace he had possessed for barely a year, after coming to Saint Winifred's festival a cripple and in pain. His year's novitiate was almost over, and soon he would be admitted as a full brother. No power or persuasion could have induced him to depart from the service of the saint who had healed him. What to Cadfael was still the serious burden and stumbling-block of obedience, Rhun embraced as a privilege, as happily as he accepted the sunlight on his face.

Cadfael turned from watching the bright head and flashing feet ascend the path, and covered the dead man's face with the corner of a scapular. Water dripped through the saturated cloth as they carried Bertred up to the road, and along the Foregate to the abbey gatehouse. Inevitably there were people abroad to halt at sight of the mournful procession, and nudge and whisper and stare as they passed. It was always a mystery where the urchins of the Foregate sprang from, as soon as there was something unusual to stare at, and how they multiplied at every step, and how the dogs, their inseparable playmates, also halted and dawdled alongside them with much the same expression of alerted curiosity on their faces. Soon guess and counter-guess would be running through the streets, but none of them would yet be able to name the drowned man. The little time before it was common knowledge who he was could be useful to Hugh Beringar, and merciful to the dead man's mother. One more widow, Cadfael recalled, as they turned in at the gatehouse and left a ring of watchers gathered at a respectable distance outside.

Prior Robert came hastening to meet the procession, with Brother Jerome scurrying at his heels, and Brother Edmund from the infirmary and Brother Denis from the guest-hall converged at the same time upon the bearers and the bier. Half a dozen brothers who had been crossing the great court variously about their own proper business lingered to watch, and to draw closer by degrees to hear and see the better.

'I have sent Brother Rhun to notify the lord abbot,' said Robert, stooping his lofty silver head over the still body on the improvised litter. 'This is a very bad business. Where did you find the man? Was it on our ground you took him ashore?'

'No, some way beyond,' said Cadfael, 'cast up on the sand. Dead some hours, I judge. There was nothing to be done for him.'

'Was it necessary, then, to bring him here? If he is known, and has family in the town or the Foregate, they will take charge of his burial rites.'

'If not necessary,' said Cadfael, 'I thought it advisable he should be brought here. I believe the lord abbot will also think so. There are reasons. The sheriff may have an interest in this matter.'

'Indeed? Why should that be so, if the man died by drowning? Surely an accident not unknown here.' He reached a fastidious hand to turn back the scapular from the bleached and bluish face which in life had glowed with such self-conscious health. But these features meant nothing to him. If he had ever seen the man, it could have been only casually, passing the gates. The house at Maerdol-head lay in the town parish of Saint Chad; neither worship nor commerce would bring Bertred into frequent contact with the Foregate. 'Do you know this man?'

'By sight, yes, though little more than that. But he is one of Mistress Perle's weavers, and lives in her household.'

Even Prior Robert, who held himself aloof from those uncomfortable worldly concerns which sometimes infiltrated into the abbey's well-ordered enclave and bred disruption there, opened his eyes wide at that. He could not choose but know what untoward things had happened connected with that household, nor quite resist the conviction that any new disaster similarly connected must be a part of the whole deplorable pattern. Coincidences do occur, but they seldom cluster by the dozen round one dwelling and one name.

'Well!' he said on a long breath, cautiously noncommittal. 'Yes, the lord abbot should certainly know of this.' And with due relief he added: 'He is coming now.'

Abbot Radulfus had emerged from his garden and was approaching briskly, with Rhun attendant at his elbow. He said nothing until he had drawn back the covering from Bertred's head and shoulders and surveyed him in sombre and thoughtful silence for a long moment. Then he again covered the dead face, and turned to Cadfael.

'Brother Rhun has told me where he was found, and how, but he does not know who the man is. Do you?'

'Yes, Father. His name is Bertred, he is Mistress Perle's foreman weaver. I saw him yesterday out with the sheriff's men, helping in the hunt for the lady.'

'Who has not been found,' said Radulfus.

'No. This is the third day of searching for her, but she has not been found.'

'And her man is found dead.' There was no need to point out to him implications which were already plain. 'Are you satisfied that he drowned?'

'Father, I need to consider that. I think he did, but also he has suffered a blow to the head. I would like to examine his body further.'

'So, I suppose, would the lord sheriff,' said the abbot briskly. 'I'll send to him at once, and keep the body here for the present. Do you know if he could swim?'

'No, Father, but there are few born here who can't. His kin or his master will tell us.'

'Yes, we must also send to them. But perhaps later, after Hugh has seen him, and made what you and he between you can of the matter.' And to the bearers of the litter, who had laid it down meanwhile and stood waiting silently, a little apart, he said: 'Take him to the mortuary chapel. You had best strip him and lay him decently. Light candles for him. However and for whatever cause he died, he is our mortal brother. I'll send a groom to look for Hugh Beringar. Wait with me, Cadfael, until he comes. I want to know everything you have gathered concerning this poor girl who is lost.'

* * *

118

In the mortuary chapel they had laid Bertred's naked body on the stone bier, and covered him with a linen cloth. His sodden clothes lay loosely folded aside, with the boots they had drawn from his feet. The light being dim in there, they had also provided candles on tall holders, so that they could be placed wherever they gave the best light. They stood close about the slab, Abbot Radulfus, Brother Cadfael and Hugh Beringar. It was the abbot who drew down the linen and uncovered the dead, who lay with his hands duly crossed on his breast, drawn out very straight and dignified. Someone had reverently closed the eyes Cadfael remembered as half-open, like someone just waking, too late ever to complete the awakening.

A youthful body and a handsome, perhaps slightly over-muscled for perfection. Not much past twenty, surely, and blessed with features regular and shapely, again perhaps a shade over-abundant in flesh or under-provided with bone. The Welsh are accustomed to seeing in the faces of their neighbours the strong solidity and permanence of bone, and are sensitive to loss where they see it pared down and over-cushioned in others. Nevertheless, a very comely young man. Face and neck and shoulders, and from elbow to fingertips, he was tanned by outdoor sun and wind, though the brown was dulled and sad now.

'Not a mark on him,' said Hugh, looking him over from head to feet, 'barring that knock on his forehead. And that surely caused him nothing worse than a headache.'

High near the hairline the skin was certainly broken, but it seemed no more than a glancing blow. Cadfael took up the head, with its thick thatch of brown hair plastered to the broad forehead, between his hands, and felt about the skull with probing fingers. 'He has another dunt, here, on the left side, here in his hair, above the ear. Something with a long, sharp edge – through all this thickness of hair it made a scalp wound. That could have knocked the wits out of him for some time, perhaps, but not killed. No, he certainly drowned.'

'What could the man have been doing?' asked the abbot, pondering. 'At that spot on that shore, in the night? There is nothing there, no path that leads anywhere, no house to be

119

visited. Hard to see what business a man could possibly have there in the dark.'

'The business he'd been on all yesterday,' said Hugh, 'is the hunt for his mistress. He was in Mistress Perle's service, of her household, he offered his help, and so far as I saw he gave it, unsparingly, and in good earnest. How if he was still bent on continuing the search?'

'By night? And there? There is nothing there but open meadow and a few groves of trees,' said Radulfus, 'not one cottage for some distance, once past our border, nowhere that a stolen woman could be hidden. Even if he had been found on the opposite bank it would have been more believable, at least that gives access to the town and the houses of the Castle Foregate. But even so – by night, and a dark night until late . . .'

'And even so, how did he come by two blows on the head and end in the river? A man might go too near on a shelving bank, and miss his footing in the dark,' said Hugh, shaking his head, 'but of a native Shrewsbury lad I doubt it. They know their river. We must find out if he was a swimmer, but the most of them learn early. Cadfael, we know where he was cast up. Is it possible he went into the water on the other side? If he tried to swim across, half-stunned after he got these injuries, might he fetch up about where you found him?'

'That we should ask of Madog,' said Cadfael. 'He'll know. The currents are certainly very strong and contrary in places, it would be possible.' He straightened the wet hair almost absently on the dead man's forehead, and drew up the linen over his face. 'There's nothing more he can tell us. It remains to tell his kin. At least they may be able to say when last they saw him, and whether he owned to having any plans for the night.'

'I've sent for Miles Coliar, but said nothing to him yet of the reason. Better he should break it to the mother, it will come easier for her there, in her own home – for I'm told she belongs there, in the kitchen. And Coliar will need to have the body taken back there to make ready for burial, if you see no need to keep it longer.'

'None,' said Cadfael, turning away from the bier with a sigh. 'At your discretion, both! I have done.' But at the door, last to leave the chapel, he cast one long glance back at the still white shape on the slab of stone. One more young man dead untimely, sad waste of the stuff of life. 'Poor lad!' said Cadfael, and closed the door gently after him.

Miles Coliar came from the town in haste and alone, uninformed of the occasion for the summons, but certainly aware that there must be a grave reason, and by the look of his face speculating anxiously and fearfully as to what that might be. They awaited him in the ante-room of the gatehouse. Miles made his reverence to abbot and sheriff, and raised a worried countenance to look rapidly from face to face, questioning their solemnity.

'My lord, is there news? My cousin ...? Have you got word of her, that you sent for me here?' His pallor blanched still more, and his face stiffened into a mask of dread, misreading, it seemed, their mute and sombre looks. 'Oh, God, no! Not ... no, she cannot be ... You have not found her ... ?' His voice foundered on the word 'dead', but his lips shaped it.

'No, no!' said Hugh in haste. 'Not that! No, there's nothing new, no word of her yet, no need to think the worst. This is quite another matter, though grim enough. The hunt for your cousin goes on, and will go on until we find her.'

Miles said: 'Thank God!' just audibly, and drew deep breath, the tense lines of his face relaxing. 'Pardon if I am slow to think and speak and understand, and too hasty to fear extremes. These few days I have hardly slept or rested at all.'

'I am sorry to add more to your troubles,' said Hugh, 'but needs must. It's not Mistress Perle we're concerned with here. Have you missed any man from your looms today?'

Miles stared, and scratched his bushy brown head, at once relieved and puzzled. 'None of the weavers are working today, the looms have been neglected since yesterday morning, we've all or most been out on the hunt. I've kept the women spinning, it's no work for them to go stravaging about with the sergeants and the men of the garrison. Why do you ask, my lord?'

'Then have you seen your man Bertred at all since last night? He lives in your household, I'm told.'

'He does,' agreed Miles, frowning. 'No, I've not seen him today, with the looms quiet there's no reason I should. He eats in the kitchen. I suppose he's out again on the hunt, though God knows we've knocked on every door and probed round every yard in the town, and not a housewife or goodman who hasn't been alerted to watch for any sign and listen for any word that could lead us to her. Yet what can we do but search and ask all over again? They're out on all the roads and asking at the hamlets for a mile round, now, as you best know, my lord. Bertred will be out raking the countryside with them, no question. He's been tireless for her, that I grant him.'

'And his mother – she's in no anxiety about him? Nothing has been said of things he may have had on his mind? She has not spoken of him to you?'

'No!' Miles was again looking bewilderedly from face to face. 'You'll hardly find a soul in our house who is not anxious, and they show it, but I've noticed nothing amiss with her more than with all the rest of us. Why? What is this, my lord? Do you know something of Bertred that I do not know? Not guilt! Impossible! He's run himself raw scouring the town for my cousin ... a decent man ... You cannot have taken *him* in any wickedness ... ?'

It was a reasonable supposition, when the lord sheriff began asking such close questions about any man. Hugh put him out of his defensive agitation, but without over-haste.

'I know no wrong of your man, no. He is the victim of harm, not the cause. This is bad news we have for you, Master Coliar.' Its purport was already implicit in his tone, but he put it into words bleak and blunt enough. 'An hour ago the brothers working on the Gaye plucked Bertred out of the river and brought him here, dead. Drowned.'

In the profound silence that followed Miles stood motionless, until finally he stirred and moistened his lips.

'Where is he?'

'Laid decently in the mortuary chapel here,' said the abbot. 'The lord sheriff will take you to him.'

In the dim chapel Miles stared down at the known face now so strangely unfamiliar, and shook his head repeatedly and vigorously, as though he could shake away, if not the fact of death, his own shock at its suddenness. He had recovered his down-to-earth calmness and acceptance. One of his weavers was dead, the task of getting him out of here and into his grave with proper rites fell to Miles as his master. What was due from him he would do.

'How could this be?' he said. 'Yesterday he came late in the evening for his meal, but there was nothing in that, all day he'd been out abroad with your men, my lord. He went to his bed soon after. He said good night to me, it must have been about the hour of Compline. The house was already quiet, but some of us were still up. I never saw him again.'

'So you don't know whether he went out again by night?'

Miles looked up sharply, the blue of his eyes at their widest startlingly bright. 'It seems that he must have done. But in God's name, why should he? He was tired out after a long day. I know no reason why he should have stirred again till morning. You said it was but an hour since you took him out of the Severn . . .'

'*I* took him out,' said Cadfael, unobtrusive in a dark corner of the chapel. 'But he had been there more hours than one. In my judgement, since the small hours of the morning. It is not easy to say how long.'

'And, look, his brow is broken!' The wide, low forehead was dry now, but for the damp fringe of hair. The skin had shrunk apart, leaving the moist wound bared. 'Are you sure, Brother, that he drowned?'

'Quite sure. How he came by that knock there's no knowing, but he surely had it before he went into the water. You can't tell us anything that may help us, then?'

'I wish I could,' said Miles earnestly. 'I've seen no change in him, he's said nothing to me that could shed any light. This comes out of the dark to me. I cannot account for it.' He looked doubtfully at Hugh across the body. 'May I take him home? I'll need to speak with his mother first, but she'll want him home.'

'Naturally,' agreed Hugh resignedly. 'Yes, you may fetch him away when you will. Do you need help with the means?'

'No, my lord, we'll do all ourselves. I'll bring down a handcart and decent covering. And I do thank you and this house for the care you've had of him.'

\* \* \*

He came again about an hour later, looking strained from the ordeal of breaking bad news to a widow now childless. Two of his men from the looms followed him with a simple, high-sided handcart used for wheeling goods, and waited mute and sombre in the great court until Brother Cadfael came to lead them to the mortuary chapel. Between them they carried Bertred's body out into the early evening light, and laid him on a spread brychan in the cart, and covered him tidily from view. They were still about it when Miles turned to Cadfael, and asked simply: 'And his clothes? She should have back with him all that was his. Small comfort for a woman, but she'll want them. And she'll need what they'll fetch, too, poor soul, though I'll see she's taken care of still, and so will Judith ... when she's found. If ...' His mind seemed to be drifting back into expectations of the worst, and fiercely rejecting them.

'I had forgot,' Cadfael owned, never having handled the clothes stripped from Bertred's body. 'Wait, I'll bring them.'

The forlorn little bundle of clothes laid aside in the chapel had been folded together as tidily as haste and their sodden condition permitted, and had drained gradually where they lay. The folds of coat and shirt and homespun hose were beginning to dry. Cadfael took the pile in one arm, and picked up in the other hand the boots that stood beside it. He carried them out into the court as Miles was smoothing the blanket neatly over Bertred's feet. The young man turned to meet him and take the bundle from him, and in the exchange, as Miles leaned to stow the clothes under the blanket, the cart tilted, and the boots, just balanced at the tail, fell to the cobbled paving.

Cadfael stooped to pick them up and restore them to their place. It was the first time he had really looked at them, and the light here in the court was clear and bright. He stood arrested in mid-movement, a boot in either hand, and slowly he turned up the left one to look attentively at the sole. For so long a time that when he did look up he found Miles standing just as still in wonder, gazing at him with open mouth, his head on one side like a puzzled hound on a lost scent.

'I think,' said Cadfael with deliberation, 'I had better get leave from the lord abbot, and come up into the town with you. I need to speak once again with the lord sheriff.'

It was but a short walk from the castle to the house at Maerdol-head, and the boy sent in haste to find Hugh brought him within the quarter-hour, cursing mildly at being side-tracked on the point of further action he had intended, but reconciled by sharp curiosity, for Cadfael would not have sent for him again so soon without good reason.

In the hall Dame Agatha, attended by a tearful Branwen, volubly lamented the rockfall of disasters which had befallen the Vestier household. In the kitchen the bereaved Alison mourned with more bitter reason the loss of her son, while all the spinning-girls formed a chorus to her threnody. But in the loom-shed, where Bertred's body had been laid out decorously on a trestle table to await the visit of Martin Bellecote, the master-carpenter from the Wyle, it was quiet to the point of oppression, even though there were three of them there conversing in low voices and few words.

'There is no shadow of doubt,' said Cadfael, holding the boot sole-up to the light of a small lamp one of the girls had set at the head of the table. The light outside was still hardly less bright than in the afternoon, but half the shed was shuttered because the looms were at rest. 'This is the boot that made the print I took from the soil under Niall's vine, and the man who wore it is the man who tried to hack down the rose-bush, the same who also killed Brother Eluric. I made the mould, I know I am not mistaken. But here is the mould itself, for I brought it with me. You will find it matches exactly.'

'I take your word for it,' said Hugh. But as one who must verify for himself every morsel of evidence, he took the boot and the waxen mould, and carried them out to the doorway to match the two together. 'There *is* no doubt.' The two fitted like seal and matrix. There was the oblique tread that had worn down outer heel and inner toe, and the crack reaching half across the sole at the ball of the foot. 'It seems,' said Hugh, 'the Severn has saved us the cost of a trial, and him a worse fate than drowning.'

Miles had remained standing somewhat apart, looking from face to face with the same baffled wonder with which he had brooded over Bertred's body in the mortuary chapel.

'I don't understand,' he said dubiously at last. 'Are you saying that it was *Bertred* who got into the smith's garden to spoil Judith's rose-bush? And *killed* . . .' The same vigorous, even violent, shaking of his head, trying to toss the unwelcome belief from him, like a bull trying to throw off a dog that had him by the soft nose. And with as little success, for slowly the conviction began to penetrate his mind, to judge by the slackening of the lines of his face, and his final resigned calm and glint of rising interest. A very eloquent face, had Miles; Cadfael could follow every change. 'Why should *he* do such a thing?' he said slowly, but rather as if his own wit was already beginning to supply answers.

'The killing he never meant, as like as not,' said Hugh reasonably. 'But as for hacking down the bush – it was you yourself gave us a good reason why a man might do so.'

'But what did it benefit Bertred? All it would have done was to prevent my cousin getting her rent paid. What was that to him? *He* had no rights in it.' But there Miles halted to reflect again. 'I don't know – it seems reaching far. I know I said he fancied he had some small chance with her. He did presume, sometimes, he had a good conceit of himself. He may even have believed he might win her favour, such things have been known. Well . . . there's no denying, if he had such vaulting ideas, the Foregate house was a good half of her property, worth a man's while trying to regain.'

'As all her suitors may have reasoned,' said Hugh, 'not merely Bertred. He slept in here?'

'He did.'

'And therefore could go in and out at will, by night or day, without disturbing any other creature.'

'Well, so he could. It seems so he did, last night, for none of us within heard a sound.'

'But granted we have the proof now that links him to the death of Brother Eluric,' said Hugh, frowning, 'we are still floundering when it comes to the vanishing of Mistress Perle. There's nothing whatever to connect him with that, and we have still a second malefactor to find. Bertred has been among the most assiduous of our helpers in the search for her. I don't think he would have spent quite so much energy if he had had any knowledge of where she was, however desirable it might be to make a show of zeal.'

'My lord,' said Miles slowly, 'I never would have believed such devious work of Bertred, but now you have shown me so far into his guilt I cannot help following further. It's a strange thing, his own mother has been pouring out to us all, since we brought him home, what he said to her last night. You may ask her yourself, my lord, she will surely repeat it to you as she has to us. I would rather not be the bearer, nor risk being suspect of mangling the purport. If it means anything, let her deliver it, not I.'

The widow, bloated with tears and surrounded by her would-be comforters, was indeed still spouting words between her bouts of weeping, and had no objection to continuing her threnody for the benefit of the sheriff, when he drove her companions away for a short while, to have the bereaved woman to himself.

'A good son he was always to me, a good worker to his mistress, and deserved well of her, and well she thought of him. But great notions he had, like his father before him, and where have they got him now? How would I like, says he to me last night, how would I like to be better than a servant in this house – a gentlewoman, fit for the hall instead of the kitchen? Only wait a day or so, says he, and you'll see, I mean to make your fortune and my own. There's not one, he says, knows what I know. If there's ought you know to the purpose, I said, why haven't you told? But would he? And spend the credit along with my breath? he says. No, you leave all to me.'

'And did he say anything about what he intended in the night?' asked Hugh, slipping his question quietly and unobtrusively into the first chink in her outpourings, while she drew breath.

'He said he must go out again when it was full dark, but he wouldn't tell me where, or why, nor what he was about at all. Wait till tomorrow, he says, and not a word to any tonight. But what does it matter now? Speak or keep silent, it does him no good now. Don't you go running your head into trouble, I told him. There may be more than you out about risky business in the night.'

Her flow of words was by no means exhausted, but its matter became repetitive, for she had told everything she knew. They left her to the ministrations of the women and the diminishing bitterness of her grief as it drained away into exhaustion. The house of Vestier, Miles assured them earnestly as they left the premises, would not let any of its old servants go short of the means of a decent life. Alison was safe enough.

# Chapter Ten

'Come with me,' said Hugh, setting off briskly up the hill towards the high cross, and turning his back with some relief on the troubled household at the clothiers' shop. 'Since you have honest leave to be out, you may as well join me on the errand you delayed for me a while ago. I was all but out of the town gate when your messenger came and Will came running after me to say I was wanted at the Vestiers'. I sent him on ahead with a couple of men, he's down there and at it by now, but I'd as lief see to it for myself.'

'Where are we going?' asked Cadfael, falling in willingly beside his friend up the steep street.

'To talk to Fuller's watchman. That's the one place outside the town walls where there'd be a waking witness even in the night, and a watchdog to alert him if anyone came prowling close by. If the fellow did by any chance go into the water this side the river, works and warehouse are only a little way upstream from where you found him. Fuller's man has both places in charge. He may have heard something. And as we go, tell me what you make of all that – Bertred's night affairs, and the fortune he was going to make.'

'By reason of knowing something no one else knew – hmm! For that matter, I noticed he stayed behind when your men left the jetty yesterday afternoon. He let you all go on well before, and then slipped back alone into the trees. And he came late for his supper, told his mother she should be a gentlewoman in the house instead of a cook, and went off again in the night to set about making his word good. And according to Miles he not only fancied his mistess, but had the assurance to feel there was no reason he should not bring her to fancy him.'

'And how persuade her?' asked Hugh, wryly smiling. 'By

abduction and force? Or by a gallant rescue?'

'Or both,' said Cadfael.

'Now truly you interest me! Those who hide can find! If by any chance the lady is where he put her, but doesn't know who put her there – for a Bertred can as easily find rogues to do his work for him as any wealthier man, it is but a matter of degrees of greed! – then who could better come to her rescue? Even if gratitude did not go so far as to make her marry him, he certainly would not be the loser.'

'It offers one way of accounting,' Cadfael acknowledged. 'And in its favour, the maid Branwen blabbed out what her mistress intended in the kitchen, so we are told. And Bertred ate in the kitchen, and was probably there to hear it. The kitchen knew of it, the hall knew nothing until next day, after she was lost. But there are other possibilities. That someone else took her, and Bertred had found out where she was. And said no word to you or your men, but kept the rescue for himself. It seems a simpler and a smaller villainy, for one surely not so subtle as to make tortuous plans.'

'You forget,' Hugh pointed out grimly, 'that by all the signs he had already committed murder, whether with intent beforehand or not, still murder. He might be forced into plans far beyond his ordinary scope after that, to cover his tracks and secure at least some of his desired gains.'

'I forget nothing,' said Cadfael sturdily. 'One point in favour of your story I've given you. Here is one against: If he had her hidden away somewhere, securely enough to baffle all your efforts to find her, why should it not be a safe and simple matter for him to effect that rescue of his without a single stumble? And the man is dead! Far more likely to come to grief in spite of all his planning, if he crossed the plans of some other man.'

'True again! Though for all we yet know, his death could have been pure mischance. True, it could be either way. If he is the abductor as well as the murderer, then we have no second villain to find, but alas, we still lack the lady, and the only man who could lead us to her is dead. If murderer and abductor are two different people, then we have still to find both the captor and his captive. And since it seems the most likely object of taking her is to inveigle her into marriage, we may hope and believe both that she is living, and that in the end he must release her. Though I own I'd rather forestall that by plucking her out of his hold myself.'

They were over the crest by the high cross, and striding downhill now, past the ramp that led up to the castle gatehouse, and still downhill alongside the towering walls, until town wall on their left and castle wall on their right met in a low tower, under which the highway passed. Once through that gateway, the level of the road opened before them, fringed for only a short way by small houses and gardens. Hugh turned right on the outer side of the deep, dry castle ditch, before the houses began, and started down towards the riverside, and Cadfael followed more sedately.

Godfrey Fuller's tenterground stood empty, the drying cloth just unhooked and rolled up for finishing. Most of his men had already stopped work for the day, and the last few had lingered to watch and listen at the arrival of the sheriff's men, before making for their homes in the town. A close little knot of men had gathered at the edge of the tenter-ground, between dye-works and wool warehouse: Godfrey Fuller himself, his finery shed in favour of stout working clothes, for he was by no means ashamed to soil his hands alongside his workmen, and prided himself on being able to do whatever he asked of them, and possibly as well or better than they could; the watchman, a thickset, burly fellow of fifty, with his mastiff on a leash; Hugh's oldest sergeant, Will Warden, bushy-bearded and massive; and two men from the garrison in watchful attendance at a few yards distance. At sight of Hugh dropping with long strides down the slope of the meadow, Warden swung away from the colloquy to meet him.

'My lord, the watchman here says there was an alarm in the night, the dog gave tongue.'

The watchman spoke up freely for himself, aware of duty properly done. 'My lord, some sneak thief was here in the night, well past midnight, climbing to the hatch behind Master Hynde's storehouse. Not that I knew then that he'd got so far, but the hound here gave warning, and out we went, and heard him running for the river. I made to cut him off, but he was past me too fast, all I got was one clout at him as he rushed by. I hit him, but did him precious little harm, surely, by the speed he made down to the bank and into the water. I heard the splash as he went in, and called off the dog, and went to look had he got into the store. But there was no sign, not to be seen in the night, and I took it he was well across and off by then, no call to make any more stir about him. I never knew till now it was a dead man came ashore on the other side. That I never meant.'

'It was not your doing,' said Hugh. 'The blow you got in did him no great damage. He drowned, trying to swim across.'

'But, my lord, there's more! When I looked round the warehouse by daylight this morning, see what I found lying in the grass under the hatch. I've just handed them over to your sergeant here.' Will Warden had them in his hands, displayed in meaning silence, a long chisel and a small clawed hammer. 'And the sill beam under the hatch broken from its nails at one end, and dangling. I reckon surely he was up there trying to break through the shutter and get in at the fleeces. A year ago when the clip was in there thieves got in and stole a couple of bales. Old William Hynde near went out of his wits with rage. Come and see, my lord.'

Cadfael followed slowly and thoughtfully as they set off round the bulk of the warehouse to the rear slope, where the shuttered hatch showed still securely fastened, though the stout beam under it hung vertically against the planks of the wall, the splintered gaps where it had broken free from its anchoring nails rotten and soft to the touch.

'Gave under his weight,' said the watchman, peering upward. 'It was his fall the dog heard. And these tools came down with him, and he had no time to pick them up, if he'd delayed a moment we should have had him. But here's good proof he was trying to break in and steal. And the best is,' said the watchman, shaking his head over the folly of the too-clever, 'if he'd got in through the hatch he couldn't have got at the fleeces.'

'No?' said Hugh sharply, turning a startled glance on him. 'Why? What would have prevented?'

'There's another locked door beyond, my lord, between him and what he came for. No, belike you wouldn't know of

132

it, why should you? William Hynde's clerk used to work in the little back room up there, it was used as a counting-house until that time thieves broke in by this back way. By then the woolman was buying here for the foreign trade, and old Hynde thought better to bid him up to his own house and make much of him. And what with their business being all transacted there, the old counting-house was out of use. He had the door locked and barred, for an extra barrier against thieves. If this rogue had got in, it would have done him no good.'

Hugh gazed and pondered, and gnawed a dubious lip. 'This rogue, my friend, was in the wool trade himself, and knew this place very well. He fetched the fleeces for the Vestiers from here, he'd been in and out more than once. How comes it that he would not know of this closed counting-house? And my deputy had them open up here two days ago, and saw the upper floor full almost to the ladder with bales. If there's a door there, it was buried behind the wool.'

'So it would be, my lord. Why not? I doubt if a soul had gone through that door since it was first shut up. There's nothing within there.'

Nothing now, Cadfael was thinking. But was there something – someone! – there only yesterday? It would seem that Bertred thought so, though of course Bertred could be wrong. He must have known of the abandoned room, he may well have thought it worth putting to the test at a venture, without special cause. If so, it cost him dear. All those dreams of bettering his fortune by a gallant rescue, of exploiting a woman's gratitude to the limit and advancing his own cause step by step with insinuating care, all shattered, swept away down the currents of the Severn. Did he really know something no one else among the searchers knew, or was he speaking only of this hidden room as a possibility?

'Will,' said Hugh, 'send a man up to Hynde's house, and ask him, or his son, to come down here and bring the keys. All his keys! It's time I took a look within here myself. I should have done it earlier.'

* * *

133

But it was neither William Hynde nor his son Vivian who came striding down the field with the sergeant after a wait of some ten or fifteen minutes. It was a serving-man in homespun and leather, a tall, bold-faced, muscular fellow in his thirties, sporting a close-trimmed beard that outlined a wide mouth and a jaunty jaw with all the dandified elegance of a Norman lordling, though his build was Saxon and his colouring reddish-fair. He made a careless obeisance to Hugh, and straightened up to measure eyes with him, ice-pale eyes with only the glittering Norse-tinge of blue in them.

'My lord, my mistress sends you these, and my services.' He had the keys in his hand on a great ring, a rich bunch of them. His voice was loud, with a brazen ring to it, though his manner was civil enough. 'My master's away at his sheepfolds by Forton, has been since yesterday, and the young master's gone up there to help them today, but he'll be back tomorrow if you need him. Will it please you command me? I'm here to serve.'

'I've seen you about the town,' said Hugh, eyeing him with detached interest. 'So you're in Hynde's service, are you? What's your name?'

'Gunnar, my lord.'

'And he trusts you with his keys. Well, Gunnar, open these doors for us. I want to see what's within.' And he added, as the man turned willingly to obey: 'When is the barge expected, if Master Hynde can spare time to go in person to his flocks?'

'Before the end of the month, my lord, but the merchant sends word ahead from Worcester. They take the clip by water to Bristol, and then overland to Southampton for shipping, it cuts off the long voyage round. A rough passage they say it is, all round the south-west.' He was busy as he talked, unfastening two massive padlocks from the bar of the warehouse doors, and drawing both leaves wide open to let in the light upon a clean-swept, slightly raised floor of boards, on which the lower-grade fleeces had been stacked. This level was empty now. From the left-hand corner within the door a wooden ladder led up through a wide, open trap to the floor above.

'You're well informed concerning Master Hynde's business affairs, Gunnar,' said Hugh mildly, stepping over the threshold.

'He trusts me. I made the journey down to Bristol with the barge once, when they had a man injured and were short-handed. Will it please you go up, sir? Shall I lead the way?'

A very self-assured and articulate person, this Gunnar, Cadfael reflected, the very image of the intelligent and trusted servant of a commercial house, capable of adapting to travel, and learning from every experience. By his stature, bearing and colouring he proclaimed his northern ancestry. The Danes had reached no further south than Brigge in this shire, but they had left a few of their getting behind when they retreated. Cadfael followed without haste as they mounted the ladder and stepped on to the upper floor. Here the light was dim, reflected up from the wide doors below, but enough to show the stacked bales stretching the full length of the storehouse.

'We could do with more light,' said Hugh.

'Wait, my lord, and I'll open.' And Gunnar made no more ado, but seized one of the bales in the centre of the array and hauled it down to set aside, and after it several more, until the stout wooden planks of a narrow door were laid bare. He flourished his ring of keys with a flurry of sound, selected one, and thrust it into the lock. There were two iron bars slotted across the door in addition, and they grated rustily as he drew them from the sockets. The key creaked as it turned. 'There's been no use made of this for a while now,' said Gunnar cheerfully. 'We'll do no harm by letting in the air for once.'

The door opened inward. He thrust it wide and made straight across to the shuttered hatch, and with a lusty banging of latches and beams released the shutters and pushed them wide to let in the slanting sunlight. 'Mind the dust, my lord,' he warned helpfully, and stood back to let them examine the whole narrow room. A rising breeze blew in, fluttering trailers of cobweb from the rough wood of the hatch.

A small, barren space, an old bench against the wall, a heap of discarded fragments of vellum and cloth and wool and wood, and indistinguishable rubbish drifted into one corner, a large ewer with a broken lip, the ancient desk leaning askew, and over all the grime and dust of abandonment, of a place two years disused, and a year sealed and forgotten.

'There was a thief got in this way once,' said Gunnar airily. 'They'd have much ado to manage it a second time. But I must make all secure again before I leave it, my master'd have my head if I forgot to shoot every bolt and turn every key.'

'There was a thief tried to get in this way only last night,' said Hugh casually. 'Have they not told you?'

Gunnar had turned on him a face fallen open in sheer astonishment. 'A thief? Last night? Not one word of this have I heard, or the mistress, either. Who says it's so?'

'Ask the watchman below, he'll tell you. One Bertred, a weaver who works for Mistress Perle. Take a look at the sill outside the hatch, Gunnar, you'll see how it came down with his weight. The hound hunted him into the river,' said Hugh, offhand, gazing musingly all round the neglected room, but well aware of the look on Gunnar's face. 'He drowned.'

The silence that followed was brief but profound. Gunnar stood mute, staring, and all his light assurance had frozen into a steely gravity.

'You'd heard nothing?' marvelled Hugh, his eyes on the dusty floor, on which Gunnar's vigorous passage had printed the only pattern of footmarks perceptible between door and hatch.

'No, my lord – nothing.' The loud, confident voice had become taut, intent and quiet. 'I know the man. Why should he want to steal fleeces? He is very well settled as he is – he was . . . *Dead?*'

'Drowned, Gunnar. Yes.'

'Sweet Christ have his soul!' said Gunnar, slowly and quietly, to himself rather than to them. 'I knew him. I've diced with him. God knows neither I nor any that I know of bore Bertred any ill will, or ever wished him harm.'

There was another silence. It was as if Gunnar had left them, and was withdrawn into another place. The ice-blue eyes looked opaque, as if he had drawn a shutter down over them, or turned their gaze within rather than without. In a few moments he stirred, and asked levelly: 'Have you done here, my lord? May I close these again?'

'You may,' said Hugh as shortly. 'I have done.'

On the way back into the town through the castle gate they were both silent and thoughtful, until Hugh said suddenly: 'If ever she was there in that dusty hole, someone has done excellent work wiping out every trace.'

'Bertred thought she was,' said Cadfael. 'Though Bertred may have been wrong. Surely he was there to try and set her free, but he may have been guessing, and guessing wrongly. He knew of the room, and knew it was not common knowledge and therefore, with care, might be used for such a purpose. And he knew that young Hynde made a very possible abductor, being vain, persistent and in urgent need of money to maintain his easy life. But was it more than a guess? Did he really discover something that made it a certainty?'

'The very dust!' said Hugh. 'No mark of any foot but Gunnar's, or none that I could see. And the young fellow, the son, this Vivian – he did ride off this morning, out of the town, that I knew already, Will reported it to me. So there's no one there but the mother now. And would *she* be lying? Hardly likely he'd tell *her* if he had a woman hidden away. If he's taken the girl elsewhere after the night alarm, it would hardly be to his mother. But I'll pay the house another visit, all the same. I fancy Bertred must have been trying his luck – but that the poor wretch had no luck! No luck with the roses, no luck with the rescue. No luck in any of his schemes.'

Another long silence, while they climbed the gradual slope within the gate, and approached the ramp to the castle entrance. 'And he did not know!' said Hugh. 'He really did not know!'

'He? And know what?'

'This man Gunnar. I had my doubts about him until then. So confident and assured, light as air, until mention was made of a man's death. That I am sure came new to him. There was no pretence there. What say you, Cadfael?'

'I say there is a man who could lie and lie, whenever the occasion needed it. But who was not lying then. His very voice changed, no less than his face. No, he did not know. He was shaken to the heart. Whatever mischief he might have a part in, he had not contemplated a death. Let alone Bertred's death!' They had reached the ramp and halted. 'I must get back,' said Cadfael, looking up into a sky just veiled and softened with the approach of twilight. 'What more can we do tonight? And what will you do tomorrow?'

'Tomorrow,' said Hugh with deliberation, 'I'll have Vivian Hynde brought to me as soon as he shows his face in the town gate, and see what's to be got out of him concerning his father's old counting-house. From all I've heard of him, he should be easier to frighten than his man shows any sign of being. And even if he's a snow-white innocent, from all accounts a fright will do him no harm.'

'And will you make it public,' Cadfael asked, 'that at least Brother Eluric's murderer is known? And is dead?'

'No, not yet. Perhaps not at all, but at least let the poor woman have what peace she can find until her son's buried. What point in blazoning forth guilt where there can never be a trial?' Hugh was looking back with a frown, and somewhat regretting that Miles had been present to witness that manifestation in the loom-shed. 'If I know the sharp ears and long tongues of Shrewsbury it may yet be common talk by morning without any word from me. Perhaps not, perhaps Coliar will hold his tongue for the mother's sake. But at any rate they shall have no official declaration to grit their teeth in until we find Judith Perle. As we will, as we must. Let them gossip and speculate. Someone may take fright and make the blunder I'm waiting for.'

'The lord abbot will have to know all that I know,' said Cadfael.

'So he will, but he's another matter. He has the right and you have the duty. So you'd best be about getting back to him,' said Hugh, sighing, 'and I'd best go in and see if any of those men of mine who've been out raking the countryside has done any better than I have.'

Upon which impeccably conscientious but none too hopeful note they parted.

Cadfael arrived back at the gatehouse too late for Vespers.
The brothers were in the choir, and the office almost over. A
great deal had happened in one short afternoon.

'There's one here been waiting for you,' said the porter,
looking out from his lodge as Cadfael stepped through the
wicket. 'Master Niall the bronzesmith. Come in to him here,
we've been passing the time of evening together, but he
wants to be on his way as soon as may be.'

Niall had heard enough to know who came, and emerged
from the gatehouse with a coarse linen bag under his arm. It
needed but one glance at Cadfael's face to show that there
was nothing to tell, but he asked, all the same. 'No word of
her?'

'None that's new. No, sorry I am to say it. I'm just back
from the sheriff himself, but without comfort.'

'I waited,' said Niall, 'in case you might bring at least some
news. The least trace would be welcome. And I can do
nothing! Well, I must be on my way, then.'

'Where are you bound tonight?'

'To my sister and her man at Pulley, to see my little girl. I
have a set of harness ornaments to deliver for one of
Mortimer's horses, though that could have waited a few days
yet. But the child will be looking for me. This is the evening
I usually go to her, else I wouldn't stir. But I shall not stay
overnight. I'll walk back in the dark. At least to be there with
the roses, if I can do nothing better for her.'

'You've done more than the rest of us,' said Cadfael
ruefully, 'for you've kept the bush alive. And she'll be back
yet to take the pick of its flowers from your hand, the day
after tomorrow.'

'Should I read that as a promise?' asked Niall, with a wry
and grudging smile.

'No, as a prayer. The best I can do. With three miles or
more to walk to Pulley, and three miles back,' said Cadfael,
'you'll have time for a whole litany. And bear in mind whose
festival it will be in two days' time! Saint Winifred will be
listening. Who more likely? She herself stood off an
unwanted suitor and kept her virtue, she'll not forsake a
sister.'

'Well ... I'd best be off. God with you, Brother.' Niall shouldered his bag of ornamental bronze rosettes and harness buckles for Mortimer's horse, and strode away along the Foregate, towards the track that led south-west from the bridge, a square, erect figure thrusting briskly into the pearly evening air cooling towards twilight. Cadfael stood looking after him until he turned the corner beyond the mill-pond and vanished from sight.

Not a man for grand gestures or many words, Niall Bronzesmith, but Cadfael was bitterly and painfully aware of the gnawing frustration that eats away at the heart from within, when there is nothing to be done about the one thing in the world of any importance.

# Chapter Eleven

Niall set out from Pulley on his return walk to Shrewsbury a little before midnight. Cecily would have had him stay, urging truly enough that if he did go back it would change nothing, and stating bluntly what Cadfael had refrained from stating, that while the woman herself was still safely out of reach there was hardly likely to be any further attack on the rose-bush, for any such attack was unnecessary. No one could deliver a rose into the hand of a woman who was missing. If someone was plotting to break the bargain and recover the house in the Foregate, as by now everyone seemed to be agreed, the thing was already done, without taking any further risk.

Niall had said very little about the affair to his sister, and nothing at all about his own deep feelings, but she seemed to know by instinct. The talk of Shrewsbury found its way out here softened and distanced into a kind of folk-tale, hardly bearing at all on real life. The reality here was the demesne, its fields, its few labourers, the ditched coppice from which the children fended off the goats at pasture, the plough-oxen, and the enshrouding forest. The two little girls, listening round-eyed to the grown-ups' talk, must have thought of Judith Perle as of one of the enchanted ladies bewitched by evil magic in old nursery tales. Cecily's two shock-headed, berry-brown boys, at home in all the woodland skills, had only two or three times in their lives, thus far, set eyes on the distant towers of Shrewsbury castle. Three miles is not so far, but far enough when you have no need to cross it. John Stury came into the town perhaps twice a year to buy, and for the rest the little manor was self-supporting. Sometimes Niall was moved to feel that he must soon remove his daughter and take her back with him to the town, for fear he

141

might lose her for ever. To a happy household, a peaceful, simple life and good company, truly, but to his own irrevocable loss and bereavement.

She was asleep long before this hour, in her nest with the other three in the loft, he had laid her there himself, already drowsy. A fair creature, with a bright sheen of gold in her cloud of hair, like her mother before her, and a skin like creamy milk, that glowed in sunny weather with the same gilded gloss. Cecily's brood were reddish-dark, after their father, with lithe, lean bodies and black eyes. She was rounded and smooth and soft. Almost from birth she had been here with her cousins, it would be hard to take her away.

'You'll have a dark walk home,' said John, peering out from the doorway. In the summer night the smell of the forest was spicy and strong, heavy in the windless dark. 'The moon won't be up for hours yet.'

'I don't mind it. I should know the way well enough by now.'

'I'll come out with you as far as the track,' said Cecily, 'and set you on your road. It's fine and warm still, and I'm wakeful.'

She walked beside him in silence as far as the gate in John's stockade, and out across the clearing of open grass to the edge of the trees, and there they halted.

'One of these days,' she said, as though she had been listening to all that he had been thinking, 'you'll be taking the little one away from us. It's only right you should, though we shall grudge her to you. As well we're not so far away that we can't borrow her back now and then. It wouldn't do to leave it too long, Niall. I've had the gift of her, and been glad of it, but yours she is, yours and Avota's, when all's said, and best she should grow up knowing it and content with it.'

'She's young yet,' said Niall defensively. 'I dread to confuse her too soon.'

'She's young, but she's knowing. She begins to ask why you always leave her, and to wonder how you do, alone, and who cooks and washes for you. I reckon you could as well take her on a visit, show her how you live and what you

142

make. She's hungry to know, you'll find she'll drink it in. And much as she joys in playing with my brood, she never likes sharing you with them. That's a true woman you'll find there,' said Cecily with conviction. 'But for all that, it might be the best thing of all you could do for her, Niall, just now is to give her another mother. One of her own, with no rival childer by. For she's sharp enough, my dear, to know that I'm none of hers, love her as I may.'

Niall said his good night to her without comment on that, and went off with a rapid stride into the trees. She knew him well enough to expect nothing more, and turned back to the house, when he had vanished from sight, aware that he had listened and been torn. It was time he should give thought to it. The life of a respected town craftsman's daughter, with property to inherit and social skills to learn, must necessarily be different from that of a country steward's girl; her betrothal prospects must be sought among a different group of people, her upbringing be aimed at a somewhat different kind of household with a different round of duties. Sharp beyond her years, the child might begin to think that a father who leaves her too long apart from him does not really want her, but visits only out of duty. Yet she was very young, very young to be taken where there was no woman to care for her. Now if only there should be some real hope in this widow woman of whom he had nothing to say! Or, for that matter, any other decent woman with a warm heart and a cool head, and patience enough for two!

Niall walked on along the narrow path between the trees, in dark-green night, full-leaved and heady with scents, with his sister's voice still in his ears. The woods were thick and well grown here, the ground so shadowed that herbal cover was scant, but the interlacing of boughs above shut out the sky. Sometimes the path emerged for a short way into more open upland where the trees thinned and clearings of heath appeared, for all this stretch of country was the northern fringe of the Long Forest, where men had encroached with their little assarts and their legal or illegal cutting of timber and pasturing of pigs on acorns and beech-mast. But even here settlements were very few. He would not see more than a couple of small, precarious holdings before he came to the hamlet of Brace Meole, nearly half his way home.

On that thought he checked to reconsider, for it might be a little quicker to turn aside to the east on a path he knew, and hit the high road, if such a track through forest could be called a high road, well before the village, instead of staying on the forest path. Every variation on this journey was familiar to him. The path of which he was thinking crossed the one on which he was walking diagonally, striking south-west, and where the ways met there was a small open clearing, the only such space in a belt of thicker woodland. Here he halted for a moment, still undecided, and stood to savour the awesome quietness of the night, just as the hush was mysteriously broken by small, persistent sounds. In such windless silence any sound, however soft, came startlingly upon the ear. Instinctively Niall drew back from the open ground, deep into the cover of the trees, and stood with head up and ears stretched to decipher the signs.

There are always some nocturnal creatures about their business in the dark, but their small rustlings keep low to the ground and furtive, and freeze when a man is scented in the night, since every man is an enemy. These sounds proceeded steadily though softly, and were gradually drawing nearer. The dull, solid but muffled thud of hooves in deep turf, drawing near at a brisk walk from the direction of the road, and a light rustling and swish of pliable twigs brushing a passing bulk. The summer growth was at its height, the trees had reached new and tender shoots just far enough to encroach upon the path with their soft tips.

What was a horseman doing, coming this way at this hour, and by the pace and the sounds heavily laden? Niall stayed where he was, well within the trees and hidden, but looking out into the clearing, where by contrast there was light enough to distinguish shapes and degrees of grey and black. No moon, and a high, faint veil of cloud between the earth and stars, a night for dark undertakings. And though masterless men seldom ventured within ten miles of Shrewsbury, and the worst to be encountered should be only a poacher, yet there was always the possibility of worse. And when did poachers go mounted about their business?

Between the dark woodland walls of the right-hand path a

vague pallor appeared. The new foliage whispered along a horse's barrel and a rider's arm. A white horse, or a pale dapple-grey or very light roan, for his hide brought with it into the clearing its own lambent gleam. The shape of the man on his back appeared at first squat and monstrously thickset, until some unevenness of the ground set up a swaying movement that showed the mount was carrying not one person, but two. A man before, a woman riding pillion behind. One shadowy bulk, without detail, became clearly two, though still without identity, as horse and riders passed by, crossed the path and continued on their cautious way south-west. The swing of the long skirt showed, there were even points of pallor mysterious in the moving darkness, a hand holding by the horseman's belt, an oval face raised to the sky, free of the hood that had fallen back on to the woman's shoulders.

There was nothing clearer to view than that, and yet he knew her. It might have been the poise of the head with its great sheaf of hair, moving against a sky almost as dark, or the erect carriage and balance of her body, or some overstrung cord within his own being that could not but vibrate to her nearness. This woman of all women could not pass by, even in the dark and unaware of him, and he not know.

And what was Judith Perle doing here in the night, three days after vanishing from her rightful place, riding pillion behind a horseman going south-west, and she under no constraint, but going with him willingly?

He stood for so long motionless and silent that the small creatures of the night seemed to have lost all awe of him, or forgotten he was there. Somewhere across the clearing, where the path by which he had come continued, something rustled hastily from one tangle of undergrowth to another, and made off westward into safety and silence. Niall stirred out of his chilled stillness, and turned to follow the sound of the muffled hooves down the grassy ride until they died into the same profound silence.

He could neither believe in nor understand what he had seen. It was not, it could not be, what it seemed. Where she was going, who was her companion, what she intended, these were mysteries, but they were her mysteries, and in her

Niall had so strong and unquestioning a faith that no strange night venture could shake it. The one certainty was that by the grace of God he had found her, and now he must not lose her again, and that was enough. If she had no need of him, if she was in no danger or distress, so be it, and he would never trouble her. But he would, he must, follow and be near to see that no harm came to her, until all this dark interlude was over and done, and she vindicated and restored to the light. The conviction was unbearably strong within him that if he lost her now she would be lost forever.

He emerged from his cover and crossed into the path they had taken. There was no danger of losing them; through the thickening forest ahead a horse must hold to the path, especially by night, and in this darkness could not press beyond a walk. A man afoot could have outrun them, provided he knew the woods as Niall knew them. But for his purpose it was enough to recover the sounds that were his guide, and if possible approach close enough to be with her in a moment if anything untoward threatened. This ground was less familiar to him than the various ways to Pulley, having left that hamlet aside on the left, but it was similar country, and he could thread his way among the trees, aside from the path, at a faster speed than the horseman was making. Soon he recovered the small, regular beat of hooves, and the light ring of the bridle as the horse tossed its head at some sudden nocturnal stir, perhaps, in the undergrowth on the other side of the track. Twice he caught that brief, abrupt peal of bells, like a summons to service, reassuring him that he was near, and could close quickly if there should be need.

They were moving steadily south-west, deeper into the recesses of the Long Forest, and here there were fewer places where the cover became more open, and patches of heath and outcrop rock appeared. Surely more than a mile past now, and still the riders pressed on, keeping the same cautious pace. The veiled sky had grown somewhat darker with thickening cloud cover. Looking up, Niall could barely distinguish the shapes of the upper branches against the heavens. He went with hands spread to touch the trees and weave his way between, but still he kept within earshot of the horse's steady progress, and once he found he had drawn abreast of it, and was aware of movement along the path on his right, by sense rather than by sight. He hung back to let the vague blur of the pale hide draw ahead again, and then took up the patient pursuit with greater care.

He had lost all idea of how long they had been engaged in this nocturnal pilgrimage through the forest, but thought it must be almost an hour, and if the riders had come from the town they must have set out an hour earlier still. As to where they were bound, he had no notion. He knew nothing in this part of the woods, barring perhaps a solitary scratched-out assart hacked recently from the waste. They must be fairly close to the source of the Meole Brook, and riding upstream. From the higher ground on the left two or three tiny tributaries came down and trickled across the path, none of them any barrier, for any one of them could be stepped over dry-shod, at least in summer. The little serpents of water made one more tiny sound, hissing drowsily between the stones. They had gone perhaps three miles, Niall reckoned, since he first began to follow.

Somewhere not too distant on the right the woods rustled and stilled. The rhythm of the horse's gait was broken, hooves shifted, at check on a harder floor where stone came near the surface, then moved more slowly back to turf and halted. Niall crept closer, feeling his way from tree to tree and putting off the hampering branches with careful quietness. It seemed by the slight easing of the darkness that the path he was approaching had widened into a grassy ride where the sky, if clouded, could at least peer in. Then he saw through the lace of leaves the dim pallor which was the body of the horse, standing still. For the first time there was a voice, a man's, in a sibilant whisper that carried clearly through the silence.

'I should take you to the gate.'

The rider was already out of the saddle. In the forest aisle where the darkness became relative there was movement upon the ground, a blacker shape shifting across the pallor of the horse like drifts of cloud across the moon.

'No,' said Judith's voice, chill and clear. 'That was not in the bargain. I do not wish it.'

By the horse's stirring and the susurration of movement

Niall knew the moment when the man lifted her down, though still, without conviction, his voice protested: 'I cannot let you go alone.'

'It is not far,' she said. 'I am not afraid.'

And he was accepting his dismissal, for again the horse stirred and trod the turf, and a stirrup rang once. The rider was remounting. Something more he said, but it was lost as his mount turned, not to go back the way he had come, but onward to the left, uphill by another track, to cut through the rough uplands the nearest way to the road. Speed rather than secrecy was his concern now. But after a few hasty paces he did check and turn to offer again what she had refused, knowing she would still refuse it.

'I'm loth to leave you so . . .'

'I know my way now,' she said simply. 'Go, get home before light.'

At that he did turn, shake his bridle, and start along a rising ride that seemed to offer better speed and a more open and smooth surface, for in a little while the receding sound of the hooves became a cautious trot, intent on making good speed away from this mysterious errand. Judith still stood where he had set her down, quite invisible in the edge of the trees, but Niall would know when she moved. He drew nearer still, ready to follow whatever move she made. She knew her way, it was not far, and she was not afraid. But he would go at her back until she reached her chosen haven, wherever that might be.

The rider was gone, the last muted sound had died into silence, before she stirred, and then he heard her turn away to the right, out of the comparative twilight of the open ride, back into the lush, leafy blackness of thick forest, for a twig snapped under her foot. He crossed the ride and followed. There was a narrow but trodden path slanting away downhill, towards some larger tributary of the Meole, for he caught the distant small whispering of water from below.

He had gone no more than twenty paces down the path, and she was perhaps twenty before him, when there was a sudden violent threshing of bushes from the right, out of the thick undergrowth, and then Judith cried out, one wild, brief cry of alarm and dread. Niall sprang forward in a reckless run towards the cry, and felt, rather than heard or saw, the night convulsed before him with the turbulence of an almost silent struggle. His spread arms embraced two bodies, blindly and clumsily, and struggled to pluck them apart. Judith's long hair, torn from its coil, streamed across his face, and he took her about the waist to put her behind him and out of danger. He felt the upward swing of a long arm reaching past him to strike at her, and some strange trick of lambent light flashed for one instant blue along the blade of a knife.

Niall caught the descending arm and wrenched it aside, hooked a knee round the assailant's knee with a wrestler's instinct, and brought them both crashing to the ground. They rolled and strained, twigs crackling under them in the blind dark, bruised shoulders against the boles of trees, wrenched and struggled, the one to free his knife arm, the other to hold the blade away from himself or get possession of it. Their breath mingled as they strained and panted face to face, and each still invisible to the other. The attacker was strong, muscular and determined, and had a fund of vicious tricks to play, using head and teeth and knees freely, but he could not break away or get to his feet again. Niall had him by the right wrist, and with his other arm wound about the man's body, pinning the upper arm so that his opponent could only claw fiercely at neck and face, drawing blood. With a grunting effort he heaved up his body and rolled them both over to make violent impact with the bole of a tree, intent on half-stunning Niall and breaking his grip to free the knife, but he succeeded all too well, and his own knife arm, already weakened with cramps from the grip on his wrist, struck the solid timber hard, jarring from elbow to fingers. His hand started open, the knife flew wide and was lost in the grass.

Niall came dazedly to his knees, to hear his enemy gasping and moaning, groping about in the turf and leaf-mould for his weapon, and muttering curses because he could not find it. And at the first lunge Niall made to grapple with him again he dragged himself to his feet and ran, breaking through the bushes, back the way he had come. The lashing of branches and rustling of leaves marked his path through the thick woods, until the last sound faded away into distance, and he was gone.

Niall clambered to his feet, shaking his ringing head, and groped for a tree to hold by. He was no longer sure which way he was facing on the path, or where to find Judith, until a still voice said, with slow, composed wonder: 'I am here!' and the barely perceptible pallor of an extended hand beckoned him, and closed on the hand he reached out to meet it. Her touch was chill but firm. Whether she knew him or not, of him she had no fear. 'Are you hurt?' she said. They drew together very gently, rather out of a startled and mutual respect than out of any caution, and their human warmth met and mingled.

'Are *you*? He struck at you before I could reach him. Did he wound you?'

'He has slit my sleeve,' she said, feeling at her left shoulder. 'A scratch, perhaps – nothing more. I'm not hurt, I can go. But you . . .'

She laid her hands on his breast, and felt anxiously down from shoulders to forearms, and found blood. 'He has gashed you – this left arm . . .'

'It's nothing,' said Niall. 'We're lightly rid of him.'

'He meant killing,' said Judith gravely. 'I didn't know there could be outlaws prowling so close to the town. Night travellers could be butchered for the clothes they wear, let alone the money they might be carrying.' Only then did she begin to quiver with the laggard disruption of shock, and he drew her into his arms to warm the chill out of her. Then she did know him. His voice had started echoes for her, his touch was certainty. 'Master Bronzesmith? How did you come to be here? So happily for me! But how?'

'No matter for that now,' said Niall. 'First let me bring you wherever you were going. Here in the forest, if there are such scum abroad, we could still come to grief. And you may take cold from the very malice and violence of it. How far have you to go?'

'Not far,' she said. 'Down to the brook here, barely half a mile. All the stranger that footpads should be loose here. I am going to the Benedictine nuns at Godric's Ford.'

He asked her nothing more. Her plans were her own, there was nothing here for him to do but see that they were not impeded. He kept an arm about her as they set off down the path, until presently it widened into a grassy ride, where a faint light came in like mist. Invisibly beyond the trees the moon was rising at last. Somewhere before them there was the elusive gleam of water in motion, in mysterious, vibrant glimpses that shifted and vanished, and emerging from the misty air on their side of it, the sharp black edges of roofs and a fence, and a little bell-turret, the only vertical line.

'This is the place?' asked Niall. He had heard of the cell, but never before questioned where it lay, or been anywhere near it.

'Yes.'

'I'll bring you as far as the gate, and see you within.'

'No, you must come in with me. You must not go back now, alone. Tomorrow, by daylight, we shall be safe enough.'

'There's no place here for me,' he said doubtfully.

'Sister Magdalen will find a place.' And she said with sudden passionate entreaty: 'Don't leave me now!'

They came down together to the high timber fence that enclosed the cell and its gardens. Though the moon was still hidden from their sight beyond the forested uplands, its reflected light was growing with every moment; buildings, trees, bushes, the curve of the brook and cushioned strips of meadow along its banks, all emerged slowly from black obscurity into subtle modulations of grey, soon to be silvered as the moon climbed. Niall hesitated with his hand on the rope of the bell at the closed gate, such a violation it seemed to break the silence. When he did rouse himself to pull, the jangle of sound went echoing along the water, and rang back from the trees of the opposite shore. But there was only a short wait before the portress came grumbling and yawning to open the grille and peer out at them.

'Who is it? Benighted, are you?' She saw a man and a woman, both unknown to her and astray here in the forest at night, and took them for what they seemed, respectable travellers who had lost their way and found themselves in unfrequented solitudes where any shelter was more than welcome. 'You want a night's lodging?'

'My name is Judith Perle.' said Judith. 'Sister Magdalen

knows of me, and once offered me a place of refuge when I needed it. Sister, I need it now. And here with me is my good friend who has stood between me and danger and brought me safely here. I pray shelter through the night for him, too.'

'I'll call Sister Magdalen,' said the portress with wise caution, and went away to do so, leaving the grille open. In a very few minutes the two returned together, and Sister Magdalen's bright, shrewd brown eyes looked through the lattice with wide-awake interest, alert even at this hour of the night.

'You may open,' she said cheerfully. 'Here is a friend, and a friend's friend is just as welcome.'

In the tiny parlour, without fuss and without questions, Sister Magdalen did first things first, mulled strong wine to warm the last chill of shock and fright out of them, rolled back Niall's bloody sleeve, bathed and bandaged the long gash in his forearm, anointed the scratch on Judith's shoulder, and briskly repaired the long tear in her bodice and sleeve.

'It is but cobbled,' she said. 'I was never a good hand with a needle. But it will serve until you're home.' And she picked up the bowl of stained water and bore it away, leaving them for the first time alone together by candle-light, gazing earnestly and wonderingly at each other.

'And you have asked me nothing,' said Judith slowly. 'Neither where I have been all these days past, nor how I came to be riding through the night to this place, in company with a man. Neither how I vanished, nor how I got my freedom again. And I owe you so much, and I have not even thanked you. But I do, from my heart! But for you I should be lying dead in the forest. He meant killing!'

'I know well enough,' said Niall steadily, 'that you never would willingly have left us all in distress and dismay for you these three days. And I know that if you choose now to spare the man who put you to such straits, you do it of good intent, and in the kindness of your heart. What more do I need to know?'

'I want it buried for my own sake, too,' she said ruefully. 'What is there to gain by denouncing him? And much to lose.

He is no such great villain, only presumptuous and vain and foolish. He has done me no violence, no lasting wrong. Better it should all be put away. You did not recognise him?' she asked, looking at him earnestly with her penetrating grey eyes, a little bruised with tiredness.

'That was he who rode with you? No, I could not tell who he was. But if I could, I would still go with your wish. Provided it was not he,' said Niall sharply, 'who came back afoot to make sure of your silence. For yes, *he* meant killing!'

'No, no, that was not he. He was gone, you heard him go. Besides, he would not. We had agreed, he knew I would keep my word. No, that other was some wretch living wild on the pickings of the roads. And we must warn Hugh Beringar so,' she said, 'when we go back. This place is very lonely. As well he should know there are masterless men abroad here.'

She had left the great waving sheaf of her hair loose on her shoulders, ready for the sleep she sorely needed. The large, high eyelids, iris-veined and translucent, hung heavily over the grey eyes. The sheen of candle-light over her tired pallor made her look like a woman fashioned in mother-of-pearl. He looked at her, and his heart ached.

'How came it,' she asked wonderingly, 'that you were there when I so needed you? I had but to cry out, and you came. It was like the grace of God, an instant mercy.'

'I was on my way home from Pulley,' said Niall, shaken and tongue-tied for a moment by the sudden sweet intensity of her voice, 'and I saw – saw, heard, no, felt in my blood – when you passed by. I never thought to trouble you, only to see that you came safely wherever it was you wished to be.'

'You knew me?' she said, marvelling.

'Yes. Yes, I knew you.'

'But not the man?'

'No, not the man.'

'I think,' she said, with abrupt and reviving resolution, 'that you may, you of all people, that you should. I think I want to tell everything to you, you and Sister Magdalen – even what the world must not know, even what I have promised to keep hidden.'

* * *

'So you see,' she said starkly, coming to the end of her story, which had taken but a few minutes to tell, 'how shamelessly I am making use of you, Sister, in coming here. I have been lost and sought, hunted high and low, for three days, and tomorrow I must go back and face all those who have laboured and agonised for me, and tell them I have been here with you, that I fled all my troubles because they fell too heavily on me, and I took refuge without a word to any, here in this retreat, where you once offered me shelter from the world. Well, it will not be quite a lie, for I am here, if only for the half of this one night. But it shames me, so to use you. Yet I must go back tomorrow.' Though it was already today, she recalled through a haze of weariness and relief. 'I cannot leave them longer than need be in doubt and anxiety, now I'm free to return. Or God knows I would stay here, and how gladly!'

'I see no need to fret over a scruple,' said Sister Magdalen sensibly. 'If this spares both you and this idiot youth you have forgiven, and shuts the mouths of gossips, then I find it as good a way of serving as any. And the need for quietness and counsel you can declare without ever a blush, for that's no lie. For that matter, you may come back again when you will, and stay as long as you will, as once I told you. But you're right, it is but fair to set their minds at rest and call off the hunt. Later, when you're rested, you shall go back and face them all, and say that you came to me when the world and the stupidity of men – saving present company, that's understood! – bore you down to despair. But creep back afoot, no, that you shan't. Would I let a woman go so poorly provided from a retreat with me? You shall have Mother Mariana's mule – poor soul, she's bedridden now, she'll do no more riding – and I'll ride with you, to give colour and body to all. I have an errand I can do to the lord abbot at the same time.'

'How if they ask how long I have been here?' asked Judith.

'With me beside you? They won't ask. Or if they do, we shall not answer. Questions are as supple as willow wands,' said Sister Magdalen, rising authoritatively to lead them to the beds prepared, 'it's easy to brush by them and slip them aside, and no one the worse for it.'

# Chapter 12

The brothers were just issuing from the church after High Mass, and the sun was climbing high into a pale blue sky, when Sister Magdalen's little cavalcade turned in at the abbey gatehouse. This was the eve of the translation of Saint Winifred, and not even for violent deaths, disappearances and disasters can the proper routine of the church be allowed to lapse into disorder. This year there would be no solemn procession from Saint Giles, at the edge of the town, to bring the relics once again to their resting-place on Winifred's altar, but there would be celebratory Masses, and day-long access to her shrine for the pilgrims who had special pleas to make for her intercession. Not so many of them this year, yet the guest-hall was well filled, and Brother Denis kept busy with provision for the arrivals, as Brother Anselm was with the new music he had prepared in the saint's honour. The novices and the children hardly realised what mortal pre-occupations had convulsed town and Foregate in the recent days. The younger brothers, even those who had been closest to Brother Eluric and deeply shaken by his death, had almost forgotten him now in the cheerful prospect of a festival which brought them extra dishes at meals, and additional privileges.

Brother Cadfael was in no such case. Try as he would to keep his mind firmly on the divine office, it would stray away at every turn to worry at the problem of where Judith Perle could be hidden away now, and whether, after so many sinister happenings, the death of Bertred could really be the random and callous accident it seemed, or whether that, too, had the taint of murder about it. But if so, why murder, and by whom? There seemed no doubt that Bertred himself was the murderer of Brother Eluric, but the signs indicated that so far from being the abductor of his mistress, he had been probing that ill deed for himself, and had intended to be her deliverer, and exploit the favour to the limit afterwards. No question but the watchman was telling the truth as far as he knew it, Bertred had fallen from the hatch, roused the mastiff, and been hunted to the river-bank, with a single clout on the head to speed his flight. Yes, but only one, and the body that was drawn out of the river on the other side showed a second, worse injury, though neither in itself could have been fatal. How if someone had helped him into the water with that second blow, after the watchman had called off his dog?

If that was a possibility, who could it have been but the abductor, alarmed by Bertred's interference and intent on covering up his own crime?

And Vivian Hynde was away helping his father with the flocks at Forton, was he? Well, perhaps! Not for long! If he did not ride into the arms of the watch at the town gates before noon, Hugh would be sending an armed guard to fetch him.

Cadfael had arrived at this precise point as they emerged into the sunlight of the morning, and beheld Sister Magdalen just riding in at the gatehouse on her elderly dun-coloured mule, at its usual leisurely and determined foot-pace. She rode with the same unhurried competence with which she did everything, without fuss or pretence, and looked about her as she entered with a bright, observant eye. Close to her stirrup walked the miller from the Ford, her trusted ally in all things. Sister Magdalen would never be short of a man to do what she wanted.

But there was another mule following, a taller beast, and white, and as he cleared the arch of the gateway they saw that his rider, also, was a woman, and not in the Benedictine habit, but gowned in dark green, and with a scarf over her hair. A tall, slender woman, erect and graceful in the saddle, the carriage and balance of her head arrestingly dignified, and suddenly, startlingly, familiar.

Cadfael checked so suddenly that the brother behind collided with him, and stumbled. At the head of their company the abbot had also halted abruptly, staring in wonder.

So she had come back, of her own will, at her own time, free, composed, not greatly changed, to confound them all. Judith Perle reined her mule alongside Magdalen's, and there halted. She was paler than Cadfael remembered her. By nature her skin was clear and translucent as pearl, but now with a somewhat dulled whiteness, and her eyelids were a little swollen and heavy from want of sleep, and blanched and bluish like snow. But also there was a calm and serenity upon her, though without joy. She had the mastery of herself, she looked back into the astonished and questioning eyes that devoured her, and did not lower her own.

John Miller went to lift her down, and she laid her hands on his shoulders and set foot to the cobbles of the great court with a lightness that did not quite conceal her weariness. Abbot Radulfus had got his breath back, and started forward to meet her as she came towards him, bent the knee to him deeply, and stooped to kiss the hand he extended to her.

'Daughter,' said Radulfus, shaken and glad, 'how I rejoice to see you restored here, whole and well. We have been in great trouble for you.'

'So I have learned, Father,' she said in a low voice, 'and I take it to my blame. God knows it was never my wish that anyone should be in distress of mind for me, and I am sorry to have put you and the lord sheriff and so many good men to such a trouble and expense on my behalf. I will make amends as best I may.'

'Oh, child, pains spent in goodwill require no payment. If you are come back to your place safe and well, what else matters? But how does this come about? Where have you been all this time?'

'Father,' she said, drawing breath in a moment's hesitation, 'you see no harm has come to me. It was rather I who fled from a burden that had become too hard to bear alone. That I never said word to any you must excuse, but my need, my compulsion, was sudden and urgent. I needed a place of quietness and peace, and a time for thought, all that Sister Magdalen once promised me if ever I needed to shut out the world for a little while, until my heart could stand it. I fled to her, and she has not failed me.'

'And you are just come from Godric's Ford?' said

Radulfus, marvelling. 'All this while that you have been thought lost, you were safe and quiet there? Well, I thank God for it! And no news of this turmoil we were in here ever came to your ears there at the Ford?'

'Never a word, Father Abbot,' said Sister Magdalen promptly. She had lighted down and approached without haste, smoothing the skirt of her habit from the creases of riding with plump, shapely, ageing hands. 'We live out of the world there, and seldom feel the want of it. News is slow to reach us. Since I was last here, not a soul has come our way from Shrewsbury until late last night, when a man from the Foregate happened by. So here I have brought Judith home, to put an end to all this doubt, and set all minds at rest.'

'As hers, I hope,' said the abbot, closely studying the pale but calm face, 'is now at rest, after those stresses that drove her into hiding. Three days is not long, to bring about the healing of a heart.'

She looked up steadily into his face with her wide grey eyes, and very faintly smiled. 'I thank you, Father, and I thank God, I have regained my courage.'

'I am well sure,' said the abbot warmly, 'that you could not have placed yourself in better hands, and I, too, thank God that all our fears for you can be so happily put away.'

In the brief, profound silence the long file of brothers, halted perforce at the abbot's back, shifted and craned and peered to get a good look at this woman who had been sought as lost, and even whispered about with sly undertones of scandal, and now returned immaculate in the blameless company of the sub-prioress of a Benedictine cell, effectively silencing comment, if not speculation, and confronting the world with unassailable composure and dignity. Even Prior Robert had so far forgotten himself as to stand and stare, instead of waving the brothers authoritatively away through the cloister to their proper duties.

'Will you not have your beasts cared for here,' the abbot invited, 'and take some rest and refreshment? And I will send at once to the castle and let the lord sheriff know that you are back with us safe and sound. For you should see him as soon as possible, and explain your absence to him as you have here to me.'

'So I intend, Father,' said Judith, 'but I must go home. My aunt and cousin and all my people will still be fretting for me, I must go at once and show myself, and put an end to their anxiety. I'll send to the castle immediately to let Hugh Beringar know, and he may come to me or send for me to come to him, as soon as he pleases. But we could not pass by into the town without first coming to inform you.'

'That was considerate, and I am grateful. But, Sister, I trust you will be my guest while you are here?'

'Today, I think,' said Sister Magdalen, 'I must go with Judith and see her safely restored to her family, and be her advocate with the sheriff, should she need one. Authority may be less indulgent over time and labour wasted than you are, Father. I shall stay with her at least overnight. But tomorrow I hope to have some talk with you. I've brought with me the altar frontal Mother Mariana has been working on since she took to her bed. Her hands still have all their skill, I think you will be pleased with it. But it's packed carefully away in my saddle-roll, I would rather not delay to undo it now. If I might borrow Brother Cadfael, to walk up into the town with us, I think perhaps Hugh Beringar would be glad to have him in council when we meet, and he could bring down the altar-cloth to you afterwards.'

By this time Abbot Radulfus knew her well enough to know that there was always a reason for any request she might make. He looked round for Cadfael, who was already making his way out from the ranks of the brothers.

'Yes, go with our sister. You have leave for as long as you may be needed.'

'With your countenance, Father,' said Cadfael readily, 'and if Sister Magdalen agrees, I could go straight on to the castle and take the message to Hugh Beringar, after we have brought Mistress Perle home. He'll have men still out round the countryside, the sooner he can call them off, the better.'

'Yes, agreed! Go, then!' He led the way back to where the mules stood waiting, with John Miller solid and passive beside them. The file of brothers, released from the porch, went its dutiful way, not without several glances over shoulders to watch the two women mount and depart. While they were about it, Radulfus drew Cadfael aside and said quietly: 'If the news came so laggardly to Godric's Ford, there may still be some things that have happened here that she does not know, and not all will be pleasant hearing. This man of hers who is dead, worse, guilty . . .'

'I had thought of it,' said Cadfael as softly. 'She shall know, before she ever reaches home.'

As soon as they were on the open stretch of the bridge, going at the dogged mule-pace that would not be hurried, Cadfael moved to Judith's bridle, and said mildly: 'Three days you've been absent. Have I to give account, before you face others, of all that has happened during those three days?'

'No need,' she said simply. 'I have had some account already.'

'Perhaps not of all, for not all is generally known. There has been another death. Yesterday, in the afternoon, we found a body washed up on our side the river, beyond where the Gaye ends. A drowned man – one of your weavers, the young man Bertred. I tell you now,' he said gently, hearing the sharp and painful intake of her breath, 'because at home you will find him being coffined and readied for burial. I could not let you walk into the house and come face to face with that, and all unwarned.'

'Bertred drowned?' she said in a shocked whisper. 'But how could such a thing happen? He swims like an eel. How could he drown?'

'He had had a blow on the head, though it would not have done more than make his wits spin for a while. And somehow he came by another such knock before he went into the water. Whatever happened to him happened in the night. The watchman at Fuller's had a tale to tell,' said Cadfael with careful deliberation, and went on to repeat it as nearly word for word as he could recall. She sat on her mule in chill silence throughout the story, almost he felt her freeze as she connected the hour of the night, the place, and surely also the narrow, dusty, half-forgotten room behind the bales of wool. Her silence and her word would be hard to keep. Here was lost a second young man, withered by the touch of some fatal flaw in her, and yet a third she might scarcely be able to save, now they had drawn so near to the truth.

160

They had reached the gate, and entered under the archway. On the steep climb up the Wyle the mules slowed even more, and no one sought to hurry them.

'There is more,' said Cadfael. 'You will remember the morning we found Brother Eluric, and the mould I made of the boot-print in the soil. The boots we took from Bertred's body, when we carried him to the abbey dead – the left boot . . . fits that print.'

'No!' she said in sharp distress and disbelief. 'That is impossible! There is here some terrible mistake.'

'There is no mistake. No possibility of a mistake. The match is absolute.'

'But why? Why? What reason could Bertred have had to try to cut down my rose-bush? What possible reason to strike at the young brother?' And in a lost and distant voice, almost to herself, she said: 'None of this did he tell me!'

Cadfael said nothing, but she knew he had heard. After a silence she said: 'You shall hear. You shall know. We had better hurry. I must talk to Hugh Beringar.' And she shook her bridle and pressed ahead along the High Street. From open booths and shop doorways heads were beginning to be thrust in excited recognition, neighbour nudging neighbour, and presently, as she drew nearer to home, there were greetings called out to her, but she hardly noticed them. The word would soon be going round that Judith Perle was home again, and riding, and in respectable religious company, after all that talk of her being carried off by some villain with marriage by rape in mind.

Sister Magdalen kept close at her heels, so that there should be no mistaking that they were travelling together. She had said nothing throughout this ride from the abbey, though she had sharp ears and a quick intelligence, and had certainly heard most of what had been said. The miller, perhaps deliberately, had let them go well ahead of him. His sole concern was that whatever Sister Magdalen designed was good and wise, and nothing and no one should be allowed to frustrate it. Of curiosity he had very little. What he needed to know in order to be of use to her she would tell him. He had been her able supporter so long now that there were things between them that could be communicated and understood without words. They had reached Maerdol-head, and halted outside the Vestier house. Cadfael helped Judith down from the saddle, for the passage through the frontage to the yard, though wide enough, was too low for entering mounted. She had barely set foot to the ground when the saddler from the shop next door came peering out from his doorway in round-eyed astonishment, and bolted as suddenly back again to relay the news to some customer within. Cadfael took the white mule's bridle, and followed Judith in through the dim passage and into the yard. From the shed on the right the rhythmic clack of the looms met them, and from the hall the faint sound of muted voices. The women sounded subdued and dispirited at their spinning, and there was no singing in this house of mourning.

Branwen was just crossing the yard to the hall door, and turned at the crisp sound of the small hooves on the beaten earth of the passage. She gave a sharp, high-pitched cry, half started towards her mistress, her face brightening into wonder and pleasure, and then changed her mind and turned and ran for the house, shouting for Dame Agatha, for Miles, for all the household to come quickly and see who was here. And in headlong haste Miles came bursting out from the hall, to stare wildly, burn up like a lighted lamp, and rush with open arms to embrace his cousin.

'Judith . . . Judith, it *is* you! Oh, my dear heart, all this time where were you? Where *were* you? While we've all been sweating and worrying, and hunting every ditch and alley for you? God knows I began to think I might never see you again. Where have you been? What happened to you?'

Before he had finished exclaiming his mother was there, overflowing with tearful endearments and pious thanks to God at seeing her niece home again, alive and well. Judith submitted patiently to all, and was spared having to answer until they had run out of questions, by which time all the spinning-women were out in the yard, and the weavers from their looms, and a dozen voices at once made a babel in which she would not have been heard, even if she had spoken. A wind of joy blew through the house of mourning, and could not be quenched even when Bertred's mother came out to stare with the rest.

'I am sorry,' said Judith, when there was a lull in the gale, 'that you have been concerned about me, that was no intent of mine. But now you see I'm whole and unharmed, no need to trouble further. I shall not be lost again. I have been at Godric's Ford with Sister Magdalen, who has been kind enough to ride back with me. Aunt Agatha, will you prepare a bed for my guest? Sister Magdalen will stay with me overnight.'

Agatha looked from her niece to the nun, and back again, with a soft smile on her lips and a shrewdly hopeful light in her blue eyes. The girl was come home with her patroness from the cloister. Surely she had returned to that former longing for the peace of renunciation, why else should she run away to a Benedictine nunnery?

'I will, with all my heart!' said Agatha fervently. 'Sister, you're warmly welcome. Pray come into the house, and I'll bring you wine and oat-cakes, for you must be tired and hungry after your ride. Use the house and us freely, we are all in your debt.' And she led the way with the conscious grace of a chatelaine. In three days, thought Cadfael, watching apart, she has grown accustomed to thinking of herself as the lady of the house; the habit can't be shaken off in an instant.

Judith moved to follow, but Miles laid a hand earnestly on her arm to detain her for a moment. 'Judith,' he said in her ear, with anxious solicitude, 'have you made her any promises? The nun? You haven't let her persuade you to take the veil?'

'Are you so set against the cloistered life for me?' she asked, studying his face indulgently.

'Not if that's what you want, but— Why did you run to her, unless . . . ? You *haven't* promised yourself to her?'

'No,' she said, 'I've made no promises.'

'But you did go to her – well!' he said, and shrugged off his own solemnity. 'It's for you to do whatever you truly want. Come, let's go in!' And he turned from her briskly to call one of the weavers to take charge of the miller and the mules, and see both well cared for, and to shoo the spinners back to their spindles, but with good humour. 'Brother, come in with us and most welcome. Do they know, then, at the abbey? That

Judith's home again?'

'Yes,' said Cadfael, 'they know. I'm here to take back some gift Sister Magdalen has brought for our Lady Chapel. And I have an errand to the castle on Mistress Perle's behalf.'

Miles snapped his fingers, abruptly grave again. 'By God, yes! The sheriff can call off this hunt now, the quest's over. But – Judith, I'd forgotten! There must be things here you don't yet know. Martin Bellecote is here, and his boy helping him. Don't go into the small chamber, they are coffining Bertred. He drowned in the Severn, two nights ago. I wish I had not to spoil this day with such ill news!'

'I have already been told,' said Judith levelly. 'Brother Cadfael would not let me return here unprepared. An accident, I hear.' There was that in the sparsity of the words and the bleakness of her voice that caused Cadfael to check and look at her closely. She shared his own trouble. She found it almost impossible to accept that anything that had happened in connection with her person and her affairs during these June days was merely accidental.

'I am going now to find Hugh Beringar,' said Cadfael, and withdrew from them on the threshold to turn back into the street.

In Judith's own private chamber they sat down together in sombre conference, Hugh, Sister Magdalen, Judith and Cadfael, greetings over, in mildly constrained formality. Miles had hovered, unwilling to be parted from the cousin he had regained, but with a respectful eye upon Hugh, half expecting to be dismissed, but with a protective hand on Judith's shoulder, as if she might need defending. But it was Judith who sent him away. She did it with a sudden flush of family tenderness, looking up into his face with a faint, affectionate smile. 'No, leave us, Miles, we shall have time later to talk as much as you wish, and you shall know whatever you need to ask, but now I would rather be without distractions. The lord sheriff's time is of value, and I owe him all my attention, after the great trouble I have caused him.'

Even then he hesitated, frowning, but then he closed his hand warmly on hers. 'Don't vanish again!' he said, and went light-footed out of the room, closing the door firmly behind him.

'The first and most urgent thing I have to tell you,' said Judith then, looking Hugh in the face, 'I didn't want him or my aunt to hear. They have been through enough anxiety for me, no need for them to know that I've been in danger of my life. My lord, there are footpads in the forest not a full mile from Godric's Ford, preying on travellers by night. I was attacked there. One man at least, I cannot answer for more, though commonly they hunt in pairs, I believe. He had a knife. I have only a scratch on my arm to show for it, but he meant to kill. The next wayfarer may not be so lucky. This I had to tell you first.'

Hugh was studying her with an impassive face but intent eyes. In the hall Miles crossed the room, whistling, towards the shop.

'And this was on your way to Godric's Ford?' said Hugh.

'Yes.'

'You were alone? By night in the forest? It was early morning when you vanished from Shrewsbury – on your way to the abbey.' He turned to Sister Magdalen. 'You know of this?'

'I know of it from Judith,' said Magdalen serenely. 'Otherwise, no, there has been no sign of outlawry so close to us. If any of the forest men had heard of such, I should have been told. But if you mean do I believe the story, yes, I believe it. I dressed her arm, and did as much for the man who came to her aid and drove off the outlaw. I know that what she tells you is true.'

'This is the fourth day since you disappeared,' said Hugh, turning his innocent black gaze again on Judith. 'Was it wise to delay so long before giving me warning of masterless men coming so close? And the sisters themselves so exposed to danger? One of Sister Magdalen's forester neighbours would have carried a message. And we should have known, then, that you were safe, and we need not fear for you. I could have sent men at once to sweep the woods clean.'

Judith hesitated only a moment, and even that rather with the effect of clearing her own mind than of considering deceit. Something of Magdalen's confident tranquillity had

165

entered into her. She said slowly, choosing her words: 'My lord, my story for the world is that I fled from a load of troubles to take refuge with Sister Magdalen, that I have been with her all this time, and no man has anything to do with my going or my returning. But my story for you, if you will respect that, can be very different. There are true things I will not tell you, and questions I will not answer, but everything I do tell you, and every answer I give you, shall be the truth.'

'I call that a fair offer,' said Sister Magdalen approvingly, 'and if I were you, Hugh, I would accept. Justice is a very fine thing, but not when it does more harm to the victim than to the wrongdoer. The girl comes well out of it, let it rest at that.'

'And on which night,' asked Hugh, not yet committing himself, 'were you attacked in the forest?'

'Last night. Past midnight it must have been, probably an hour past.'

'A good hour,' said Magdalen helpfully. 'We had just gone back to bed after Lauds.'

'Good! I'll have a patrol go out there and quarter the woods for a mile around. But it's unheard-of for any but occasionally the lads from Powys to give trouble in those parts, and if they move we usually have good warning of it. This must be some lone hand, a misused villein gone wild. Now,' said Hugh, and suddenly smiled at Judith, 'tell me what you see fit, from the time you were dragged into a boat under the bridge by the Gaye, to last night when you reached the Ford. And for what I shall do about it you will have to trust me.'

'I do trust you,' she said, eyeing him long and steadily. 'I believe you will spare me, and not force me to break my word. Yes, I was dragged away, yes, I have been held until two nights ago, and pestered to agree to a marriage. I will not tell you where, or by whom.'

'Shall I tell you?' offered Hugh.

'No,' she said in sharp protest. 'If you know, at least let me be sure it was not from me, neither in word nor look. Within two days he was repenting what he did, bitterly, desperately, he could see no way out, to escape paying for it, and it had gained him nothing, and never would, and he knew it. Very heartily he wished himself safely rid of me, but if he let me go

166

he feared I should denounce him, and if I was found it would equally be his ruin. In the end,' she said simply, 'I was sorry for him. He had done me no violence but the first seizing me, he had tried to win me, he was too fearful, yes, and too well conditioned, to take me by force. He was helpless, and he begged me to help him. Besides,' she reasoned strongly, 'I also wanted the thing ended without scandal, I wanted that far more than I wanted any revenge on him. By the end I didn't want revenge at all, I *was* avenged. I had the mastery of him, I could make him do whatever I ordered. It was I who made the plan. He should take me by night to Godric's Ford, or close, for he was afraid to be seen or known, and I would return home from there as if I had been there all that time. It was too late to set out that night, but the next night, last night, we rode together. He set me down barely half a mile from the Ford. And it was after that, when he was gone, that I was attacked.'

'You could not tell what manner of man? Nothing about him you could recognise or know again, by sight or by touch, scent, anything?'

'In the woods there, before the moon, it was raven-dark. And over so quickly. I have not told you yet who it was who came to my aid. Sister Magdalen knows, he came back with us this morning, we left him at his house in the Foregate. Niall Bronzesmith, who lives in the house that was mine once. How everything I am, and know, and feel, and everyone who draws near me,' she said with sudden passion, 'spins around that house and those roses. I wish I had never left it, I could have given it to the abbey and still been its tenant. It was wrong to abandon the place where love was.'

Where love is, Cadfael thought, listening to the controlled voice so abruptly vibrant and fierce, and watching the pale, tired face blaze like a lighted lantern. And it was Niall who was by her when it came to life or death!

The flame burned down a little and steadied, but was not quenched. 'Now I have told you,' she said. 'What will you do? I promised that I would not urge any charge against – him, the man who snatched me away. I bear him no malice. If you take him and charge him, I will not bear witness against him.'

'Shall I tell you,' asked Hugh gently, 'where he is now? He is in a cell in the castle. He rode in at the eastern gate not half an hour before Cadfael came for me, and we whisked him into the wards before he knew what we were about. He has not yet been questioned or charged with anything, and no one in the town knows that we have him. I can let him go, or let him rot there until the assize. Your wish to bury the affair I can understand, your intent to keep your word I respect. But there is still the matter of Bertred. Bertred was abroad that night when you made your plans . . .'

'Cadfael has told me,' she said, erect and watchful again.

'The night of his death, which may or may not be mere accident. He was prowling with intent to break in and – steal, shall we say? And it is possible that he was helped to his death in the river.'

Judith shook her head decidedly. 'Not by the man you say you are holding. I know, for I was with him.' She bit her lips, and considered a moment. There was hardly anything left unsaid but the name she would not name. 'We both were within there, we heard his fall, though we did not know then what was happening. We had heard small sounds outside, or thought we had. So we did again, or so he did, afterwards. But by then he was so fraught, every whisper jarred him from head to heel. But he did not leave me. Whatever happened to Bertred, he had no hand in it.'

'That's proof enough,' agreed Hugh, satisfied. 'Very well, you shall have your way. No one need know more than you care to tell. But, by God, *he* shall know what manner of worm he is, before I kick him out of the wards and send him home with a flea in his ear. That much you won't grudge me, he may still count himself lucky to get off so lightly.'

'He is of no great weight,' she said indifferently, 'for good or ill. Only a foolish boy. But he is no great villain, and young enough to mend. But there is still Bertred. Brother Cadfael tells me it was he who killed the young monk. I understand nothing, neither that nor why Bertred himself should die. Niall told me, last night, how things had been here in the town after I vanished. But he did not tell me about Bertred.'

'I doubt if he knew,' said Cadfael. 'It was only in the

afternoon we had found him, and though the word was going round in the town, naturally, after he was brought back here, I doubt if it had reached Niall's end of the Foregate, and certainly I did not mention it to him. How did he come to be there at hand, close by Godric's Ford, when you needed him?'

'He saw us pass,' said Judith, 'before we were into the forest. He was on his way home then, but he knew me, and he followed. Well for me! But Niall Bronzesmith has always been well for me, the few times ever we've met or touched.'

Hugh rose to depart. 'Well, I'll have Alan take a patrol down into the forest, and make a thorough drive there. If we have a nest of wild men in those parts, we'll smoke them out. Madam, there shall be nothing made public of what has been said here. That matter is finished as you would have it. And thank God it ended no worse. Now I trust you may be left in peace.'

'Only I am not easy about Bertred,' Judith said abruptly. 'Neither about his guilt nor his death. So strong a swimmer, born and raised by the river. Why should his skill fail him that night, of all nights?'

Hugh was gone, back to the castle to call off his hunters as fast as they came in to report, and either to deal faithfully with the wretched Vivian Hynde, or, more probably, leave him sweating and worrying overnight or longer in a chilly cell. Cadfael took the carefully rolled altar frontal Sister Magdalen had extracted from her saddle-roll, and set off back to the abbey. But first he looked in at the small bare room where Bertred's coffined body lay on trestles, and the master-carpenter and his son were just fitting the lid, and said a prayer for a young man lost. Sister Magdalen came out with him as far as the street, and there halted, still silent and frowning in intense thought.

'Well?' said Cadfael, finding her so taciturn.

'No, not well. Very ill!' She shook her head dubiously. 'I can make nothing of this pattern. Plain enough what happened to Judith, but the rest I cannot fathom. You heard what she said of Bertred's death? The same doubts I feel about what so nearly might have been her own, but for the smith. Is there anything in all this coil that has happened by pure chance? I doubt it!'

He was still pondering that as he started uphill towards the High Street, and as he neared the corner, for some reason he slowed and turned to look back, and she was still standing in the mouth of the passage, gazing after him, her strong hands folded at her girdle. Nothing by pure chance, no, surely not, even those happenings that seemed wanton carried a false echo. Rather a sequence of events had set off each the following one, and called in motives and interests until then untouched, so that the affair had come about in a circle, and brought up the hapless souls involved in it facing where they had never intended to go. A deal more rapidly and purposefully than he had left her, Cadfael started back towards Sister Magdalen.

'I did wonder,' she said without apparent surprise, 'what was going on in your mind. I've seldom known you sit through such a conference saying so little and scowling so much. What have you thought of now?'

'There's something I should like you to do for me, since you'll be staying in this house,' said Cadfael. 'What with the youngster's burial and Judith's return, it shouldn't be too difficult to filch a couple of things for me, and send them down to me at the abbey. By Martin's boy Edwy, if they're still here, but not a word to anyone else. Borrowing, not stealing. God knows I shan't need them for long, one way or the other.'

'You interest me,' said Magdalen. 'What are these two things?'

'Two left shoes,' said Cadfael.

# Chapter Thirteen

Now that his mind was stringing together a thread of abhorrent sense out of details which hitherto had seemed to make none, he could not turn his thoughts to anything else. Throughout Vespers he struggled to concentrate on the office, but the lamentable sequence of disasters connected with the rose rent marched inexorably through his mind, gradually assembling into a logical order. First there was Judith, still deprived and unhappy after three lonely years, thinking and sometimes speaking of retreating into a nunnery, and vexed by a number of suitors both old and young, who had had an eye on her person and her wealth all this time, and wooed and pleaded without reward, and were now beginning to get desperate in case she carried out her design to become a religious. Then the attempt on the rose-bush, to retrieve at least the possibility of regaining the gift-house, and the resultant death of Brother Eluric, probably, indeed almost certainly, unplanned and committed in panic. After that, however bitterly regretted, one man at least had murder already against him, and would be far more likely afterwards to stick at nothing. But then, to confound and complicate, came the abduction of Judith, another panic measure to prevent her from making her gift unconditional, and try to persuade or threaten her into marriage. Even if he had not been named, the perpetrator of that enormity was known. And the nocturnal death of Bertred might have been logical enough, had the abductor brought it about, but plainly he had not. Judith vouched for that, and so, probably, could Vivian Hynde's mother, since it seemed clear that once the bargain was made between captive and captor, Judith had been removed to the greater comfort of a house which had already been visted in search of her, and the buried room in

171

the warehouse hurriedly and ingeniously cleared of all traces of her presence. So far, well! But there had been listeners outside in the night, Bertred first and possibly another afterwards, unless Vivian had reached a state in which every stirring of a spider or a mouse in the roof could alarm him. The plan might well have been overheard, and the horse with the double load might have had another follower, besides Niall Bronzesmith. And that would round off the whole disastrous circle, all the more surely if he who began it was also the one who sought to end it.

For consider, thought Cadfael, while his mind should have been on more tranquil and timeless things, what an excellent scapegoat Vivian Hynde makes for whoever attacked Judith in the forest. The man who had snatched her away and tried in vain to force marriage upon her, now riding away with her into the forest by night, and perhaps not trusting to her promise not to betray him, but preferring, once he had set her down, to dismount and hurry back to put an end to her. True, as things were, Judith vindicated him, she was quite certain he had not turned back, but made all haste away home, or up to Forton, to his father's flocks. But how if the attempt had succeeded, and Judith had been left dead in the forest, and there had been no witness to do him justice?

A scapegoat provided for one murder beforehand, Cadfael pursued. How if there had been another provided for the first murder, not beforehand, since that killing was not premeditated, but afterwards? A scapegoat suddenly presented helpless and vulnerable and already trussed for execution, bringing with him in an instant the inspiration of his usefulness, and the certainty of his death? Still not chance, but the bitterly ironic consequence of what had gone before.

And all this complication of logic and guilt depended upon two left shoes, which as yet he had not seen. The older the better, he had said, when Magdalen, intelligent and immune from surprise, questioned him on detail, I want them well worn. Few but the rich own many pairs of shoes, but one of the wearers of those he had in mind had no further use for whatever he did possess, and the other must surely have more than one pair. Not the new, Cadfael had said firmly, for he surely has some that are new. His oldest he'll hardly miss.

Vespers was over, and Cadfael spared time to pay a visit to his workshop in the herb-garden before supper, in case the boy was waiting for him there. The master-carpenter's son knew his way about very well, from old acquaintance of some years past, and would certainly look for him there. But all was cool and quiet and solitary within, a single wine-jar bubbling contentedly on its bench, in a slow, drowsy rhythm, the dried bunches of herbs rustling softly overhead along the eaves without and the beams within, the brazier quenched and cold. These were the longest days of the year, the light outside was barely subdued from its afternoon brightness, but in another hour it would be mellowing into the level beams of sunset and the greenish glow of twilight.

Nothing yet. He closed the door on his small inner kingdom, and went back to supper in the refectory, and bore with Brother Jerome's unctuous reproof for being a moment late without comment or complaint. Indeed, without even noticing it, though he made appropriately placating answer by instinct. The household at Maerdol-head must be too busily awake and in motion for Sister Magdalen to manage her depredations as easily and quickly as he had hoped. No matter! Whatever she took in hand she would complete successfully.

He evaded Collations, but went dutifully to Compline, and still there was no sign. He retired again to his workshop, always a convenient excuse for not being where according to the horarium he should have been, even thus late in the evening. But it was full dark, and the brothers already in their cells in the dortoir, before Edwy Bellecote came, in haste and full of apologies.

'My father sent me on an errand out to Frankwell, and I had no leave to tell him what I was about for you, Brother Cadfael, so I thought best to hold my tongue and go. It took me longer than I thought for, and I had to pretend I'd left my tools behind as an excuse for going back to the house so late. But the sister was on the watch for me. She's quick, that one! And she had what you asked for.' He produced a bundle rolled in sacking from under his coat, and sat down comfortably, uninvited but sure of his welcome, on the bench by the wall. 'What would you be needing two odd shoes for?'

Cadfael had known him well since the boy, turned eighteen now, was a lively imp of fourteen, tall for his years and lean and venturesome, with a bush of chestnut hair, and light hazel eyes that missed very little of what went on about him. He was using them now to good effect, as Cadfael unwrapped the sacking, and tipped out the shoes on the earth floor.

'For the proper study of two odd feet,' he said, and viewed them for a moment without touching. 'Which of the two is Bertred's?'

'This. This one I purloined for her from where his few things were laid by, but she had to wait for a chance to get at the other, or I should have been here before ever I got sent out to Frankwell.'

'No matter,' said Cadfael absently, and turned the shoe sole-upward in his hands. Very well worn, the whole-cut upper rubbed thin at the toe and patched, the single-thickness sole reinforced with a triangular lift of thick leather at the heel. It was of the common sort that have no fastening, but are simply slipped on the foot. The leather thonging that seamed the instep at the outer side was almost worn through. But after all its probable years of wear, the sole was trodden straight and true from back of heel to tip of toe. No pressure to either side, no down at heel nor oblique wear at the toe.

'I should have known,' said Cadfael. 'I can't recall seeing the man walking more than half a dozen times, but I should have known. Straight as a lance! I doubt if he ever trod a sole sidelong or ground down a heel askew in his life.'

The other shoe was rather a low-cut ankle boot, made on the same one-piece pattern as to the upper, and similarly seamed at the instep, with a slightly pointed toe, a thicker lift of leather at the heel, and a thong that encircled the ankle and was fastened with a bronze buckle. The outer side of the back of the heel was trodden down in a deep segment, and the same wear showed at the inner side of the toe. The light of Cadfael's small lamp, falling close but sidelong over it, accentuated the lights and shadows. Here there was only the faint beginning of a crack under the big toe, but it showed in the same spot as on the boot that had been taken from Bertred's dead foot, and it was enough.

'What does it prove?' wondered Edwy, his bright shock-head bent curiously over the shoe.

'It proves that I am a fool,' said Cadfael ruefully, 'though I have sometimes suspected as much myself. It proves that the man who wears a certain shoe this week may not be the man who wore it last week. Hush, now, let me think!' He was in two minds whether there was any need to take further action immediately, but recalling all that had been said that afternoon, he reasoned that action could wait until morning. What could have been more reassuring than Judith's simple assumption that the attack on her had been a mere matter of the hazards of forest travel, an opportunist blow at a woman benighted, any woman, simply for the clothes she wore if she proved to have nothing else of value about her? No, no need to start an alarm and rouse Hugh again before morning, the murderer had every cause to believe himself safe.

'Son,' said Cadfael, sighing, 'I am getting old, I miss my bed. And you had better be off to yours, or your mother will be blaming me for getting you into bad ways.'

When the boy had gone, with his curiosity still unsatisfied, Cadfael sat still and silent, at last admitting into his thoughts the realisation of which even his mind had been fighting shy. For the murderer, so well persuaded now of his own skill, feeling himself invulnerable, would not give up now. Having come so far, he would not turn back. Well, his time was short. He had only this one night left, though he did not know it, and he neither would nor could attempt anything against Judith now, in her own home, with Sister Magdalen keeping her formidable company. He would prefer to bide his time, unaware that tomorrow was to see an ending.

Cadfael started erect, causing the lamp to flicker. No, not against Judith! But if he was so sure of himself, then he had still this one night to try again to conserve the house in the Foregate, for tomorrow the rose rent would be paid, and for another year the abbey's title would be unassailable. If Judith was not vulnerable, the rose-bush still was.

He told himself that he was being a superstitious fool, that no one, not even a criminal at once lulled and exhilarated by success, would dare venture anything again so soon, but by the time he had completed even the thought he found himself halfway across the garden, heading at a hasty walk out into the great court, and making for the gatehouse. Here on familiar ground darkness was no impediment, and tonight the sky was clear, and there were stars, though fine as pinpricks in the midnight blackness. Along the Foregate it was very quiet, nothing moving but the occasional prowling cat among the alleys. But somewhere ahead, near the corner of the abbey wall at the horse-fair ground, there was a small, vibrating glow in the sky, low down behind the house-roofs, and its quivering alternately lit them into black silhouette and quenched them again in the common darkness. Cadfael began to run. Then he heard, distant and muted, the flurry of many voices in half-unbelieving alarm, and suddenly the glow was swallowed up in a great burst of flame, that fountained into the sky with a crackling of wood and thorn. The babble of voices became an uproar of men shouting and women shrilling, and all the Foregate dogs baying echoes from wall to wall along the highway.

Doors were opening, men running out into the roadway, pulling on hose and coats as they came and breaking into shuffling, entangled motion towards the fire. Questions flew at random, and were not answered because no one as yet knew the answers. Cadfael arrived among the rest at the gate of Niall's yard, which already stood wide. Through the wicket into the garden the poppy-red glow glared, quivering, and above the crest of the wall the column of fire soared, breathing upward a whirlwind of burning air and spinning flakes of ash, double a tall man's height, to dissolve into the darkness. Thank God, thought Cadfael at sight of its vertical ascent, there's no wind, it won't reach either the house or the farrier's toft on the other side. And by the fury and noise of it, it may burn out quickly. But he knew already what he would see as he stepped through the wicket.

In the middle of the rear wall the rose bush was a great globe of flames, roaring like a furnace and crackling like the breaking of bones as the thorns spat and writhed in the heat. The fire had reached the old, crabbed vine, but beyond that there was nothing but the stone wall to feed it. The fruit trees were far enough removed to survive, though their nearer branches might be scorched. But nothing, nothing but blackened, outspread arms and white wood-ash, would be left of the rose-bush. Against the blinding brightness of the flames a few helpless figures circled and flinched away, unable to approach. Water thrown from a safe distance exploded into steam and vanished in a frantic hissing, but did no good. They had given up the attempt to fight it, and stood back, dangling buckets, to watch the old, gnarled bole, so many years fruitful, twist and split and groan in its death-agony.

Niall had drawn back to the wall opposite, and stood watching with a soiled, discouraged face and drawn brows. Cadfael came to his side, and the brown head turned to acknowledge his coming, and nodded brief recognition before turning back again to resume his interrupted watch.

'How did he get this furnace going?' asked Cadfael. 'Not with simple flint and steel and tinder; that's certain, and you in the house. It would have taken him a good quarter-hour to get beyond the first smoulder.'

'He came the same way,' said Niall, without removing his bleak gaze from the tower of smoke and spinning ash surging up into the sky 'Through the paddock at the back, where the ground's higher. He never even entered the garden this time. He must have poured oil over the wall on to the bush and the vine – drenched them in oil. And then he dropped a torch over. Well alight ... And he away in the dark. And there's nothing we can do, nothing!'

Nothing any man could do, except stand back from the heat and watch, as very gradually the first fury began to slacken, and the blackened branches to sag from the wall and collapse into the blazing heart of the fire, sending up drifts of fine grey ash that soared upwards like a flight of moths. Nothing except be thankful that the wall behind was of solid stone, and would not carry the fire towards either human habitation.

'It was dear to her,' said Niall bitterly.

'It was. But at least she has her life still,' said Cadfael, 'and has rediscovered its value. And she knows who to thank for the gift, next after God.'

Niall said nothing to that, but continued grimly to watch

as the fire, appeased, began to settle into a bed of crimson, and the flying moths of ash to drift about the garden, no longer torn headlong upward by the draught. The neighbours stood back, satisfied that the worst was over, and began gradually to drift away, back to their beds. Niall heaved a great breath, and shook himself out of his daze.

'I had been thinking,' he said slowly, 'of bringing my little girl home here today. We were talking of it only the other night, that I should do well to have her with me, now she's no longer a babe. But now I wonder! With such a madman haunting this house, she's safer where she is.'

'Yes,' said Cadfael, rousing, 'yes, do that, bring her home! You need not fear. After tomorrow, Niall, this madman will haunt you no more. I promise it!'

The day of Saint Winifred's translation dawned fine and sunny, with a fresh breeze that sprang up only with the light, and drifted the stench of burning across the roofs of the Foregate as inevitably as the first labourer to cross the bridge brought the news of the fire into the town. It reached the Vestier shop as soon as the shutters were taken down and the first customer entered. Miles came bursting into the solar with a face of consternation, like someone charged with bad news and uncertain how to convey it delicately.

'Judith, it seems we're not done yet with the ill luck that hangs around your rose-bush. There's yet one more strange thing happened, I heard it just this moment. No need for you to trouble too much, no one is dead or hurt this time, it's not so terribly grave. But I know it will distress you, all the same.'

So long and deprecating a preamble was not calculated to reassure her, in spite of its soothing tone. She rose from the window-bench where she was sitting with Sister Magdalen. 'What is it now? What was there left that could happen?'

'There's been a fire in the night – someone set fire to the rose-bush. It's burned, every leaf, burned down to the bole, so they're saying. There can't be a bud or a twig left, let alone a flower to pay your rent.'

'The house?' she demanded, aghast. 'Did that take fire? Was there damage? No harm to Niall? Only the bush?'

'No, no, nothing else touched, never fret for the smith, nor for the house, they're safe enough. They'd have said if anyone had been harmed. Now, be easy, it's over!' He took her by the shoulders, very gently and brotherly, smiling into her face. 'Over now, and no one the worse. Only that plaguey bush gone, and I say just as well, considering all the mischief it's caused. Such a queer bargain to make, you're well rid of it.'

'It need never have brought harm to anyone,' she said wretchedly, and slowly sat down again, drawing herself out of his hands quite gently. 'The house was mine to give. I had been happy in it. I wanted to give it to God, I wanted it blessed.'

'It's yours again to give or keep, now,' said Miles, 'for you'll get no rose for your rent this year, my dear. You could take your house back for the default. You could give it as your dowry if you do go so far as to join the Benedictines.' He looked sidelong at Sister Magdalen with his blue, clear eyes, smiling. 'Or you could live in it again if you're so minded – or let Isabel and me live in it when we marry. Whatever you decide, the old bargain's broken. If I were you, I would be in no hurry to make such another, after all that's happened in consequence.'

'I don't take back gifts,' she said, 'especially from God.' Miles had left the door of the solar open behind him; she could hear the murmur of the women's voices from the far end of the long room beyond, suddenly and sharply cut across by other voices at the hall door, a man's first, courteous and low, then her aunt's, with the sweet social note in it. There might be a number of neighbourly visits this day, as Bertred went to his burial. At mid-morning he would be carried to Saint Chad's churchyard. 'Let it rest,' said Judith, turning away to the window. 'Why should we be talking of this now? If the bush is burned . . .' That had an ominous biblical ring about it, the burning bush of revelation. But that one, surely, was not consumed.

'Judith, my dear,' said Agatha, appearing in the doorway, 'here is the lord sheriff to visit you again, and Brother Cadfael is come with him.'

They came in quietly, with nothing ominous about them,

but for the fact that two sergeants of the garrison followed them into the room and stood well withdrawn, one on either side the doorway. Judith had turned to meet the visitors, anticipating news already known.

'My lord, I and my affairs are causing you trouble still. My cousin has already told me what happened in the night. With all my heart I hope this may be the last ripple of this whirlpool. I'm sorry to have put you to such shifts, it shall end here.'

'That is my intent,' said Hugh, making a brief formal reverence to Magdalen, who sat magisterial and composed by the window, an admirably silent woman when the occasion demanded. 'My business here this morning is rather with Master Coliar. A very simple question, if you can help us.' He turned to Miles with the most amiable and inviting of countenances, and asked, on a silken, rapid level that gave no warning: 'The boots we found on Bertred, when he was taken out of the river – *when did you give them to him?*'

Miles was quick in the wits, but not quick enough. He had caught his breath momentarily, and before he could release it again his mother had spoken up with her usual ready loquacity, and her pride in every detail that touched her son. 'It was the day that poor young man from the abbey was found dead. You remember, Miles, you went down to bring Judith home, as soon as we heard. She'd gone to collect her girdle—'

He had himself in hand by then, but it was never an easy matter to stop Agatha, once launched. 'You're mistaken, Mother,' he said, and even laughed, with the light note of an indulgent son used to tolerating a woolly-witted parent. 'It was weeks ago, when I saw his shoes were worn through into holes. I've given him my cast-offs before,' he said turning to confront Hugh's levelled black eyes boldly. 'Shoes are costly items.'

'No, my dear,' Agatha pursued with impervious certainty, 'I recollect very well; after such a day how could I forget? It was that same evening, you remarked that Bertred was going almost barefoot, and it showed very ill for our house to let him run abroad so ill-shod on our errands . . .'

She had run on as she always ran on, hardly paying heed to anyone else, but gradually she became aware of the way her son was standing stiff as ice, and his face blanched almost to the burningly cold blue-white of his eyes, that were fixed on her without love, without warmth, with the cold, ferocious burning of death. Her amiable, silly voice faltered away into small, broken sounds, and fell silent. If she had done nothing to help him, she had delivered herself in her blind, self-centred innocence.

'Perhaps, after all,' she faltered, her lips shaking, fumbling for words better calculated to please, and to wipe away that look from his face. 'Now I'm not sure – I may be mistaken . . .'

It was far too late to undo what she had done. Tears started into her eyes, blinding her to the aquamarine glare of hatred Miles had fixed upon her. Judith stirred out of her puzzled, shocked stillness and went quickly to her aunt's side, folding an arm about her trembling shoulders.

'My lord, is this of so great importance? What does it mean? I understand nothing of all this. Please be plain!' And indeed it had happened so suddenly that she had not followed what was said, nor grasped its significance, but as soon as she had spoken understanding came, sharp as a stab-wound. She paled and stiffened, looking from Miles, frozen in his bitter, useless silence, to Brother Cadfael standing apart, from Cadfael to Sister Magdalen, from Magdalen to Hugh. Her lips moved, saying silently: 'No! No! No . . .' but she did not utter it aloud.

They were in her house, and she had her own authority here. She confronted Hugh, unsmiling but calm. 'I think, my lord, there is no need for my aunt to distress herself, this is some matter that can be discussed and settled between us quietly. Aunt, you had much better go and help poor Alison in the kitchen. She has everything on her hands, and this is a most unhappy day for her, you should not leave her to carry all alone. I will tell you, later, all that you need to know,' she promised, and if the words had a chill of foreboding about them, Agatha did not hear it. She went from the room docilely in Judith's arm, half-reassured, half-daunted, and Judith returned and closed the door at her back.

'Now we may speak freely. I know now, all too well, what this is about. I know that two people may look back on events no more than a week past, and recall them differently. And I know, for Brother Cadfael told me, that the boots Bertred was wearing when he drowned made the print left behind by Brother Eluric's murderer in the soil under the vine, when he climbed back over the wall. So it matters indeed, it matters bitterly, Miles, who was wearing those boots that night, you or Bertred.'

Miles had begun to sweat profusely, his own body betraying him. On the wax-white, icy forehead great globules of moisture formed and stood, quivering. 'I've told you, I gave them to Bertred long ago . . .'

'Not long enough,' said Brother Cadfael, 'for him to stamp his own mark on them. They bear your tread, not his. You'll remember, very well, the mould I made in wax. You saw it when you came to fetch Mistress Perle home from the bronzesmith's. You guessed then what it was and what it meant. And that same night, your mother bears witness, you passed on those boots to Bertred. Who had nothing to do with the matter, and who was never likely to be called in question, neither he nor his possessions.'

'No!' cried Miles, shaking his head violently. The heavy drops flew from his forehead. 'It was not then! No! Long before! Not that night!'

'Your mother gives you the lie,' said Hugh quite gently. 'His mother will do no less. You would do well to make full confession, it would stand to your credit when you come to trial. For come to trial you will, Miles! For the murder of Brother Eluric . . .'

Miles broke then, crumpling into himself and clutching his head between spread hands, at once to hide it and hold it together. 'No!' he protested hoarsely between rigid fingers. 'Not murder . . . no . . . He came at me like a madman, I never meant him harm, only to get away . . .'

And it was done, so simply, at so little cost in the end. After that admission he had no defence, whatever else he had to tell would be poured out freely at last, in the hope of mitigation. He had trapped himself into a situation and a character he could not sustain. And all for ambition and greed!

'. . . perhaps also for the murder of Bertred,' went on

182

Hugh mercilessly, but in the same dispassionate tone.

There was no outcry this time. He had caught his breath in chilling and sobering astonishment, for this he had never foreseen.

'. . . and thirdly, for the attempt to murder your cousin, in the forest close by Godric's Ford. Much play has been made, Miles Coliar, and reasonably enough, seeing what happened, with the many suitors who have plagued Mistress Perle, and the motive they had for desiring marriage, and marriage to her whole estate, not the half only. But when it came to murder, there was only one person who had anything to gain by that, and that was you, her nearest kin.'

Judith turned from her cousin lamely, and slowly sat down again beside Sister Magdalen, folding her arms about her body as if she felt the cold, but making no sound at all, neither of revulsion nor fear nor anger. Her face looked pinched and still, the flesh hollowed and taut under her white cheekbones, and the stare of her grey eyes turned within rather than without. And so she sat, silent and apart, while Miles stood helplessly dangling the hands he had lowered from a face now dulled and slack, and repeating over and over, with strenuous effort: 'Not murder! Not murder! He came at me like a madman – I never meant to kill. And Bertred drowned; he drowned! It was not my doing. Not murder . . .' But he said no word of Judith, and kept his face turned away from her to the last, in a kind of horror, until Hugh stirred and shook himself in wondering detestation, and made a motion of his hand towards the two sergeants at the door.

'Take him away!'

## Chapter Fourteen

When he was gone, and the last receding footstep had sunk into silence, she stirred and breathed deeply, and said rather to herself than to any other: 'This I never thought to see!' And to the room in general, with reviving force: 'Is it true?'

'As to Bertred,' said Cadfael honestly, 'I cannot be sure, and we never shall be quite sure unless he tells us himself, as I believe he may. As to Eluric – yes, it is true. You heard your aunt – as soon as he realised what witness he had left behind against himself, he got rid of the boots that left it. Simply to be rid of them, not then, I think, with any notion of sloughing off his guilt upon Bertred. I think he had come to believe that you really would take the veil, and leave the shop and the trade in his hands, and therefore it seemed worth his while to try and break the abbey's hold on the Foregate house, and have all.'

'He never urged me to take vows,' she said wonderingly, 'rather opposed it. But he did somehow touch on it now and then – keeping it in mind.'

'But that night made him a murderer, a thing he never intended. That I am sure is truth. But it was done, and could not be undone, and then there was no turning back. What he would have done if he had heard in time of your resolve to go to the abbot and make your gift absolute, there's no knowing, but he did not hear of it until too late, and it was someone else who took action to prevent. There was no question but his desperation then was real enough, he was frantic to recover you, fearing you might give way and commit your person and estate to your abductor, and he be left out in the cold, with a new master, and no hope of the power and wealth he had killed to gain.'

'And Bertred?' she asked. 'How did Bertred come into it?'

'He joined my men in the hunt for you,' said Hugh, 'and

by the look of things he had found you, or had a shrewd notion where you were hidden, and said never a word to me or any, but set out by night to free you himself, and have the credit for it. But he took a fall, and roused the dog – you'll have heard. The next of him was being fished out of the Severn on the other bank, next day. What happened between, and just how he came by his death, is still conjecture. But you'll recall you heard, or thought you heard, sounds as of someone else abroad in the night, after Bertred was gone. While you were making your plans to ride to Godric's Ford the next night.'

'And you think that must have been Miles?' She spoke her cousin's name with a strange, lingering regret. She had never dreamed that the man who was her right hand could strike at her with mortal intent.

'It makes sense of all,' said Cadfael sadly. 'Who else had such close opportunity to note some suspect complacency about Bertred, who else could so easily watch and follow him, when he slipped out in the night? And if your cousin then crept close, after Bertred was hunted away, and overheard what you intended, see how all things played into his hands! In the forest, well away from the town, once the other man parted from you, how simple a matter it was to leave you dead and plundered, and the blame would fall first on outlaws, and if ever that was brought in question, on the man who had held you prisoner and brought you there into remote forest, to make sure you should never betray him. I do not think,' said Cadfael with careful consideration, 'that the idea of murder had ever occurred to him until then, when chance so presented it that it must have seemed to him the perfect solution. Better than persuading you into a nunnery. For he would have been your heir. Everything would have fallen into his hands. And how if then, with this intent already filling his mind, he came upon Bertred, already half-stunned from one blow, and was visited by yet another fearful inspiration – for Bertred alive could possibly meddle with his plans, but Bertred dead could tell nothing, and Bertred dead would be found to be wearing the boots of Eluric's murderer. Thus he was provided with a scapegoat even for that.'

185

'But this *is* conjecture,' said Judith, wringing at disbelief. 'There is nothing, nothing to bear witness to it.'

'Yes,' said Cadfael heavily, 'I fear there is. For it so happened that when your cousin came down to the abbey with a cart, to bring home Bertred's body, he found that those who had stripped off the boy's sodden clothes had paid no heed to his boots, and neither did I pay any heed, or give a thought to them, when I brought out the bundle of clothing to the cart. Miles had to tilt the cart and spill the boots at my feet for me to pick up, before I looked at them, and knew what I was seeing. He did not intend that that infallible proof should be overlooked.'

'It was not so clever a move,' she said doubtfully, 'for Alison would have been able to tell you that her son had the boots from Miles.'

'True, if ever she was asked. But bear in mind, this was a dead murderer discovered – no trial to come, no mystery, no point in asking questions, and none in hounding a dead body, let alone a wretched, bereaved woman. Even if I had had no doubts,' said Hugh, 'and somehow a crumb of doubt there always was, I should not have kept his body from peaceable burial, or put her to any more grief than she already bore. Nevertheless, it was a risk, he might have had to brazen it out. But not even the shrewdest schemer can think of everything. And he,' said Hugh, 'was new to such roguery.'

'He must have gone in torment,' said Judith, marvelling, 'all night long since I escaped him, knowing I should return, not knowing how much I might be able to tell. And then I made it plain enough I had no notion who it was who had struck at me, and he felt himself safe . . . Strange!' she said, frowning over things now beyond help or remedy. 'When he went out, he did not seem to me evil, or malicious, or aware of guilt. Only bewildered! As though he found himself where he had never thought or meant to be, in some place he could not even recognise, and not knowing how he made his way there.'

'In some sort,' said Cadfael soberly, 'I think that is truth. He was like a man who has taken the first slippery step into a marsh, and then cannot draw back, and at every step forward sinks the deeper. From the assault on the rose-bush to the attempt on your life, he went where he was driven. No wonder if the place where he arrived was utterly alien to him, and the face that waited for him in a mirror there was one he did not even know, a terrible stranger.'

They were all gone, Hugh Beringar back to the castle, to confront and question his prisoner now, while the shock of self-knowledge endured and the cold cunning of self-interest had not yet closed in to reseal a mind and conscience for a while torn open to truth; Sister Magdalen and Brother Cadfael back to the abbey, she to dine with Radulfus, having assured herself affairs in this house were in no need of her presence for a few hours, he back to his duties within the enclave, now that all was done and said that had to be done and said, and silence and time would have to be left to take their course, where clamour and haste were of no help. They were all gone, even the body of poor Bertred, gone to a grave in Saint Chad's churchyard. The house was emptier than ever, half-depeopled by death and guilt, and the burden that fell back upon Judith's shoulders was the heavier by two childless widows for whom she must make provision. Must and would. She had promised that she would tell her aunt all that she needed to know, and she had kept her promise. The first wild lamentation was over, the quiet of exhaustion came after. Even the spinning-women had deserted the house for today. The looms were still. There were no voices.

Judith shut herself up alone in the solar, and sat down to contemplate the wreckage, but it seemed rather that what she regarded was an emptiness, ground cleared to make room for something new. There was no one now on whom she could lean, where the clothiers' trade was concerned, it was again in her own hands, and she must take charge of it. She would need another head weaver, one she could trust, and a clerk to keep the accounts, able to fill the place Miles had held. She had never shirked her responsibilities, but never made a martyrdom out of them, either. She would not do so now.

She had almost forgotten what day this was. There neither would nor could be any rose rent paid, that was certain. The bush was burned to the ground, it would never again bear the little, sweet-scented white roses that brought the years of her marriage back to mind. It did not matter now. She was free and safe and mistress of what she gave and what she retained; she could go to Abbot Radulfus and have a new charter drawn up and witnessed, giving the house and grounds free of all conditions. All the greed and calculation that had surrounded her was surely spent now, but she would put an end to it once for all. What did linger on after the roses was a faint bitter-sweetness of regret for the few short years of happiness, of which the one rose every year had been a reminder and a pledge. Now there would be none, never again.

In mid-afternoon Branwen put her head in timidly at the door to say that there was a visitor waiting in the hall. Indifferently Judith bade her admit him.

Niall came in hesitantly, with a rose in one hand, and a child by the other, and stood for a moment just within the doorway to get his bearings in a room he had never before entered. From the open window a broad band of bright sunlight crossed the room between them, leaving Judith in shadow on one side, and the visitors upon the other. Judith had risen, astonished at his coming, and stood with parted lips and wide eyes, suddenly lighter of heart, as though a fresh breeze from a garden had blown through a dark and gloomy place, filling it with the summer and sanctity of a saint's festival day. Here without being summoned, without warning, was the one creature about her who had never asked or expected anything, made no demands, sought no advantages, was utterly without greed or vanity, and to him she owed more than merely her life. He had brought her a rose, the last from the old stem, a small miracle.

'Niall . . .' she said on a slow, hesitant breath, and that was the first time she had ever called him by his name.

'I've brought you your rent,' he said simply, and took a few paces towards her and held out the rose, half-open, fresh and white without a stain.

'They told me,' she said, marvelling, 'there was nothing left, that all was burned. How is this possible?' And in her turn she went to meet him, almost warily, as though if she touched the rose it might crumble into ash.

Niall detached his hand very gently from the child's grasp,

as she hung back shyly. 'I picked it yesterday, for myself, when we came home.'

The two extended hands reached out and met in the band of brightness, and the opened petals turned to the rosy sheen of mother-of-pearl. Their fingers touched and clasped on the stem, and it was smooth, stripped of thorns.

'You've taken no harm?' she said. 'Your wound will heal clean?'

'It's nothing but a scratch. I dread,' said Niall, 'that you have come by worse grief.'

'It's over now. I shall do well enough.' But she felt that to him she seemed beyond measure solitary and forsaken. They were looking steadily into each other's eyes, with an intensity that was hard to sustain and harder to break. The little girl took a shy step or two and again hesitated to venture nearer.

'Your daughter?' said Judith.

'Yes.' He turned to hold out his hand to her. 'There was no one with whom I could leave her.'

'I'm glad. Why should you leave her behind when you come to me? No one could be more welcome.'

The child came to her father in a sudden rush of confidence, seeing this strange but soft-voiced woman smile at her. Five years old and tall for her age, with a solemn oval face of creamy whiteness with the gloss of the sun on it, she stepped into the bar of brilliance, and lit up like a candle-flame, for the hair that clustered about her temples and hung on her shoulders was a true dark gold, and long gold lashes fringed her dark-blue eyes. She made a brief dip of the knee by way of reverence, without taking those eyes or their bright, consuming curiosity from Judith's face. And in a moment, having made up her mind, she smiled, and unmistakably held up her face for the acceptable kiss from an accepted elder.

She could as well have put her small hand into Judith's breast and wrung the heart that had starved so many years for just such fruit. Judith stooped to the embrace with tears starting to her eyes. The child's mouth was soft and cool and sweet. On the way through the town she had carried the rose, and the scent of it was still about her. She had nothing to say, not yet, she was too busy taking in and appraising the room and the woman. She would be voluble enough later, when both became less strange.

'It was Father Adam gave her her name,' said Niall, looking down at her with a grave smile. 'An unusual name – she's called Rosalba.'

'I envy you!' said Judith, as she had said once before.

A slight constraint had settled upon them again, it was difficult to find anything to say. So few words, and so niggardly, had been spent here throughout. He took his daughter's hand again, and drew back out of the bar of light towards the door, leaving Judith with the white rose still sunlit on her breast. The other white rose gave a skipping step back, willing to go, but looked back over her shoulder to smile by way of leave-taking.

'Well, chick, we'll be making for home. We've done our errand.'

And they would go, both of them, and there would be no more roses to bring, no more rents to pay on the day of Saint Winifred's translation. And if they went away thus, there might never again be such a moment, never these three in one room together again.

He had reached the door when she said suddenly: 'Niall . . .'

He turned, abruptly glowing, to see her standing full in the sunlight, her face as white and open as the rose.

'Niall, don't go!' She had found words at last, the right words, and in time. She said to him what she had said in the dead of night, at the gate of Godric's Ford:

'Don't leave me now!'

Eight and a half centuries have passed since Brother Cadfael walked the streets of Shrewsbury but you can still follow in his footsteps.

The Abbey of Saint Peter and Saint Paul and Shrewsbury Council have joined together to create a series of walks round this ancient town that will allow you, literally, to stand in the steps of Brother Cadfael. You can see the castle, the Meole Brook, St Giles' Church and many other locations that have survived from mediaeval times.

These walks have been created by the Abbey Restoration Project, which is dedicated to the upkeep of the Abbey of Saint Peter and Saint Paul and the excavation and preservation of the monastery ruins.

If you would like further details, or even to make a contribution to the horrendous cost of preservation, please contact:

> Shrewsbury Abbey Restoration Project,
> Project Office,
> 1 Holy Cross Houses,
> Abbey Foregate,
> Shrewsbury SY2 6BS